AGILE PERFORMANCE IMPROVEMENT

THE NEW SYNERGY OF AGILE AND HUMAN PERFORMANCE TECHNOLOGY

Bob Winter

technologies
CA Press
Apress®

Agile Performance Improvement: The New Synergy of Agile and Human Performance Technology

ISBN-13 (pbk): 978-1-4842-0893-9

ISBN-13 (electronic): 978-1-4842-0892-2

Managing Director: Welmoed Spahr
Acquisitions Editor: Robert Hutchinson
Technical Reviewer: Joseph R. Richer
Editorial Board: Steve Anglin, Mark Beckner, Gary Cornell, Louise Corrigan, James DeWolf, Jonathan Gennick, Robert Hutchinson, Michelle Lowman, James Markham, Susan McDermott, Matthew Moodie, Jeffrey Pepper, Douglas Pundick, Ben Renow-Clarke, Gwenan Spearing, Matt Wade, Steve Weiss
Coordinating Editor: Rita Fernando
Copy Editor: Laura Poole
Compositor: SPi Global
Indexer: SPi Global

Distributed to the book trade worldwide by Springer Science+Business Media LLC, 233 Spring Street, 6th Floor, New York, NY 10013. Phone 1-800-SPRINGER, fax (201) 348-4505, e-mail orders-ny@springer-sbm.com, or visit www.springeronline.com.

For information on translations, please e-mail rights@apress.com, or visit www.apress.com.

Apress and friends of ED books may be purchased in bulk for academic, corporate, or promotional use. eBook versions and licenses are also available for most titles. For more information, reference our Special Bulk Sales–eBook Licensing web page at www.apress.com/bulk-sales.

Apress Business: The Unbiased Source of Business Information

Apress business books provide essential information and practical advice, each written for practitioners by recognized experts. Busy managers and professionals in all areas of the business world—and at all levels of technical sophistication—look to our books for the actionable ideas and tools they need to solve problems, update and enhance their professional skills, make their work lives easier, and capitalize on opportunity.

Whatever the topic on the business spectrum—entrepreneurship, finance, sales, marketing, management, regulation, information technology, among others—Apress has been praised for providing the objective information and unbiased advice you need to excel in your daily work life. Our authors have no axes to grind; they understand they have one job only—to deliver up-to-date, accurate information simply, concisely, and with deep insight that addresses the real needs of our readers.

It is increasingly hard to find information—whether in the news media, on the Internet, and now all too often in books—that is even-handed and has your best interests at heart. We therefore hope that you enjoy this book, which has been carefully crafted to meet our standards of quality and unbiased coverage.

We are always interested in your feedback or ideas for new titles. Perhaps you'd even like to write a book yourself. Whatever the case, reach out to us at editorial@apress.com and an editor will respond swiftly. Incidentally, at the back of this book, you will find a list of useful related titles. Please visit us at www.apress.com to sign up for newsletters and discounts on future purchases.

The Apress Business Team

This book is dedicated to the memory of my mother,
whose aspirations for me always preceded my
own by a decade or so. May His peace
be with you, until we meet again.

Contents

About the Author

Bob Winter is an internal Principal Education Consultant and Practice Lead at CA Technologies, a software company of 13,000 employees. His unique perspective, supporting the enterprise Agile transformation while being the product owner for an education scrum, has provided him with opportunities to infuse education with Agile, while teaching an engineering community the importance of the human component of everything. Winter is the only person to hold both the Certified Performance Technologist and Certified Scrum Professional designations. With 20+ years of experience in large-scale instructional design and program management, he has deep expertise in all disciplines of the learning profession. He is a member of the International Society for Performance Improvement (ISPI) and the ScrumAlliance. He is the author of the It Ain't Training blog, and he tweets as `@TheBobWinter`.

Winter's educational background includes a BA in English from Cornell University and an MA in education from Seton Hall University. In his spare time, he likes to sail, run, play the piano, and coach youth sports.

Winter resides in Marblehead, MA with his wife, Monica, and their children, Hadley and Griffin.

About the Technical Reviewer

Joe Richer is a Senior Principal Education Consultant and Agile Coach at CA Technologies. With more than 30 years of experience, he lives at the intersection of corporate education and Agile software development. Richer has worked with large global firms like Motorola, Fidelity Investments, and CA Technologies, as well as with startups such as Zaiq Technologies and Amicore.

Richer brings a passion for business results to his work and is often been heard during planning and coaching sessions to exclaim, "Outcomes, outcomes, outcomes! It's all about outcomes!" He holds dear a philosophy of learning support for the goals of the business, rather than support of learning for learning's sake.

An experienced agilist, Richer has played all of the Agile scrum roles at one time or another: team member, product owner, and scrum master. Today as an Agile coach, Joe promotes self-organizing teams as a means to accomplish knowledge work. He believes that determining what to do and how to do it are easy for most teams once they have learned to communicate with mutual trust in order to articulate and realize a common vision.

Richer is a veteran of the US Navy. He resides in Cranston, RI, with his wife, Kathy, and their children, Ellen and Sean.

Acknowledgments

There are many people to thank who made this work possible.

Monica, Hadley, and Griffin Winter, for allowing me to carve out the time and space within our bustling household to write this book. They realized I was serious when I said that I needed to change the cat litter two days before garbage day, so that I could work on my writing.

The crew at Apress, including Robert Hutchinson, Rita Fernando, and Laura Poole, for their patience and guidance. In addition to ably guiding me through the book development process, they taught me lifelong lessons in the nuances of the em dash, the semicolon, and copyright law.

Joe Richer, for carrying out his duties as technical editor with more zeal than I could have reasonably expected.

Current and former colleagues who lent their expertise in providing detailed feedback on the first drafts of various chapters or sections: Heather Ackerly, Nicole Cleckley, Mark Grover, Matt Hopf, Todd Meigs, Tammy Scandalis, Michael Stricklen, Scott Weersing, and David Youssefnia.

Ken Klein, who converted my scribbles into the illustrations that appear in Chapters 4, 5, 6, and 8.

Tom Dalley and J. B. Braun, who provided clarifying technical detail for Chapter 8's anecdote about the 2013 America's Cup.

Loretta Lang, proprietor of Maddie's Sail Loft in Marblehead, Massachusetts, who allowed me to take a picture in the kitchen to illustrate an example in Chapter 2.

Guy di Lella, who sponsored the book on behalf of CA Technologies, and Meagan Gregorczyk, who performed the executive sponsor review.

Sinead Condon, my manager at CA Technologies, who supported this endeavor wholeheartedly before I could even finish explaining it to her.

Harlan Protass, who provided legal review of the contracts that I would have otherwise blindly signed.

Karen Sleeth, who encouraged me as I undertook the book proposal process for CA Press.

Everyone I list here has contributed to any goodness to be found within these pages. All mistakes or misguided assertions belong to me.

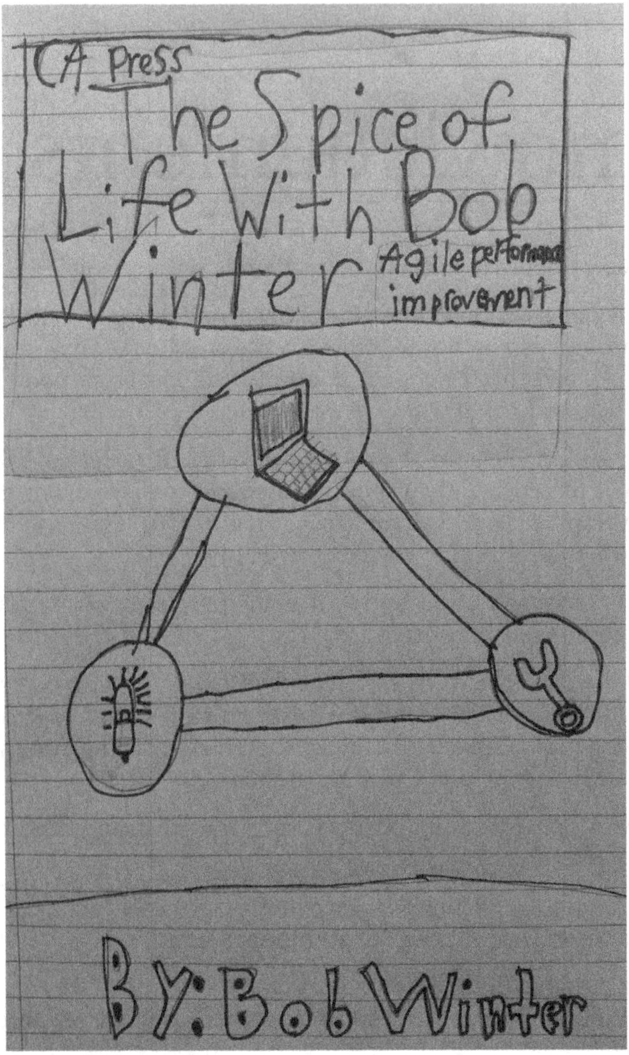

Rejected Book Cover Idea. My nine-year old son took an impressive interest in the development of this book. He drafted a cover design and suggested a title, *The Spice of Life with Bob Winter*, which didn't quite make it past the editorial review.

Introduction

This book addresses a pervasive and potentially devastating work problem: failure to deliver value. As an advisor or consultant, do you find yourself recast by your client as an order taker? As a project manager, do you struggle to deliver high-quality output in a timely manner? As a member of a development team, do you find yourself being industrious in the pursuit of delivering things that nobody cares about? As a product owner, do you seek better ways to articulate the impact of your team's output?

For answers I turn to the colorful histories, foundational principles, and practices from two disciplines: Agile and human performance technology. The hybrid is ***agile performance improvement***, which embraces a collaborative approach to the pursuit of business results that the two professions share.

You don't have to be a corporate training person or a software engineer to apply the lessons of agile performance improvement. Any individual or team producing creative output can apply it. I draw from a variety of pursuits to illustrate the method—from running a restaurant to running a car rental agency, from home improvement to skateboarding and beyond.

As well as being a foundational exposition of agile performance improvement, this book is a call to action for like-minded people to band together to change the way we work.

There is some serious business in here, but I consciously keep the tone lighthearted. After all, learning to work together toward shared success is some of the most fun you can have.

CHAPTER

1

Agile and Human Performance Technology

The Twain Shall Meet

This book is dedicated to those who by their daily acts of courage sustain the advance of freedom and bring closer the day of its absolute triumph.

—Jim and Michele McCarthy, *Software for Your Head*[1]

Agile performance improvement blends the best of agile software development methods with the best of *human performance technology* (HPT).[2] The two systems share an ambition to remedy the most profound failures of popular methods.

[1]Jim McCarthy and Michele McCarthy, *Software for Your Head: Core Protocols for Creating and Maintaining Shared Vision* (Boston: Addison-Wesley, 2002).
[2]Also known as *human performance improvement.*

Traditionally, software development projects cover time horizons stretching to months and years. Such "waterfall" projects typically run over budget and late, often missing the window for usefulness. Agile methods promise to deliver value through small, potentially shippable product features developed within short iterations.

Corporate learning consultants (and other service providers) constantly battle expectations from their customers to be "order takers." Following this well-worn but unfortunate path is to consign their teams to a cycle of industriousness in the pursuit of producing worthless things. The application of principles and methods of HPT ensures rigorous front-end analysis and defines solutions that achieve a clear and quantifiable outcome.

Everyone in software engineering knows about Agile, and most practice it. They don't know much about HPT. When practicing Agile faithfully and well, they deliver faster. Imagine if, by applying the practices of HPT, they could more often deliver features their customers cared about?

Human resources and learning professionals know about HPT, and most practice it. Most don't know much of Agile. Imagine if, by applying the practices of Agile, they could deliver their products within weeks rather than months?

Agile performance improvement enables teams to focus on the highest-value work, continuously improving its ability to frequently produce high-quality output.

Objectives of This Book

> *An objective is a description of a performance you want learners to be able to exhibit before you consider them competent. An objective describes an intended result of instruction, rather than the process of instruction itself.*
>
> —Robert Mager, *Preparing Instructional Objectives*[3]

In the learning business, we talk about objectives all the time. Mager's definition emphasizes a focus on performance leading to results, which will be a theme in this text. Let's discuss how the reader can hope to improve performance and get better outcomes.

[3]Robert F. Mager, *Preparing Instructional Objectives, 2nd ed.* (Belmont, CA: Fearon, 1975).

After reading this book, business executives, team members, Agile practitioners, and performance consulting practitioners should be able to do the following:

- Apply agile engineering practices to the design and development of learning solutions and nonsoftware products
- Apply the analytical techniques of HPT to the solution of any business problem involving human capabilities, including software development
- Leverage the agile performance improvement model to maximize the value of interactions among product owners, work teams, and customers in any product or process area
- Avoid the common pitfalls faced by teams transitioning from traditional work methods to Agile

This book primarily appeals to professionals from the worlds of software development and human performance improvement, but any work team that creates things of value can apply the ideas presented here.

The idea of examining the two practices in this way came to me several years ago when I found myself in a new position as an internal learning consultant supporting a large software engineering function. My professional background was primarily in HPT, but Agile was about to take over my life. The company was in the midst of a multiyear initiative to transform hundreds of teams to agile methods, and our learning department was working in Agile as well. So my constituency, my team, and I were all learning Agile at once.

On my first day of work at the company, a veteran colleague greeted me: "Bob, welcome. I would like to spend some time today introducing you to our department and the agile transformation initiative. But before we get started, take that tie off." I wasn't at the software company for five minutes before I had learned my first lesson.

A Tale of Two Conferences

> *All I ask is that one may be compared with the other; that they may be placed side by side and fairly examined. That which is of heaven will then be confessed. That which is not so, must naturally be condemned.*
>
> —Edward Kenealy

It's spring 2014. I'm fairly certain that I'm the only person who attended both THE Performance Improvement Conference in Indianapolis and the Global Scrum Gathering in New Orleans (Figure 1-1). These are the signature annual gatherings for the International Society for Performance Improvement (ISPI) and the ScrumAlliance, respectively. The conferences themselves were comparable in size, conference format, and cost. Both were more of an educational event than a trade show, and I learned a lot at each. Both were well run, and I plan to return to them again.

Figure 1-1. A panel discussion at ScrumAlliance's 2014 Global Scrum Gathering in New Orleans.

My observations from those two conferences, held just three weeks apart, crystallized the idea for this book. Agile and HPT, as two distinct principle-based approaches, are appealing, sensible, and surprisingly compatible. Important distinctions do jump out, and I will examine them along the way.

Who Are These People?

To understand agile performance improvement is to understand the typical profiles of people in these two disciplines. The agilists and the performance improvement professionals draw on their own rich histories and grow through the cultures of their respective professions.[4] After attending enough of these conferences (or any recurring gathering of like-minded people), you

[4]An *agilist* is one who practices the techniques of agile software development. There is no equivalent pithy term to describe the practitioner of HPT.

start to see the people converge around a common *ethos* and terminology. Table 1-1 compares the professional profile of a typical ScrumAlliance conference attendee with that of a typical ISPI conference attendee.

Table 1-1. Profiles of Typical ScrumAlliance and ISPI Conference Attendees Compared

Theme	ScrumAlliance	ISPI
Field	Software development	Corporate learning and development
Current profession	External Agile consultant, trainer, or coach	Internal performance consultant or academic
Before becoming a consultant, I spent years as a(n)....	Software engineer	Instructional designer
Impressive credentials	Certified Scrum Trainer (CST)	ISPI Certified Performance Technologist (CPT)
	Certified Scrum Coach (CSC) (from ScrumAlliance)	Academic degree (PhD)
Primary source of credibility	Experience	Research
The authoritative PDF everyone has read or pretends to have read	*The Scrum Guide*, by Ken Schwaber and Jeff Sutherland	*The Certified Performance Technology Standards*, by ISPI

The ScrumAlliance crowd included software development professionals from large and small work environments. There were quite a few people who actually develop software using Scrum, but most attendees seemed to be Agile trainers, coaches, or consultants. Most presenters came from the ranks of the latter, touting their credibility as hardened veterans of the software business and ScrumAlliance certifications. The ISPI attendees were primarily consultants and other professionals from learning or other human resources disciplines. The presenters are a balanced mixture drawn from academia, corporations, and the military. In addition to ISPI credentials, most presenters express their credibility through their academic qualifications.

ScrumAlliance and ISPI are not the largest professional societies in the respective fields; they are more specialized and cast a less wide net than the largest affiliations, the AgileAlliance and the Association for Talent Development (ATD). ScrumAlliance focuses on Scrum, which is the most popular Agile development framework but only one of many methods of Agile. ISPI is specific to the practice of human performance improvement, as opposed to ATD, which covers all of the disciplines of learning and development.

Name-Dropping at the Conferences

Common to the respective histories of Agile and HPT are pantheons of brilliant and sometimes colorful characters. You will meet a few of them as I introduce concepts and techniques throughout this book. These prominent figures have one thing in common: they all have books. Table 1-2 lists the signature books of a few innovative and influential thought leaders from each field. These names and titles are often invoked at the respective conferences.

Table 1-2. Comparison of Revered Figures of Agile and HPT

Contribution	Agile	HPT
Awesome keynote speaker at 2014 conference	Kenny Rubin, author of *Essential Scrum, A Practice Guide to the Most Popular Agile Process*	Aubrey Daniels, author of *Bringing Out the Best in People: How to Apply the Astonishing Power of Positive Reinforcement*
Wide-ranging and well-done introduction to the discipline	*Succeeding with Agile*, by Mike Cohn	*Serious Performance Consulting According to Rummler*, by Geary Rummler
Breakthrough treatment of essential interpersonal skills	*Coaching Agile Teams*, Lyssa Adkins	*Performance Consulting*, by Dana Gaines and James Robinson
For the hard-core student	*Refactoring: Improving the Design of Existing Code*, by Martin Fowler	*Preparing Instructional Objectives*, by Robert Mager
Seriously deep book	*Agile Software Development: Principles, Patterns, and Practices*, by Robert C. Martin	*Human Competence: Engineering Worthy Performance*, by Thomas F. Gilbert

The short list of distinguished figures in Agile might surprise nonsoftware readers. They have all written great books and are popular conference speakers, but they are not household names. There are a number of figures in technology who have achieved pop-culture status. Steve Jobs, Bill Gates, and Larry Ellison come to mind, but you will not hear their names at ScrumAlliance conferences as often as you will those of the Agile luminaries.

The elders of Agile started their groundbreaking work only two or three decades ago, so just about all of them are alive and active. ISPI has been around for more than 50 years, so many of the founding fathers of HPT are deceased or retired. Their names and work carry on.

The ISPI conference has a warm family feel, with a notable amount of hugging and laughing. The most distinguished presenters are extraordinarily approachable and collegial. There are no household names here, either.

History

Throughout this book, I introduce just enough history for the reader to be conversational about how Agile and HPT came to be. Table 1-3 compares the historical themes of Agile and HPT in broad terms. The common lore for each field includes a watershed event. For Agile, the most talked-about pivot point was the 2001 release of the *Manifesto for Agile Software Development* (commonly known simply as the *Agile Manifesto*), which codified the values and principles of Agile. HPT's defining hour came in 1978 with the publication of *Human Competence: Engineering Worthy Performance* by Thomas F. Gilbert, "the father of HPT."[5] The ideas presented therein are the foundation for agile performance improvement.

Table 1-3. Historical Themes of Agile and HPT Compared

Theme	Agile	HPT
View of the past	Failed software projects	Skinnerian behavioral science
Essential 20th-century innovation that people don't talk about so much anymore	Extreme programming (XP)	Instructional systems design (ISD)
Most quoted artifact	Agile Manifesto	ISPI Certified Performance Technologist Standards
Current industry conundrum	Scaling Agile to the enterprise	Pursuit of strategic influence

Those seminal moments were not beginnings but culminations of evolving thought leadership in each profession. As each field matured, some of the important ideas and people that led to the release of the *Agile Manifesto* or *Human Competence* moved into the background.

In studying the field of human performance improvement, we learn of its roots in behavioral psychology. This research dates back to the early 20th century and the operant conditioning work of B. F. Skinner, whose research at Harvard was well known for how he learned to control the behavior of mice and pigeons. Skinner's theories and practices were applied to human behavior via the military and school teaching. His legacy propelled several generations of research psychologists to make a science out of engineering human performance. The methods and principles gained influence in the corporate workplace through the work of psychologists and consultants. Now performance consulting is a profession. In this book, you will meet some of the most influential figures in the growth of HPT.

[5]Thomas F. Gilbert, *Human Competence: Engineering Worthy Performance, Tribute Edition* (New York: Pfeiffer, 1995).

The roots of Agile go back to the dawn of the PC era (the 1980s), starting with people who were sick and tired of failing software projects. They were tired of large preplanned projects running late and yielding low quality. The Agile Manifesto authors are well recognized, and deservedly so, but I hear little anymore of some of the other contributors to the genesis of the Agile idea. For example, Eric S. Raymond was invited to the Utah ski weekend that resulted in the publication of the Agile Manifesto, but he was unable to attend. He certainly would have joined the original seventeen signatories in Agile immortality had he accepted the invitation. Raymond wrote *The Cathedral and the Bazaar* (1999),[6] a collection of essays that detail his role in the open-source movement and the Linux story. He also compiled the *New Hacker's Dictionary (1991)*,[7] which offered the lexicon of software development, then a mysterious subculture, to the masses.

Also underrated these days is the work of Jim and Michele McCarthy, authors of *Software for Your Head* (2002).[8] The book compiles findings from dozens of teams who participated in their week-long boot camp. Teams learned collaboration and high performance through an assignment to "design, implement, and deliver a course that teaches you [the team] everything you need to know to ship great software on time, every time." This idea makes as much sense to me as any other method I've seen to teach Agile.

Agile's Other Agenda? The McCarthys also give us the epigraph of this chapter, a glimpse into the political agenda of Agile. For some, the story of technology—from the emergence of the personal computer to the today's debate over net neutrality—is the story of freedom for individuals to have the same access to and control of information as do the governments and corporations. Furthermore, the idea of Agile threatens the nature of authoritarian rule over employees within the workplace. For Agile to deliver on its promise, executives need to reconsider a range of deeply entrenched non-Agile practices, from heavy-handed governance structures to compensation and appraisal systems that value individual heroics over team performance. They will also need to abandon command-and-control management personas that tell teams not only *what* work they should do but *how* to do it. Whether the political agenda is of any concern to today's typical agilist is open to speculation. As Agile becomes increasingly mainstream (and lucrative)—and it's there already in the software world—it can be accepted without any fear of a hippie uprising.

---

[6]Eric S. Raymond, *The Cathedral and the Bazaar: Musings on Linus and Open Source by an Accidental Revolutionary* (Beijing: O'Reilly, 1999).
[7]Eric S. Raymond, *The New Hacker's Dictionary, Third Edition* (Cambridge, MA: MIT Press, 1996).
[8]Jim McCarthy and Michele McCarthy, *Software for Your Head: Core Protocols for Creating and Maintaining Shared Vision* (New York, NY: Addison-Wesley Professional, 2002).

Weltanschauung

At the intersection of these Agile and HPT, I observe ways of thinking at once profound and incomplete. (Table 1-4) One of the fascinating aspects of sitting through the ISPI and ScrumAlliance conferences was recognizing patterns in the quirks, pet peeves, and triggers on display.

Table 1-4. Worldviews at the Conferences Compared

Theme	Agile	HPT
Management types are....	Adversaries who don't understand us and how we want to work	Leaders who don't yet realize how much we can help them
Cross to bear	Dealing with non-agile people, exemplified by the very existence of management, finance, project management, and human resources	Having to scratch and claw to have a strategic voice ("a seat at the table") with the executives they serve
Actual quote overheard about human resources (HR)	"HR is a problem, or rather the problem."	"Beware of false prophets, the HR people, who would rank and rate you, but don't really understand the organization."
They are snarky about the idea of implementing ...	Manual testing processes	Training as a standalone solution
Typical model	Circular and repeating	Horizontals and verticals
About measurement	A lot of talk about things that should not be measured (defects, release cadence)	A lot of talk about what can and should be measured

As you read this book, you will observe me replicating and analyzing some of these soapbox moments to elucidate the principles and values of Agile and HPT.

These few observations from the conferences highlight the worldview, the lens if you will, of each practitioner. They also highlight the blind spots. My presentation of agile performance improvement should help remediate those blind spots.

Fancy Words

Every profession (and hobby) has its own language and its own fancy words. (Table 1-5) This book defines just enough terminology for Agile and HPT practitioners to understand one another. If you want to get the most out of the ScrumAlliance and ISPI conferences, beforehand you will want to read the books, watch the YouTube videos, and have a dictionary nearby.

Table 1-5. The Jargon

Theme	Agile	HPT
People love to talk about how nobody talks about ...	Continuous integration	Cause analysis
Fancy word to describe most problems	Recursive	Unaligned
Fancy word to describe solutions	Automated	Holistic
Language of success	Defect-free Minimum viable product Value flow	Improved performance Retention Employee satisfaction
You'll never get anywhere without addressing ...	Culture	Work environment
Unenlightened practice	Waterfall	Order-taking
People are ...	Resources	Performers

At these conferences, I found amusement in the straw man arguments. I hear Agile coaches talk about how nobody talks about continuous integration, but really, as a novice agilist, it seems like all I ever hear Agile people talk about is continuous integration. The learning people gripe that people don't do enough root cause analysis, but it's all they talk about. After I discuss both of these terms later in this book, you may become amused by this notion. Nonetheless, the idea that I could cobble together such a comparison in Table 1-5 shows some obvious compatibility between the two methods.

What Each Should Know about the Other

Throughout this book, I highlight what Agile and HPT can and should learn from one another. This is where agile performance improvement becomes necessary. What each gleans from the other remediates blind spots and completes the skill set. Table 1-6 reflects (in broad strokes) the contrasting thought processes of typical Agile and HPT workers.

Table 1-6. Comparing the Lenses through Which Agile and HPT People View Work

Outlook	Agile	HPT
On training	One capable person can pollinate specific skills within a specific team	Scalable solutions and support structures are required to reinforce formal learning events
Software is...	A muse through which we hear the angels of heaven singing	Something we use to make e-learnings
Agile is...	What we do; what we are	Something technology people talk about that I should learn more about
Performance consulting is...	Some HR crap	The keys to the kingdom
Performance improvement means...	Applications working better	People working better
If attendees attended the opposite conference, they would gain an appreciation for...	The human component of success	The great learning agility that exists within work teams
And they would also learn	To quantify value, you need more sophisticated measurement techniques	People on teams don't care about corporate learning interventions unless they have immediate *prima facie* value

In sum, Table 1-6 highlights fundamental distinctions in how Agile and HPT folks view work. The differences are not irreconcilable. Ultimately, Agile and HPT share a rigorous quest to deliver business value. They use different terminology to describe that value, and they use different methods to measure it, but they share a focus.

After introducing the basics and toolkits for the two professions, I address how to measure success, not just in terms of value delivered to the customer but through the efficacy of the team. The reader will see the key to success is in the agile performance improvement system, which is composed of the customer, the product owner, and the team. It is the team's ability to foster collaboration and maintain flow while minimizing the effect of outside disruption that leads to the best results for the customer.

Although Agile methods are nearly ubiquitous in the software industry, we have this book because Agile is spreading to fields beyond software engineering. According to a 2013 VersionOne survey,[9] 81 percent of Agile practitioners worked in the software or IT area of their company. This means that 19 percent of agilists work in nontechnology areas. The latter percentage is expected to grow in the coming years.

There is much goodness in Agile and HPT, and they are mutually enriching. As a mashup of the two fields, agile performance improvement has general applicability to agilists and HPT people, but it will be most instructive for product owners and performance consultants, respectively. If you are a product owner, you can learn from the performance consultant. If you are a performance consultant, you can learn from the product owner. Ultimately the performance consultant and product owner become one.

The Performance Consultant as Product Owner

> *I shall not today attempt further to define the kinds of material I understand to be embraced within that shorthand description, and perhaps I could never succeed in intelligibly doing so. But I know it when I see it.*
>
> —Potter Stewart[10]

My functional profession is *internal performance consultant*. There is no standard definition for this role, but effectively it is an HPT practitioner. I consult with business partners within my company to help them figure out how to remediate human capability needs. My interaction with executives and middle managers frequently starts off as a request for training. If things go well, we bring the conversation around to the question, "What are you trying to accomplish?"

[9]VersionOne, *2013 State of Agile Survey*, 2014. Retrieved March 2, 2015, from http://www.versionone.com/pdf/2013-state-of-agile-survey.pdf.
[10]In his concurring opinion of *Jacobellis v. Ohio* (1964), US Supreme Court Justice Stewart famously declined to define parameters for "obscenity" in filmmaking. See https://www.law.cornell.edu/supremecourt/text/378/184.

When working in Scrum, the internal performance consultant becomes the *product owner*. Clearly defined in the *Scrum Guide*[11] and elsewhere, the major responsibilities of the product owner are to

- Populate the product backlog with work items
- Put the work items in rank order
- Ensure that development team members understand the specifications for each work item before they commit to it

The "what" of the product owner is clear and simple: the highest ranked items are those that "maximiz[e] the value of the product and the work of the Development Team."[12] A significant gap in the definition is the "how." How does one determine what the highest value work is? Consultants, analysts, executives, process improvement professionals, all refer to a body of knowledge dedicated to determining what value is for their profession. HPT teaches us the practice of performance consulting, the skillset of which includes relationship building and front-end analysis techniques underrepresented in the Agile canon.

The principles of Agile and HPT are compatible, with only nuanced distinctions. The methods and practices are made whole by blending them as agile performance improvement.

Before revealing the details of agile performance improvement, I introduce the history and basics of Agile and HPT. Along the way, I delineate the compatibility and potential synergies between the two trades through anecdotes and principle-driven approaches. I outline the application of a rigorously outcomes-focused mind-set that yields measurable results.

Let's start with the basics of human performance improvement.

---

[11]The *Scrum Guide* is the authoritative document for the rules of Scrum. See Chapter 4.
[12]Ken Schwaber and Jeff Sutherland, *Scrum Guide*, 2013. Retrieved March 2, 2015, from `http://www.scrumguides.org/scrum-guide.html`.

CHAPTER

2

The Basics of Human Performance Improvement

An ounce of analysis is worth a pound of objectives.

—Joe Harless[1]

In the 1970s, Joe Harless coined the term *front-end analysis*, now known as *needs assessment*. Front-end analysis refers to the activities done before addressing a solution to a human performance problem. Analysis of needs comes before everything else, including the establishment of objectives. That idea sums up the essence of human performance improvement (also known as *performance improvement, human performance technology*, or *performance engineering*) generally and performance consulting specifically.

[1]J. Harless, *An Ounce of Analysis Is Worth a Pound of Objectives* (Newnan, GA: Harless Performance Guild, 1975).

This chapter provides an overview of the history and core ideas of performance improvement. You will be introduced to the most widely accepted set of professional standards as defined by the International Society for Performance Improvement (ISPI), which refers to the practice as *human performance technology* (HPT). In applying the standards, the agile consultant will need to navigate blind spots and misconceptions that plague both Agile and performance improvement practitioners.

Before introducing the basics, let's look at the two schools of thought about training. Do you ♥ training? Or do you do everything possible to avoid it?

- **The "I ♥ training" school.** The "I ♥ training" school of thought reinforces mantras such as "Training is fun!" and "All curious and inquisitive people ♥ training!" "I ♥ training" is an understandable and even healthy point of view for classroom facilitators and, to some degree, instructional designers. It is common among executives (training and otherwise) who measure the success of training by volume of content produced, course evaluation feedback, and usage (participation).
- **The "I-do-everything-I-can-to-avoid-instruction" school.** William Coscarelli recalled Harless opening a 1977 talk with the provocative maxim: "I do everything I can to avoid instruction."[2] Harless went on to explain how front-end analysis directs clients to the root causes of their issues, and those root causes are only occasionally matters of training.

The Harlessian "avoid instruction" attitude carries with it a whole other set of assumptions than those of the "I ♥ training" school. Instead of training for the sake of training, with a goal of simply getting butts in seats, the measure of training success is business impact. Instead of more training being better, adherents to this school recognize that training is expensive to produce and deploy. Instead of trumpeting favorable mean responses on "smile sheets,"[3] the Harlessians know that training has limited utility: it can only be relied on to help build skills.

Harlessians, join me in a journey through the history and key concepts of HPT.

---

[2]William Coscarelli, "Harless, Mom, and ISPI," *Performance Improvement*, vol. 51, no. 6, July 2012; doi: 10.1002/pfi.21270.

[3]Training course feedback forms are referred to as "smile sheets," because people generally give high marks about the classroom training that they attend.

Human Performance Technology (HPT)

In 1962, the first meeting of the Programmed Learning Society met at the Randolph AFB Officers' Club in San Antonio, Texas. The group later became the National Society for Performance and Instruction (NSPI), and it is known today as ISPI.[4]

Programmed learning was a term suggested in the 1950s by behaviorist B. F. Skinner as a way to apply his principles of *operant conditioning* (learning that occurs as reward or punishment is provided for behavior) to the pursuit of human learning. Around the same time, *instructional systems design* (ISD) became the standard term for a systematic approach to workplace learning.[5] HPT grew out of a need to tie results more closely to business objectives.

The Two Worlds of Education In the corporate learning world, we see a lot of instructional designers who come from the ranks of corporate trainers and trainers from the field of school teaching. However, there does not appear to be much shared history between corporate learning and school education. I entered the world of corporate education after a short, not-so-great stint as a high school English teacher.[6] I remain surprised that in all of my years in the corporate world, I have never heard invoked the names of John Dewey, the father of progressive education, or Horace Mann, the Secretary of Education who helped professionalize teaching. Conversely, I have never heard school teachers talk about Thomas F. Gilbert or Donald Kirkpatrick, whom you will meet in this chapter. Even though school teaching and corporate learning have a shared heritage in psychology and pedagogy and to some extent attract the same talent, the two worlds rarely collide.

---

[4]See `http://www.ispi.org/pl/history/ispi.swf`.

[5]When I first entered this industry in the 1990s, one still heard the term *ISD* quite a bit. That term has since been replaced by the term *instructional design*, although it is not perfectly synonymous inasmuch as it specifically refers to the creation of training solutions.

[6]A book that I never wrote was going to be called something like *So You Want to Be an Inner-City School Teacher?* If you get me in the mood, I have many stories from that one year in Jersey City, New Jersey. Those tales are variously funny, poignant, and troubling. Bottom line: God bless the teachers, especially those who try to help the kids in the inner city.

Defining HPT

ISPI defines HPT as follows[7]:

> *Human Performance Technology (HPT), a systematic approach to improving productivity and competence, uses a set of methods and procedures—and a strategy for solving problems—for realizing opportunities related to the performance of people. More specific [sic], it is a process of selection, analysis, design, development, implementation, and evaluation of programs to most cost-effectively influence human behavior and accomplishment. It is a systematic combination of three fundamental processes: performance analysis, cause analysis, and intervention selection, and can be applied to individuals, small groups, and large organizations.*

This definition refers to the ideas pioneered by the early practitioners and sets the stage for introducing the skill set of the profession. HPT describes the role and guiding principles of the performance consultant. In traditional training functions, this role might have been called a *program director* or *project manager*. In recent years, however, the role has evolved as businesses demand more than fulfillment from their learning partners.

Professional Standards

There are a number of professional associations that bring together people under the umbrella of performance technology, performance consulting, performance improvement, and related fields. Many of these organizations provide their members with sets of standards and offer respected credentials to their practitioners. The two best-known organizations are ISPI and the Association for Talent Development (ATD):

- **ISPI.** ISPI defines the Certified Performance Technologist (CPT) Performance Standards and provides the CPT designation.
- **ATD.** ATD defines the ATD Competency Model and provides two designations related to its application: Certified Professional in Learning and Performance (CPLP) and the Human Performance Improvement (HPI) certificate. ATD's name until 2014 was the American Society for Training and Development (ASTD).

---

[7]International Society for Performance Improvement, "What Is HPT?" (2014), retrieved from `http://www.ispi.org/content.aspx?id=54`. The terms *analysis, design, development, implementation,* and *evaluation* in the second sentence of the definition are the key words for the *ADDIE model,* about which you will hear more later in this chapter.

There is merit in both approaches. The ATD Competency Model is holistic in nature, covering a broad skill set across all learning functions. The CPT Performance Standards, which emphasize performance improvement across the skill set, are a better vehicle for presenting the foundational concepts of HPT in this chapter.

Full Disclosure I am an ISPI person. I hold the CPT designation and learned the practice of performance consulting through my mastery of the CPT Performance Standards.

ATD Competency Model

The ATD Competency Model defines the following "10 Areas of Expertise for the Training and Development Profession": (ATD n.d.)[8]

- performance improvement
- instructional design
- training delivery
- learning technologies
- evaluating learning impact
- managing learning programs
- integrated talent management
- coaching
- knowledge management
- change management

Several of these competencies—including learning technologies, managing learning programs, and training delivery—are outside of the consulting focus of HPT and have no equivalents in ISPI.

ATD's heritage is in the training field, and its membership includes practitioners from all of these important disciplines. ATD's focus on the skill set of performance improvement has strengthened considerably in recent years, and it is fairly represented in the model.

---

[8]https://www.td.org/~/media/Files/Certification/Competency%20Model/031271-ASTDCompModel.pdf.

CPT Performance Standards

ISPI defines ten standards that competent practitioners follow in the practice of HPT.[9] The first four standards are sometimes called *principles* because they are fundamental to every standard.

The first four standards are:

1. Focus on results or outcomes.
2. Take a systemic view.
3. Add value.
4. Work in partnership with clients and stakeholders.

Competent practitioners follow a systematic process represented by the remaining six standards:

5. Determine need or opportunity.
6. Determine cause.
7. Design solutions, including implementation and evaluation.
8. Ensure solutions' conformity and feasibility.
9. Implement solutions.
10. Evaluate results and impact.

Now I will describe what each standard means in practice.

The Four Principles of ISPI

The first four CPT Standards are the principles of ISPI. The expectation is that practitioners will strive to apply these principles in all situations.

Note In Chapter 4, you will read of the principles of Agile. To work at the intersection of HPT and Agile is, in some sense, to serve two masters. Think of them as your mom and dad. You love them both, each for different reasons.

---

[9] http://www.ispi.org/pl/cpt/CPT-Performance-Standards.pdf.

One common misperception about the CPT Standards is that you have to be in a certain role to apply them. That idea is simply not true. Any person at any level can apply the principle-based Standards 1 through 4: focus on results, build partnerships, view things systemically, and add value. For the process-based Standards 5 through 10, the skill set applies to different stages or disciplines involved in the development of solutions. So it is fair to say that it is rare for an individual to apply all ten standards in a single project, whereas a team will routinely apply all of them.

Standard 1: Focus on Results or Outcomes

> *Competent practitioners are focused on results throughout their assignments. They are not predisposed to a set of solutions.*

This standard deserves to be number one. The focus on outcomes or results is always the first and most important thing. As I mention continually in this book and in my work life, the work of connecting a training request to a business outcome is never finished. The maxim "Always start at the end" is the most important concept but probably also the most neglected.

In reality, sometimes a training request is just a training request, and sometimes you cannot draw a straight line between a solution and some business value.

When a Training Request Is Just a Training Request Design, development, and implementation of required training on compliance and legal topics is such a case. These projects can be expensive, consuming untold dollars against a finite training budget. There is no saying no to the internal security and legal people. But as an advisor to the business, you are obliged to try. Except in cases of a regulatory requirement, such as you see in financial services, there is some leeway in what topics are trained. So ask: "Why are you doing this training on sexual harassment? Is there a problem with sexual harassment here at the company? What will happen if you do *not* do the training? What will be the benefit if we do? Do they really need an elaborate e-learning, or could they just sign off that they read the policy? What else are you doing to fix the problem besides training?" The same way you can tell a lot about a household by looking at its garbage, you can tell a lot about an organization by the compliance training they require their employees to take.

Standard 2: Take a Systemic View

Competent practitioners take a systemic view of their work. This requires them to identify the subsystems that make up the total organization. They look for and recognize that a change in one area will affect other areas. They consider how the dynamics in society, the marketplace, workplace, work, and workers affect the desired outcomes.

Hoping to solve a business problem by providing training to people is usually a fool's errand. In most cases, there is a problem in the system, or process, or environment, or culture. Taking a systemic view means that the consultant needs to look at all components of the system, as in the following illustration.

Changing Behavior at the Coffee Shop Figure 2-1 shows what customers see when entering a coffee shop. Just inside the door, you find yourself at a low counter where you can place a food order. Behind the counter are friendly employees, an enticing menu, and lots of delicious food. To the right of the counter, also facing the incoming customer, are coffee urns and a full bar of accouterments. You see the sign.

Figure 2-1. CPT Standard 2. This is what happens when you try to modify behavior without looking at the system.

The situation was exactly as the sign described it. If you head in the direction of the arrow, you can purchase a coffee cup and pay for your food from a cashier, on the other side of the store. Then you proceed upstream to get your coffee and pick up your food.

In this case, you have a *systemic problem* (store design) that employees tried to solve by *training* (that is, modifying the behavior of) customers.

> "That's a beautiful sign. Did you draw it?" I asked, after purchasing my coffee cup.
>
> "No. Suzy did it. She's not here right now, but she's is a great artist," the friendly barista replied.
>
> "Wow. It's lovely. Does it work?"
>
> "Not really. People don't read it."
>
> "I could see that."
>
> "The owners know about this problem. They are planning to remodel later this year."
>
> "That's probably a good idea."

Shortly after we sat down to eat our bagels and drink our coffee, the place got busier, and it was absolute chaos. Annoyed customers were bumping into each other, stressed-out employees had to repeatedly explain the nonsensical flow of the store, and it was taking an eternity to purchase anything. I felt bad for the people who work there.

In retrospect, it was disingenuous of me to suggest to the barista that remodeling was a good idea. If I was consulting with them, I would encourage an agile approach toward fixing the problem. Instead of an expensive remodeling job, I would start with small changes and see how it went. It would take little time and little money to move the cash register to the place where you currently order food, and move the coffee urns to the place where the cash register is now. Those moves alone would make all of the traffic flow in one direction.

If we selected some baseline measure, then we could make a fair assessment of the effectiveness of the changes. For example, we could look for an improvement in one of these key success measures:

- Amount of time it takes a customer to purchase a bagel and coffee
- Percentage of customers who ask a question about how to buy a cup of coffee
- Frequency of customer expletives coupled with the word *stupid*

There's a chance that moving the cash register and coffee urns would solve the problem, saving the owner lots of money on the remodel. If it doesn't work, or makes things worse, they can try something else. My idea is all right, but I guess that the employees could come up with better ones.

Standard 3: Add Value

> *Competent practitioners add value by using their expertise to facilitate the process in ways that result in better decisions, higher quality work by their team, and a higher quality end product.*

The use of the term *value* is interesting here, and you will read later that it is a key word in Agile as well. In Standard 3, *value* refers to the practitioner (consultant) more than the work. In Agile, *value* refers to what the work itself contributes to the business mission.

Having said that, this standard is very important to consider for one working from a support function, like learning. The effective performance consultant is always finding ways to add value besides what is directly requested from a client. "Facilitating the process" means helping the client look at a situation holistically. It means helping them make better decisions for solving a problem for which training is not the entire solution. Once we get past the initial consulting phase, the performance consultant (or HPT professional) is responsible for overseeing that the work itself is done right, resulting in a higher quality end product—higher, that is, than would have resulted in his absence.

Standard 4: Work in Partnership with Clients and Stakeholders

> *Competent practitioners collaborate with clients and stakeholders.*

Partnership refers to working side by side with clients and stakeholders. The implication is that the HPT practitioner is more than a service provider, more than an order-taker. The business's goals are our goals. If they succeed, we succeed. Becoming this type of trusted advisor takes time.

When an HPT professional is doing things right, they earn a seat at the table and become a trusted advisor to executives. When starting a new relationship with a client, it is important to demonstrate an ability to be responsive, professional, and competent. Trust builds over time.

In my most successful engagements, being viewed as a partner means that I am asked to do things beyond the scope of what one would expect as someone with the word *education* or *training* in their job title. Some examples:

- Being asked to participate in special strategic projects.
- Forming an alliance with a critical function in the group not related to my function.
- Being brought in to vet specific business situations without a training goal in mind.

- Permission to proceed with whatever activity—data gathering or other—that you recommend.
- Being told by an executive to stop asking permission.

Standards 5–10: Systematic Process

> *Standards 5 through 10 describe the systematic processes competent practitioners follow.*[10]

Depending on their roles, practitioners will specialize in one or more of these process areas.

Standard 5: Determine Need or Opportunity

> *Competent practitioners design and conduct investigations to find out the difference between the current and the desired performances (the performance gap).*

Here is where we learn about gap analysis. Analysis of the situation, before any training is designed or delivered, focuses on identifying performance indicators with which we can compare the current performance and the desired performance. It's a very simple idea but is often neglected in the name of expediency.

Standard 6: Determine Cause

> *Competent practitioners design and conduct investigations to find out why a gap exists between the current and desired performances. They look for the underlying causes.*

After the consultant identifies the gap, he or she needs to find out the reasons that the performance gaps exists in the first place.

Standards 5 and 6 are essential to the performance consultant as guidance around front-end analysis. I explain the skill set around these two standards at length in Chapter 3.

---

[10]CPT Standards 5–10 map to the ADDIE Model as follow: Analysis (Standards 5, 6), Design (Standard 7), Develop (Standard 8), Implement (Standard 9), and Evaluate (Standard 10).

Standard 7: Design Solutions Including Implementation and Evaluation

> *Competent practitioners design solutions and the plan to implement them.*

Instructional designers design the solution based on established learning objectives. They create engaging learning experiences by applying scientifically proven principles of learning.

According to this standard, the instructional designers also create the plans for how to implement the solution. In larger organizations, however, there will be implementation specialists.

Standard 8: Ensure Solutions' Conformity and Feasibility

> *Competent practitioners oversee the development of the solutions. They may develop some or all of the solutions or be a member of the development team.*

There are technicians who specialize in development. These days, they are the people who take the design created by the instructional designers and produce an e-learning course, a reference piece, a web page, or other electronic learning resource.

To "ensure solutions' conformity and feasibility," *quality assurance* and *formative evaluation* are performed.

Quality assurance involves proofreading classroom materials or testing the functionality of e-learning. One opportunity in our field is to find ways to automate the testing and implementation of electronic learning materials. An emerging topic in this area is DevLearn.

Formative evaluation tests learning efficacy. In lay terms, this is a pilot program. Pilot participants are selected from the population to which the intervention is targeted. There are three significant mistakes that I see in this area. Any of them can put an entire development project at great risk:

- Testing or piloting in nonrealistic settings
- Selecting pilot participants from the ranks outside of the target audience
- Not doing formative evaluation at all

Standard 9: Implement Solutions

> *Competent practitioners develop strategies that allow clients to sustain change.*

This standard refers to two activities: the implementation (rollout) and the sustainment plan. Large training departments will have an operations area that provides infrastructure and implementation services.

Sustainment is always a risk. Once a solution is rolled out, people are ready to move onto the next thing. An effective instructional designer will create a sustainment plan. For example, if a new compliance course is created, and everyone needs to take it, there needs to be an accommodation for the course being offered annually or for new joiners. Otherwise, the course will die on the vine after the initial rollout.

Standard 10: Evaluate Results and Impact

> *Competent practitioners help clients measure the impact of the solutions.*

Some larger companies employ evaluation specialists, but for the most part, instructional designers are responsible for evaluating results and impact. These activities are known as *summative evaluation*. Presumably the measurements will tie back to the outcomes and results established before the solution was designed. Too often (that is, most of the time), I see the outcomes defined *after* a project is done, or evaluation not done at all.

Chapter 7 explores some of techniques I have applied to establish the business impact of learning interventions.

Now that we have looked at the CPT Performance Standards, let's turn back the clock and meet the father of HPT.

Human Competence

Thomas F. Gilbert (Figure 2-2) was a colleague of B. F. Skinner at Harvard University before becoming a professor of behavioral psychology at the University of Alabama. Today, he is known as the father of human performance technology.

Figure 2-2. Thomas F. Gilbert (1927–1995). He is the father of human performance technology. (Photo courtesy of Marilyn Gilbert and Aubrey Daniels)

It is no exaggeration to say that Gilbert is the most distinguished thought leader in the history of HPT. You can't read an issue of *Performance Improvement* journal without seeing a reference to one of his concepts. ISPI's most prestigious annual award is named in his honor. Based on the accounts of his contemporaries, he was a great guy and a mentor to many.

Gilbert came and went before my time in this business, so learning about him stirs up in me the same feelings I got when I first discovered the greatness of Babe Ruth, George Gershwin, or Mark Twain. There's a reason Gilbert is still remembered, and exploration of his ideas causes me only to admire him further. There have been many great thought leaders in the field over the past three decades, but none has surpassed Gilbert.

For me, the seminal moment in the history of HPT was the 1978 publication of Gilbert's famous book *Human Competence: Engineering Worthy Performance*. It introduced a variety of memorable and enduring ideas, including ACORN (a model for creating a mission for aligning organizational actions with its mission), PIP (performance improvement potential), and his leisurely theorems. The book is beautifully written, replete with such deep nuggets of wisdom as this one[11]:

> *Over and over we shall see that only when we have made a proper analysis of accomplishments and their measures will we have any sensible reason to concern ourselves with behavior.*

[11]T. F. Gilbert, *Human Competence: Engineering Worthy Performance (Tribute Edition)* (New York: McGraw-Hill, 1986), p. 73.

Elsewhere in *Human Competence*, Gilbert discusses the "great cult of behavior"—the tendency for a lamentably large number of people to jump immediately to past performance measures and focus only on teaching to behavior. The entire system, including consideration of the repertory of the individual and the environmental factors, works in harmony to produce what Gilbert calls *worthy performance*.

Worth is value of an accomplishment in consideration of the cost of implementing a solution,

$$Worth = Value / Cost.$$

To say that performance is worthy is to say that the change is net contributing to profitability.[12]

Gilbert's Unfinished Autobiography *Human Incompetence: Confessions of a Psychologist* was published in 2011 with the help of Aubrey Daniels, another luminary in the HPT field. In this delightfully entertaining little book, discovered by Gilbert's wife, Marilyn, years after his passing, we learn about the life experience that led to Gilbert's pioneering work. We gain further insight into his brilliance, as he modestly spins yarns about childhood, his work in a behavioral scientist's lab, and the ill-fated invention of a teaching machine. Hear him opine, decades ahead of the world, on the folly of performance appraisals and the implications of the impending information age. If you want to learn more about Gilbert the man, pick up this book.

For all of his memorable nuggets of wisdom and analytical constructs, Gilbert is most remembered for the *behavior engineering model* (BEM), which he introduced in the first section of *Human Competence*. Over the succeeding 35 years, people have tried to expand it, modify it, or create a new proprietary models derived from it (with and without attribution to Gilbert). No one has improved on its elegance, depth, and utility. I discuss the original in detail and how it informs the performance consultant's analytical practice unlike any other single concept.

The Behavior Engineering Model

> *The behavior engineering model classifies different ways to look at a single phenomenon we call behavior. Performance cannot exist at all unless all six aspects of behavior are present.*
>
> —Thomas Gilbert, *Human Competence*

---

[12]Worthy accomplishment is very similar to the more modern term, *return on investment* (ROI).

The BEM (Table 2-1) lays out the categorization of individual and environmental factors that influence behavior. As a framework for analysis, the BEM helps the analyst pinpoint causes of behavior or performance deficiencies, so that impactful solutions can be designed to remediate them.

Table 2-1. Gilbert's Behavior Engineering Model (BEM)

	Information	Instrumentation	Motivation
Environmental supports	**Data (1)** Relevant and frequent feedback about the adequacy of performance Descriptions of what is expected of performance Clear and relevant guides to adequate performance	**Instruments (2)** Tools and materials of work designed scientifically to match human factors	**Incentive (3)** Adequate financial incentives made contingent on performance Nonmonetary incentives made available Career development opportunities
Person's repertory of behavior	**Knowledge (4)** Scientifically designed training that matches the requirements of exemplary performance Placement	**Capacity (5)** Flexible scheduling of performance to match peak capacity Prosthesis Physical shaping Adaptation Selection	**Motives (6)** Assessment of people's motives to work Recruitment of people to match the realities of the situation

Gilbert sequences the six BEM boxes (also known as "the six boxes" or "Gilbert's boxes") in the order in which they should be diagnosed. He finds (and my own experience attests) that the three environmental factors are more likely to be primary causes of poor performance (or the biggest opportunities to improve performance) than the personal repertory factors. Some estimate that environment causes 85 percent of poor performance. The "85 percent rule" will be discussed later in this chapter.

Let's take a look at each of Gilbert's boxes, considering associated questions to ask and who can help in each area.

Environment

1. Data

Key Questions: Do the people know what is expected of them? Do they know how they are performing against what is expected?

Who Can Help? Management; human resources; employee communications

In addition to being number 1 in Gilbert's stack ranking, failure against these questions is far and the way the most common problem I see. Readers would be stunned how much mileage I get out asking executives this question: Do they know they are supposed to be doing this?

2. Instruments

Key Questions: Do the people have the tools, resources, and defined processes to perform the job? Is the environment safe and free of hazards?

Who can help? Procurement; management

You see this problem often as well. Ever order a gin and tonic that doesn't come with a lime? It's not because the person is not trained in making a mixed drink. It's probably because the bar doesn't have any limes.

3. Incentives

Key Questions: Are the incentives designed to be contingent on how well they perform the job? Is the correct performance being reinforced through incentives, both monetary and nonmonetary?

Who can help? Compensation (HR); management

Wisdom on this topic from Gilbert[13]:

> *Money is a beautifully honed instrument for recognizing and creating worthy performance. It is the principal tool for supplying incentives for competence and therefore deserves great respect. Any frivolous use of money weakens its power to promote human capital—the true wealth of nations.*

Misalignment of incentives with performance is not unusual. One example that I have seen in many venues: The company asks everyone to do more for the common good, such as mentoring, delivering classes, and working on special projects. Then people with a high degree of variable compensation

[13]Gilbert, ibid., p. 307. I struggled to restrain my use of Gilbert quotes in this chapter. Every time I open up *Human Competence* or *Human Incompetence*, I find new words of wisdom. Finish reading this book, and then start reading Gilbert.

(such as salespeople or securities traders) are unwilling to take time to participate in these activities because it will take away time focused on their individual goals. It's understandable. People in staff functions, who generally are inclined to do what is asked of them, get frustrated because these types won't participate.

If you want people to do those other things besides relentlessly focusing on sales results or trading profit, you have to structure their compensation accordingly. Easier said than done. Fidelity Investments is an example of a company that uses incentives to drive behaviors and attitudes they want to see. Look at what they disclose to customers about how their registered investment reps are compensated[14]:

> *Our compensation plans are designed to encourage representatives to establish and maintain strong customer relationships, and deliver personalized guidance, which emphasizes and promotes the benefits of long-term investing and sticking to a financial plan throughout market cycles. They are also designed to ensure that our representatives are motivated and compensated appropriately to provide you the best possible service.*

The disclosure goes on to talk about their compensation being derived more from customer experience and customer loyalty measures than assets under management (that is, sales). It's refreshing.

Repertory

4. Knowledge

Key Questions: Do they know enough to perform the responsibilities of the job? Do they have the skills to perform the mechanics of the job?

Who can help? Learning (HR); communications; management

Here's where we move into the "repertory of the individual" and the world of training. If analysis is undertaken in Gilbert's sequence, it is rare to reach "knowledge" without having identified more pressing issues related to the work environment.

[14]See https://www.fidelity.com/bin-public/060_www_fidelity_com/documents/representative-compensation.pdf.

Millennial Trend In recent years, there has been an interesting swing in methods for delivering knowledge. In the olden days, training happened live in a classroom. Then in the past couple of decades, web-based training (or e-learning) took over. Now I see the pendulum swinging back to live training. The fact of the matter is, the methodology is dictated by what is being taught. Certain topics are well suited for self-paced (asynchronous) study, and some topics are more effectively delivered with participants learning together (synchronous). In any case, the delivery method is a high-class worry when you haven't determined if training is going to help solve your problem. As you see in the examples I present, by the time people contact me, often they have decided (1) that they need training and (2) the methodology they envision. A key part of the performance consultant's job is the reframing technique (presented in Chapter 3), which helps the client unwind their thinking.

---

5. Capacity

Key Questions: Are the employees (literally) able to do the job? Do they have the intelligence, physical ability, personality traits that are required?

Who can help? Recruiting (HR), HR generalists, management

Sometimes, you just have the wrong person in a job. Sometimes, the collective capabilities of a team are not adequate to do a job. However, this is rare.

6. Motives

Key Questions: Are they willing to work for the available rewards?

Who can help? Recruiting (HR); management

Willingness is an interesting question. Motivation is internally driven, whereas incentive is externally driven (Table 2-2). An employee needs to find a reason within himself to work hard in exchange for the payoff. If the economic exchange doesn't make sense for the worker, he will decide at some point to not make that exchange.

Table 2-2. Motivation versus Incentive

	Definition	Source	Examples
Motivation	The reasons that people do things, in the absence of management	Internal	Desire to do a good job. Pride. Work ethic. Love of the work. Other things that we can't imagine.
Incentive	Action taken by management to influence behavior	External	Money, perks, prizes, praise, career growth. The prospect of being punished or laid off.

In considering the question of willingness, consider the image of an underperforming restaurant kitchen worker (Figure 2-3) standing over a deep fryer muttering, "I am not doing this @&()$#!^ for $8 an hour!" Managers can sympathize with this point of view. Doing an entry-level job for a minimal amount of money is a bummer. But let's face it—that same worker who doesn't like making french fries for $8/hour will eventually be unhappy making french fries for $50/hour, especially in the same work environment. Rather than raise wages, the consultant or manager should seek to find the sources of this disgruntlement and underperformance, particularly if it is a condition that is widespread across the kitchen staff. Chances are, modifications to the environment could make the job of fry cook more palatable at any price.

Figure 2-3. An underperforming and disgruntled kitchen worker dropping some french fries into the deep fryer. (Actually, it's the author, happily moonlighting.)

Too often, managers are quick to blame performance deficiencies on the individual. Countless times I have heard managers explain away poor performance with one of these facile, cynical refrains:

- Motivation deficiency: "He doesn't care." "She's lazy."
- Capacity deficiency: "He's useless." "She's stupid."
- Knowledge deficiency: "He doesn't know what the hell he's doing." "She needs more training."

Not only are those assessments likely to be wrong, they are dangerous. As Geary Rummler, a protégé of Gilbert, famously said: "If you pit a good performer against a bad system, the system will win almost every time."

What happens if you proceed as if there is a performance problem with an individual, when really you have a broken system? You send people to pointless, time-consuming, and expensive training. You go around blaming the workers for what is wrong. You lay off and fire people and generally kill morale. No good can come of it. It is always best to assume the best of employees. It's the right thing to do, and it's the most expedient thing to do. The vast majority of employees try hard, want to do a good job, and want to get better. Go with that feeling, management! Work with them, not against them.

The performance consultant contributes by advising managers to avoid these dangerous ways of thinking. Do this by considering other environmental variables in the BEM.

Looking back at the fry cook example, consider the possible conditions in the work environment that have the worker discouraged and underperforming.

Information: Does the cook know what is expected? Does he know what a good french fry looks like and tastes like? Has he seen or heard the feedback from customers and other employees about the quality of the french fries?

Instrumentation: Does the cook have the equipment that will make it possible to consistently create good fried food? What if the fryolator machine does not maintain the oil at the appropriate temperature? What if the oil is dirty and the deep fryer splatters and smokes when fries are down, annoying the employee and putting him in harm's way? What if following the menu specifications yields unpleasing fries?

Incentives: What are the rewards for making consistently excellent fried food? What are the consequences of not consistently producing high-quality output?

We might also look at other factors in the work environment that are under management's purview. What if the supervisor is a jerk? What if the other people in the kitchen dislike the employee? What if the employee just ended a romantic relationship with one of the waitresses?

As you can see, the performance of human beings in the job is the product of all of the six boxes of the BEM. This situation makes it difficult to isolate the impact of training on business results. An axiom helps us to explain that idea. It is the *85 percent rule*.

The 85 Percent Rule

HPT's heritage is research. Since the days of Gilbert, Rummler, and the other trailblazers, great research has been done, much of it by PhDs in the areas of learning transfer, motivation, systems engineering, and the like. For the most part, the measures are confined to the efficacy of training on performers.

One of the most quoted statistics in HPT-land is the 85 percent rule (Figure 2-4): 85 percent of the time, the cause of performance deficiencies is related to environmental factors. Only 15 percent are related to the individual factors, including knowledge. The message? Training alone will rarely solve your problem.

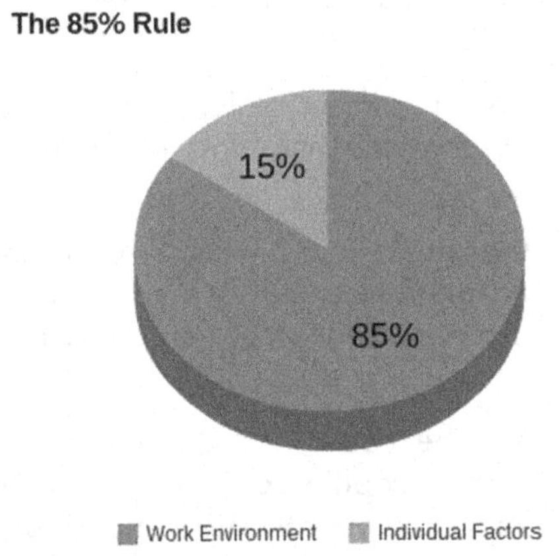

Figure 2-4. The 85 percent rule. Among the factors related to a performance deficiency, 85 percent are related to the work environment, and 15 percent are related to matters of the individual. This statistic is often presented as a fact, but I cannot find any research basis for it.

As lovely and simple as the 85 percent rule is, I'm convinced that it's apocryphal. I have conducted exhaustive Internet searches; I have emailed colleagues; I have asked questions in conference sessions; I have looked for the rule within the works of Gilbert, Rummler, Mager, and other authors to whom the rule is sometimes ascribed. I cannot find a primary source of the rule or a study positing the rule.

Just because it's not proven does not make the 85 percent rule bad. It's consistent with the empirical evidence I've seen in my career, and I will continue to cite it. Why argue? Think of other widely cited statistics that are still useful but may not be 100 percent accurate, such as, "Men think about sex every seven seconds."

Now that we are familiar with the history and ideas of HPT, let's look at what we can learn from the corporate learning practices.

Lessons of Corporate Learning

The world of corporate learning is at once more broad and more specialized than the scope of this book. A learning function includes at least ten different professional disciplines, as represented in the ATD Standards. This book focuses on the performance consulting skill set, with examples and connections to other related activities.

The perspective I present is a reflection of my immersion in the learning field, and the work we do revolves around the improvement of human performance. This book is about having the learning people learn the lessons of agility, and agile people learn the lessons of HPT.

Now let's look at selected terminology, history, and reflections on the common knowledge for the learning profession. We'll start with the ADDIE model, the most popular model applied for the development of training.

The ADDIE Model

The ADDIE (Figure 2-5) model presents five phases and subordinate tasks. It lays out the steps necessary to create solutions that are focused on defined learning objectives that are instructionally sound and thoroughly tested and evaluated.

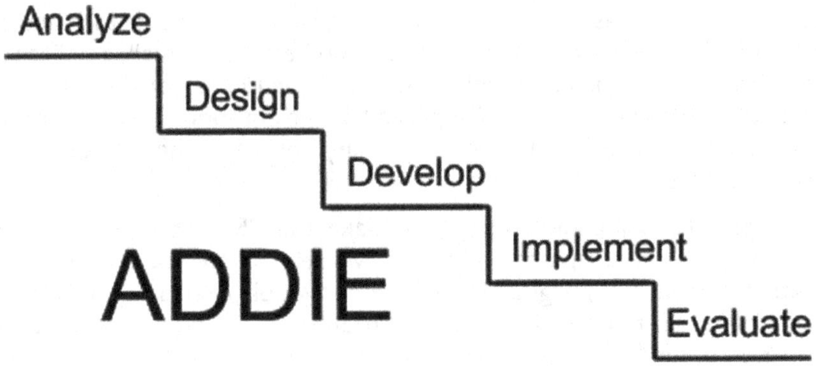

Figure 2-5. ADDIE model. This is the classic instructional design process. It is also classic waterfall. When approached as a linear process, it is incompatible with Agile.

In recent years, ADDIE has come under fire for a variety of reasons, not least of which is its similarity to waterfall. But most learning functions return to it, due to inertia, comfort, or ignorance. There is still goodness in ADDIE, and this is a worthy discussion.

What Is Waterfall? *Waterfall* refers to a sequential design process where each phase is completed before the next one begins. I explain at various points why waterfall is a dirty word to agilists. Here's a summary: The base assumption of waterfall is that large projects can be preplanned months (or years) in advance with some degree of accuracy. The scope and timeline are fixed. Any changes to the plan cause inconvenience, delays, and the invocation of more process. The agilist critique is that it is impossible to know enough before starting a project to plan with the precision that waterfall project management demands. The Agile Manifesto values responding to change over sticking with a plan.

For me, the goodness of ADDIE is its ability to define and organize the skills and practices that a learning function collectively needs to complete a thorough engagement. In ISPI-land, Standards 5–10 match up with ADDIE neatly, with the A split in two.

However, following ADDIE as an end-to-end process causes serious conflict with the rules, spirit, and principles of Agile and Scrum.[15] This remains true even when someone comes up with an iterative framework within each

[15]ADDIE is sometimes presented as a cyclical (not linear) process, where the E loops back to the A. There is no consensus on how the model is presented. The stair-step model I created for Figure 2-6 highlights the notion that ADDIE can reinforce a tendency for folks to make projects too big and too linear.

phase of ADDIE, such as Michael Allen's *successive approximation model* (SAM). The same critique applies to the CPT Performance Standards, which reinforce ADDIE as a process.

There are different practices and models that we adapt to the instructional design process that can help us work around the potential potholes that ADDIE digs in the Agile road. As you address those specific skills and practices, it is worthwhile to talk about whether they contribute to "being Agile" and "doing Scrum." The answers will probably be different for every team. (There are no *best* practices, right?)

It is important to understand ADDIE if you want to understand the learning profession. Now I turn to Don Kirkpatrick, a household name in the learning field.

The Kirkpatrick Model

In my estimation, the work of Donald L. Kirkpatrick (Figure 2-6) is the most discussed in the history of the corporate learning profession. Kirkpatrick's passing in 2014 at age 90 caused a moment of reflection for me. I never met the man, but his ideas have been an ongoing subject of discussion and debate in my professional life.

Figure 2-6. Donald L. Kirkpatrick, inventor of the Kirkpatrick Model of learning evaluation. (Photo courtesy of Wendy Kirkpatrick and Kirkpatrick Partners)

In a dark and smoke-filled office at a place called Chemical Bank, near Wall Street in Manhattan, I was first told of Kirkpatrick. It was in my first months as a training person, after my stint as a school teacher. A senior member of the training staff explained his expectations for me to design the evaluation of a new hire training program. He explained to me the four levels of the Kirkpatrick Model[16]:

> **Level 1: Reaction.** To what degree participants react favorably to the training
>
> **Level 2: Learning.** To what degree participants acquire the intended knowledge, skills, attitudes, confidence, and commitment based on their participation in a training event
>
> **Level 3: Behavior.** To what degree participants apply what they learned during training when they are back on the job
>
> **Level 4: Results.** To what degree targeted outcomes occur as a result of the training event and subsequent reinforcement

The beautiful order and simplicity of the model immediately appealed to me and set off a lengthy moment of clarity. It was then that I first understood the difference between what we do as school teachers (teach people content, for no apparent reason, other than knowing all of the stuff that all educated people know) and what we do in corporate training functions (teach people skills for the purpose of doing a job).

Over the years I participated in a number of task teams charged with implementing a Kirkpatrick-esque system of evaluation. Typically, the task team would spend 6–12 months meticulously crafting a standard Level 1 Evaluation instrument (smile sheet, if you will), before running out of steam and disbanding. This tendency points to the peril of Kirkpatrick—people get so focused on following the levels one at a time, starting with Level 1, that they lose sight of why they were pursuing them in the first place. My experience is supported by copious research that repeatedly shows that almost all organizations have Level 1 instruments in place, but almost none of them have Level 4 systems in place. This reinforces the instinct within training types to expend too much energy thinking first of how to make their classes or e-learnings aesthetically appealing—or, even better, fun!

My conception of why we train people has evolved considerably in the intervening 20 years. I prefer to think of the Kirkpatrick levels as taxonomy, rather than a sequence. All evaluative activities fall into two categories: measures

---

[16]Kirkpatrick Partners, "The Kirkpatrick Model" (2014), retrieved December 9, 2014, from `http://www.kirkpatrickpartners.com/OurPhilosophy/TheKirkpatrickModel/tabid/302/Default.aspx`.

that training people care about and measures that business people care about. Although there is value in the former, we should emphasize the latter.

Today, his family's company, Kirkpatrick Partners, has clarified the presentation of the original concept in the form of the "New World Kirkpatrick Model." This updated version addresses the common critique of the original.

Being misunderstood and oversimplified is a fate that Kirkpatrick shares with Dr. Winston W. Royce, an engineer who "invented" the waterfall method of managing large software development projects. In 1970, Royce wrote a highly influential paper that is often cited as the basis of the *software development life cycle* (SDLC), which today is routinely massacred by Agile development enthusiasts.[17] His paper explicitly denounces the end-to-end, one-way street that is waterfall planning, yet it spawned a multimillion-dollar cottage industry.

Royce and Kirkpatrick both gave the world ideas that were almost too elegant for their own good—so much so that many of those espousing the method only considered the ideas themselves in a superficial manner.

By any measure, Kirkpatrick was a giant in the field of learning and development. His evaluation concept was his dissertation topic in 1959, and it was refined in many articles and books in the ensuing 50 years. To those of us steadfastly pursuing the holy grail of correlating training to business outcomes, he has been a constant inspiration.

The Logical Fallacy of Learning

Post hoc ergo propter hoc is a fancy Latin phrase that defines a logical fallacy translated as "after this, therefore because of this." The fallacious argument is that if X occurs after Y, then Y must have been caused by X.

We see this argument in action often when consulting with clients and business leaders, and we even see it slip into the thinking of learning people. I recently read an otherwise intelligent article that provided a perfect example: employees are not following a procedure, and the assumption is that a lack of knowledge is causing this failure to follow to procedure. Leaping off from there, an elaborate business case follows that if we could just improve retention of learning, improved performance would follow.

Correlating a performance failure ("the employee fails to follow proper customer-service principles and ends up driving a loyal customer away") with poor learning transfer is fallacious, because the root cause of that failure is

[17]W. W. Royce, "Managing the Development of Large Software Systems," Proceedings, WESCON, August 1970, retrieved from http://leadinganswers.typepad.com/leading_answers/files/original_waterfall_paper_winston_royce.pdf.

much more likely to be related to nontraining factors. How many times do we see training promised as a panacea for performance problems? Excellent training is provided to employees, and Kirkpatrick-style multilevel evaluation is used to establish the efficacy of the training. Then, somehow, the performance indicators don't move, and the failure is attributed to a flaw in the training, instead of the business executive who is ultimately accountable for the result. Now we have a situation where not only did the performance *not* improve but the training department is the scapegoat. It's a lose-lose situation.

In Shakespeare's *Julius Caesar,* the nobleman Cassius says to Brutus: "The fault, dear Brutus, is not in our stars, / But in ourselves." We could adapt that notion for an executive to say: "The fault, dear comrades, is not in our supporting staff functions, but in ourselves." As we saw earlier, the point of the BEM is that the causes of employee performance problems are far more likely to be factors that will not be fixed by training. "Before we throw training at a problem," the enlightened business leader continues, "let's make sure that we understand the causes of the performance problem."

Learning professionals, take heed: Seek the causes of the performance issues before moving toward a (very expensive, time-consuming) training solution. Business people don't automatically think this way, so we, as advisors, need to teach them. When training is implemented, a useful metric beyond knowledge transfer would be to see a correlation between the effectiveness of knowledge transfer to the job (Kirkpatrick Level 3, if you will) and performance. Don't make an assumption of root cause. Otherwise, you fall into the trap of *post hoc ergo propter hoc.*

This type of thinking can change the game. The game for the "I ♥ training" contingent has been to drive usage of training, creating the illusion of learning function as indispensable. Training departments struggle to prove that although results are still poor, everyone went to the training and loved it. Closer to the truth: "Results are still poor so we wasted money building training that people went to and liked but clearly didn't work in improving performance."

The game that Gilbert, Rummler, and Harless want us to play is to create worthy performance with as much business value as possible and as little training as possible.

Outside of the cubicle walls of the corporate world, there are learning environments that just allow learning and performance happen naturally. Let's visit Ann Arbor, Michigan.

The Organic Learning Environment

The Ann Arbor Skatepark (Figure 2-7) opened in 2014. It is a $1 million, 30,000-square-foot wonderland of, well, all sorts of things that are great for skateboarders. As described by the City of Ann Arbor website[18]:

> *Skateboarders will enjoy features such as kidney pools from 5 feet to 9.5 feet deep, a snake run, clover and flow bowls, rock ride, and a slappy curb. Landscape features being incorporated into the design include native plants and bioswales and retention areas that exceed standard stormwater requirements.*

Figure 2-7. The Ann Arbor Skatepark. Corporations and youth sports organizations are well advised to consider how kids develop their skills in this organic learning environment.

I can't really describe how cool this place is. On a sunny mild Saturday afternoon, my son joined around 50 kids of all ages (well, every age from 5 to 30, notwithstanding my bruising five-minute foray) having an absolute blast on skateboards, inline skates, and scooters.

[18]City of Ann Arbor, "Skatepark," September 28, 2014, retrieved from `http://www.a2gov.org/departments/Parks-Recreation/play/Pages/Skatepark.aspx`.

What struck me was the park as an organic learning environment. The skater ethos and indeed the park's official etiquette and rules emphasize that there is no structure, no competition, and especially no coaching by parents. I struggle to build even a flimsy metaphor or analogy to suggest how we might create more effective corporate (or for that matter, youth sports) learning environments. There are many clichés to describe the aspirational learning dynamic of the more controlled corporate setting. The clichés become beautiful realities in the skatepark, without a whiff of irony or cynicism.

Forming communities. The vast majority of kids were riding skateboards, with a few on scooters and inline skates. Three of the better scooter riders found each other and began traveling as a group through the park. They would stop together and confer about how to do a trick or navigate the next feature. Nobody had to formally identify them as the best practitioners of their craft or bring them together so they could learn from one another. They just did it.

Raising the bar. A group of four skaters was flying repeatedly over a set of stairs. Clearly, they were among the few that could do the trick, with grabs, ollies, and other variations thrown in. When that trick became easy, they set up their own challenge. They put down a plastic garbage barrel at the top of a ramp and started trying to jump over it on their boards. If these kids were under the direct supervision of a manager, they wouldn't be allowed to move the garbage can, and they would also be less safe practicing a comparable difficult trick using an existing park feature (a cement barrier).

Meaningful coaching and mentoring. For a few minutes, I observed the skateboarding of one young man I'll call the Smooth Skater wearing a Knit Cap on an 80-Degree Day. He was rolling along by himself all around the park, and I was struck by the fluidity of his skating and his occasional tricks. In my eyes, he was the best skater there, but he was by no means a show-off. All of a sudden, Smooth Skater stopped next to a kid half his age, and gave him some coaching. "Hey, Lil' Bro," he seemed to be saying, "you need to get more springiness in your knees as you go over the slopes, like this." Smooth Skater provided a quick demonstration of what he meant by springiness in the knees, and watched as Lil' Bro tried it. Then Smooth Skater showed him how one would apply the springy knees technique on a small slope about five feet away. He tapped Lil' Bro on the chest with the back of his hand and skated away. The whole thing took no more than 15 seconds. Lil' Bro started practicing the springy knee thing, statically at first, then down some easy ramps. It was a beautiful interaction, initiated by someone I'm sure never went to a corporate coaching class and never entered into a formal mentoring agreement with Lil' Bro or anyone else.

An environment of trust, where mistakes are okay. Without a delineated path and dozens of kids doing their own thing in a relatively small space, there were collisions, near collisions, and other mishaps occurring every few seconds. If one kid bumped into or cut off another, they both got up and someone said "Are you okay?" and someone said "Sorry, bro." They shared a fist bump or a laugh (often both) and moved on. You know what I did not see any of, in a full hour of observing the skatepark? Injuries, flaring tempers, hurt feelings, or interventions by authority figures.

How do these things just happen at the skate park, yet they happen only through great effort or divine providence in the large workplace? Is it the design of the environment? Is it the bringing together of like-minded people? Is it the passion? Is it the wider culture of this hobby?

Peter Senge's 1990 book *The Fifth Discipline: The Art and Practice of the Learning Organization,* introduced the concept of the learning organization, and for a decade the idea of applying systems thinking to improve performance launched a thousand meetings and conference presentations. That beautifully descriptive term, "the learning organization," has fallen out of the lexicon of business buzzwords. Let me bring it back: The community of the Ann Arbor Skatepark is a learning organization, the product of a design perfectly coupled with individual capabilities.

Are There Any Drawbacks to HPT?

When I first considered putting this book together, my overall hypothesis was that the HPT people care more about people than the software engineers do, that they understand the human component as being critical to any change.

Indeed, HR functions routinely consider employee satisfaction and levels of engagement and their impact on turnover and productivity. Nonetheless, there are several aspects of HPT that cause trouble for the agilist.

- End to-end waterfall-ness is still prevalent in project management via the ADDIE model, which is well represented in the CPT Performance Standards.
- Practitioners favor extensive analysis, which can be counter to the rapid cycles of Agile and Scrum.
- Even with the best of intentions and rigorous discipline, one cannot reasonably expect to demonstrate measurable business impact on even half of training projects. Alas, sometimes training is just training.
- Some of the language and heritage of HPT seem (ironically) to dehumanize employees: the idea that their performance can be "engineered"; the legacy of Skinnerian behaviorism, which conjures up images of rats and pigeons doing things for food; and the continual reference to employees as "performers," especially in the old videos from the 1970s and 1980s.

Nonetheless, agilists can learn a lot from HPT. When I introduce the agile performance improvement system in Chapter 6, you will see that the skills of the performance consultant can make agile frameworks work better. As a product owner, the consultant applies rigorous analysis that keeps the focus on defining outcomes and considering the importance of human performance in team efficacy.

So What?

Decades after Harless and Gilbert told us what to focus on, carrying the torch is still much easier said than done.

There is no end to making the case for defining demonstrable performance improvement and not squandering resources on the development of useless training. When in doubt, remember Gilbert's law of training: "The very best training is always the shortest training."[19]

We must seek true partnership with clients to help them see how our work can support their goals. If we cannot consistently demonstrate value and focus on outcomes, our function will cease to exist.

This chapter surveyed the history and concepts of human performance improvement. The next chapter will examine how the performance consultant applies the lessons learned in this chapter.

[19]T. F. Gilbert, *Human Incompetence: Confessions of a Psychologist* (Atlanta: Performance Management Publications, 2011).

CHAPTER

3

The Performance Consultant's Toolkit

Over and over, we shall see that only when we have made a proper analysis of accomplishments and their measures will we have any sensible reason to concern ourselves with behavior.

—Thomas F. Gilbert[1]

As an agilist working out of an internal support function, the performance consultant is the product owner. The performance consultant learns from Scrum, SAFe, and other Agile frameworks the importance of backlog refinement and prioritization, so that items of the highest value to the customer are done first. Conversely, the product owner in traditional Agile fields such as software engineering can learn from the performance consultant. The *what* of the product owner is clear, but there is a gap in the Agile thought leadership around the *how.*[2] The performance consultant's toolkit as presented in this chapter provides direction for how to field requests, how to interact with customers, and how to approach analysis of human performance.

[1]Thomas F. Gilbert, *Human Competency: Engineering Worthy Performance*, Tribute ed. (Washington, DC: International Society for Performance Improvement, 1996), p. 72.
[2]Product owners can also turn to the fields of product management and sales for methods for interacting with customers.

Gilbert's quote provides insight into the performance consultant's mindset in doing the *how*. Many performance consultants began as instructional designers and human resources generalists. We were all conditioned to focus on behavioral objectives. A model of performance[3] is built, and training is developed around the behaviors described in the model. What is missing most of the time, and Gilbert pointed this out to us 40 years ago, was that analysis of "accomplishments and their measures" (that is, human performance) needs to be nailed down before we start talking about what behaviors support that performance. The behavioral lens focuses on the learner, and the performance lens focuses on the end-user.

In the world of corporate learning, everything that happens after a work item is undertaken by a team is generally considered instructional design. This skill set includes design, development, implementation, and evaluation. Depending on the size of the organization, these areas can all be specialties, but generally speaking, experienced instructional designers are proficient at all of these activities.

The performance consultant uses analytical techniques to establish a performance outcome and recommends solutions that address the causes of a performance gap. The output of the consultant's work, recommendations to improve performance, will find a place in the backlog, to be prioritized according to its potential value to the customer.

This chapter introduces the skill set of the performance consultant, which includes:

- Responding to requests
- Reframing the conversation
- Identifying the performance gaps
- Determining the cause
- Recommending solutions

I illustrate each of these activities with axioms and anecdotes. The reader will see how effective consulting is a combination of interpersonal and analytical skills.

---

[3]A model of performance is documentation that describes standards for behaviors and other environmental support that a person needs to exhibit to do a job. Most workers and managers are familiar with various presentations of the behavioral component of performance. These include competency models, job descriptions, procedure manuals, step-action tables, and the like.

Responding to Requests

Beware the solution in search of a problem.

—Bob's Axiom No. 1

Before we make the decision to undertake a project, the performance consultant assists the client with front-end analysis.[4] Front-end analysis is the work that we do before undertaking a project, looking at data that describe the current situation. The better the front-end analysis, the better the odds of providing a solution that enables improved performance. Although our proactive analysis routinely aligns efforts with business strategy, most work comes to us by way of specific requests, putting us in a reactive mode. It is important to be able to effectively field and respond to these requests from colleagues.

When someone approaches their education or human resources liaison with a solution in mind, they typically do so without examining the problem in terms of performance outcomes. The requester is not trying to waste anyone's time; they just do not think the way that performance consultants do. That's why we are here.

Without solid front-end analysis, the consultant risks putting the business in a position where they are providing a solution that does not address the problem. What good is it to train a cook to fry an egg, when what we really need is to satisfy the craving for sweets?

Let's start from the beginning. How the consultant responds to a request sets the stage for the interactions that follow.

Select a Response Mode

Establish some good will before getting fancy.

—Bob's Axiom No. 2

Performance consultants often take one of several approaches in responding to a training request:

- Fulfilling the request as stated
- Empowering the requester
- Deflecting the request

[4]When referring to the people to whom service is provided, HPT people usually say "client," and Agile people usually say "customer." Throughout this book, consider the two terms interchangeable.

About the word *training* Most people in my profession have purged their vocabulary of this word, but many outside of it have not. Euphemisms include *learning, education, performance support, intervention, course*, and *curriculum*. There are nuanced distinctions among these terms, but sometimes the word *training* is the right one. *Training* means to teach someone a repeatable, rote skill to a specified standard. Teaching a dog to fetch a stick or a cashier to ring up groceries are examples where *training* is the correct word. If you are gathering a team for four hours in a classroom with a goal of getting them to trust one another, I would not call that *training*. Making people read and sign off on corporate compliance rules? I wouldn't call that *training* either; I would call it *memorization*. There is still a place for the word training when used precisely. In this book, I apply a flexible usage of the word, which splits the difference between how the training person uses it and how other people use it.

There is merit to these three response modes, but generally they are flawed because they assume that the analysis by the requester is robust.

Fulfilling the request as stated. This is known as "order-taking." In Classic Scenario I that follows, the consultant investigates the suggested training solution from Bunkysoft, shepherding the acquisition of a training course through the internal procurement process and ensuring that employees are scheduled or directed to take the training. There are numerous benefits to this approach. Efficiently bringing the training courses in house demonstrates goodwill and responsiveness on the part of the learning partner. It also (temporarily, at least) relieves the client of having to worry about the situation. In addition, approving requests without scrutiny provides an opportunity to create workflow efficiencies that lead to impressive yet meaningless learning metrics like employee training hours and hours of training produced. Focusing on front-end analysis and crafting a holistic solution in response can cause the production factory to slow down. Practicing an Agile method such as Scrum, discussed in detail in Chapter 4, will ensure the prioritization of those backlog items that potentially show the most immediate value to the customer.

Empowering the requester. This is also known as "giving permission." Here the education person will give the requester permission to pursue a training solution on his own. The basic thinking is: If you are sure about your analysis, and you think training is the solution, then go for it. The benefit to this approach is that the business partner can pursue the training without being encumbered by gatekeeping processes of the training department or corporate policy. We find this behavior enticing because it empowers the requester and preserves precious production capacity for other high-priority efforts. The risk is that the training the requester suggests may do nothing to improve the performance of the humans doing the job. Another risk is that the requester spends a lot of money hiring the vendor to give the training to the users. You know that giving permission is telling them, "Go ahead—it's your money."

Deflecting the request. This is known as "putting it in the backlog." The learning partner will make a conscious decision about how helpful to be. Sometimes she will decline to assist based on some overall mandate to focus on other predetermined matters, or she will cite some long list of projects that are already identified as more important. In terms of Agile, this is telling them you will "put it in the backlog."

After you "put it in the backlog" a product backlog item might end up on any of several alternative pathways. It might become a blockbuster project, if it has a great case for providing value to the customer. Or the item might never rise to the top of the priority list. Usually, if you add an item to the backlog after minimal discovery, you have a chuckle over it: "Yeah, he wants us to design and deliver a five-day training class about Confucianism as the pathway to software wisdom. I told him we'd 'put it in the backlog.' Ha ha ha!"

"Putting it in the backlog" will almost always be received as unhelpful by the client. This is not good for the future of your relationship or your career. In the long run it will reduce the chances of receiving any future requests from that person, thus reducing your workload and lessening your potential relevance at the company. Being an outcome-focused, helpful, and trusted advisor to executives is a matter of survival. When things get tough with the economy, the big companies are looking for places to trim the fat. Showing that you contribute to improving the performance of the workforce is the best way to stay off of a list.

It's still much too common a notion that there is implicit value in producing and deploying training content. Delivering new courses, measuring reaction (Kirkpatrick Level 1, see Chapter 2), and counting course completions only prove that money has been spent. Showing that money has been spent without showing actual business value labels your work as simply "cost."

While there are benefits to each of these response modes, none are satisfactory. Each provides what the client expects in fulfillment of an explicit request, but none of them actually strengthen the partnership between the consultant and the business.

The effective professional consultant employs a fourth response mode: focusing on business results over dutiful implementation. Requests usually originate unconnected to business results, but the consultant sets up a transition to outcomes-based discussion by considering the request type.

Consider the Request Type

Training requests come from a good place.

—Bob's Axiom No. 3

All requests fall into one of four categories. I introduce these terms to describe them:

- Legitimation
- Grassroots
- Emergent analysis
- Executive

The thinking and approach for each is different. Later in this chapter, you will see the consultant at work, navigating classic scenarios that elucidate each of the four.

"Legitimation requests" seek to convert content (training developed in the field or purchased from a vendor) and into an official course. This situation can involve a range of support, which could include uploading the course to the learning management system, polishing the piece of content with professional instructional design, developing a scalable delivery capacity around a course, or all three. Some program managers in the learning function do not like legitimation requests because they put the learning function in a position where they must allocate resources to professionalizing the instructional design or finding a strategic justification for the content. On the contrary, these projects are potentially labor-saving efforts for the learning function, and supporting them potentially provides a lot of bang for the buck. Along the way, I can do my front-end analysis, ex post facto, and truly legitimate the training by making it focused on enabling improved performance. To a performance improvement person, "I need help putting a training together" sounds like the beginning of a beautiful partnership.

"Grassroots requests" come from the field, accommodating a team- or domain-level need. This is the most common type of request, often focusing on the support of an initiative. From that standpoint, these requests are enticing, because the requester is deeply embedded in the nuts and bolts of the business and close to the work. Often these situations present opportunities to find a straight line between the focus of the initiative and the performance output of individuals and teams. If the initiative is sponsored by an executive, then the consultant can readily find strategic alignment. If not, there is still usually a possibility of monetizing the performance value of training. In my business, I like to have perfect strategic alignment, but in reality, just making a connection between the effort and some result is pretty good.

"Emergent analysis requests" are proactively proposed as the consultant identifies patterns and performance opportunities. The performance consultant enters any situation with an open mind. Hypotheses may develop, but the conclusions are based on analysis of empirical evidence. Although the methods of a practitioner may not always be wholly valid, what comes out of the analysis is closer to the truth than other sources of information. Sometimes the consultant, as an objective third party, is the person on whom the burden to share the truth falls.

About the validity of methods We do the best we can to make the data analysis valid, but not at the expense of expediency. As an agilist, I mine and analyze data just enough to provide face validity on which to base decisions. The extensive analytical methods that you see from the world of industrial and organizational psychology provide rigor but often constitute overkill.

"Executive requests" come straight from the leader of a business unit, who is typically the sponsor or stakeholder. A request from an executive obviously carries more weight than one from anyone else, due to the expected strategic alignment and the accountability associated with the relationship. However, the odds of the solution-based request being off-base are at least as great as for requests from the field. Happily, touch points with an executive are wonderful opportunities to explicitly discuss and collaborate on holistic, strategic approaches that focus on delivering value to the organization.

We may be busy, we may have high priorities, and we may have the business executive on speed dial, but we still have an obligation to respond appropriately to requests. The winning response mode comes from a desire to help managers focus on outcomes that support their goals, before we talk in detail about a training solution. The first step in shifting the conversation from the latter to the former is the reframing discussion.

Reframing the Conversation

Don't forget why they called you in the first place.

—Bob's Axiom No. 4

Saying "no" to a request is damaging to the trusted relationship you have built up over time. No is not the answer; helping the customer look at the request in a different way is good consulting. This is *reframing*. Instead of starting with the solution, we will initiate a discussion that looks at what the business situation is and what capability[5] needs exist.

About the term reframing The reframing discussion technique was given to us by Dana Gaines Robinson and James C. Robinson in their wonderful book called *Performance Consulting*, which was first published in 1996.[6] A reframing asks the requester to look at the business problem from a performance point of view. In the book the authors divide all requests into reactive and proactive. Three of the four Classic Scenarios to follow are reactive situations, where the consultant is reacting to a specific request. *Classic Scenario III* is a proactive effort by the consultant that leads to emergent analysis.

As a liaison between the learning department and business executives, I regularly field requests for specific training classes. The majority of the time, the client provides the request in response to a business problem. However, the training solution that they suggest will not help them fix their problem. In some cases the client may even establish learning objectives based on the behaviors they want to see. But failure to link the objectives to a performance outcome will put the project at risk of wasting time and missing the real opportunity.

Holding a successful reframing conversation with a client requires significant practice and involves many nuances. Let us look now at Classic Scenario I. Notice how the performance consultant executes the reframing conversation to shift attention away from the solution and toward a focus on the business problem at hand.

Classic Scenario I: Legitimation Request

> *Only in rarest of circumstances will training alone adequately address a performance problem.*
>
> —Bob's Axiom No. 5

[5]By *capability*, we mean the total skill set that the workers possess—all of the performance they are able to deliver. It's more than behavior. As Gilbert showed (Chapter 2), work environment factors contribute heavily to enabling performance.

[6]Dana Gaines Robinson and James C. Robinson, *Performance Consulting*, 2nd ed. (San Francisco: Berrett-Koehler, 2008).

This email is typical of legitimation requests that come to me on a weekly basis.

> *To: Bob Winter*
>
> *From: William Jones*
>
> *Subject: Bunkysoft Training*
>
> *Hi Bob,*
>
> *I was given your name as a contact so I hope you can either assist or point me in the right direction...*
>
> *We have a new distributed team (hence online training*[7] *may be better) and are in the process of planning a new development project on a platform that none of the team members have any knowledge of. The platform in question is Bunky, and they have some virtual training available (see descriptions at* `Bunkysoft.com`*) but I wanted to reach out to see how we can get this training set up for the team. From what I've heard, some of the teams have already done similar training and indicated that they got some value from it. We want to track that people have taken the training, and we want all new hires to take the class going forward.*
>
> *Any insight appreciated,*
>
> *Will*

Let's look at what Will asked for, as this will color our approach with him.

Craft an Initial Response

> *Always acknowledge and respect a request.*
>
> —Bob's Axiom No. 6

I know right away that I do not want to make any decisions on this matter via email. My goal is to acknowledge the request and suggest a face-to-face meeting. I proceed with an eye toward reframing the conversation as one about

[7]I realize you haven't even read the email in its entirety yet, much less heard my analysis, but I have to point out something in this email that I love. Will is unambiguous about wanting a training course, which is fine. But he speculates on the methodology ("online") before he has told me anything other than the fact that he has a "new" team. You have to respect the request, but this positioning is a reminder of why people like Will need me. I can help here.

performance rather than training. If things go well, we will discuss the situation over the course of several meetings and several emails. I want to set the stage for the conversations that will follow. I position myself as helpful, competent, and curious to know more.

> *From: Bob Winter*
>
> *To: William Jones*
>
> *Subject: RE: Bunky training*
>
> *Hi Will,*
>
> *Thanks for reaching out. I am not familiar with Bunky or the available training, but I can help you evaluate them. I would also like to talk through your plans to help create the most effective learning experience, which could include this Bunkysoft training and likely some other structured activities as well. Additionally, we can talk through administrative items (such as scheduling and tracking) with which we can assist.*
>
> *Let me know if you'd like to meet, and we can set up some time to discuss all of this.*
>
> *Bob*

The following week we meet. The opening moments of the conversation are about respecting the request and establishing rapport. I want to find out all about Will's intentions with the Bunky training.

> *Bob: I understand you want to bring in training on the Bunky tool for your all of your employees. Is that right?*
>
> *Will: Yes. We are very eager to get everyone trained on Bunky. I have been looking at different options, and I like the webinar training that Bunkysoft offers. They call it "virtual training." I talked to the salesperson over there last week. I figure the virtual training will cost about $400 per person for a full day, which sounds reasonable to me. Multiply that times 800 people, and the whole thing will cost around $320,000. I have that money in the budget, so we have no problems there.*
>
> *Bob: So you want to bring in the training from Bunkysoft then?*
>
> *Will: That's correct.*

Bob:And you said in one of your emails that you also looked the courses offered by the Giant IT Training company (GITT)?

Will: I did. Overall, I looked into five or six training vendors. The GITT training seems very good also, but it's considerably more expensive than any of the others. Overall, I like the Bunkysoft training the best. It covers everything you could want to know about Bunky. A couple of our guys took the virtual training, and they said that it was really good.

Bob: Wow, it sounds like you have done your homework. I looked up Bunky as well after I got your email, and the training looked like it should be pretty good.

Will: Excellent. I'm glad you like it as well.

Bob:Tell me more about the audience. Which roles or teams or whatever need to take the training? How many different sites are we talking about?

And so it goes. I'm supportive and helpful, and we haven't yet discussed whether the training is a good idea. I continue along this discussion thread for some time until I see an opening to shift from talking about the training situation to talking about the business situation.

Will: So I really want to get everyone trained on Bunky by March 15, which is five weeks from now. I think we can do that.

Bob: March 15. Okay, that sounds doable. What happens on March 15?

Will:What happens on March 15? What do you mean?

Bob:Why do you want to finish the training by March 15? Is that the day that everyone has to start using Bunky, or something?

Will: No. My goal is to get the training done as soon as possible, before annual budget planning season starts. I get really tied up with the budget starting in April. If we push it, I think we can get everyone trained up in five weeks.

Now we're getting somewhere. If I was in order-taking mode, I would have potentially signed my education team up for a five-week fire drill. I don't mind rallying my team around a deadline, but Will's deadline is arbitrary and pointless. Further in the conversation, I learn the tool is going to be rolled out in phases over many months.

Bob: You know what is really helpful sometimes? We can try to time the training so that people get it right before or after they start using the tool.

Will: Of course. That's a great idea.

So, I'm still with him, pounding through the details of his request. In suggesting the staggered rollout, we provide the training "just in time." This approach will be more effective, without costing any more money. In my estimation, Will is still not ready to talk about outcomes, but the discussion cues an avalanche of potential areas of inquiry (and Will's somewhat predictable responses).

Bob: How many people know how to use Bunky now?

Will: The tools team plus about five pilot testers are all up to speed. I'd say a dozen people altogether.

Bob: How proficient are these dozen people with the Bunky tool now?

Will: I'd say we're all pretty comfortable with it at this point.

Bob: How did you all learn how to use it?

Will: How did I learn it? The whole tools team attended a one-hour demo from the engineering manager at Bunkysoft. Then we just sort of figured it out.

Bob: Could others learn it the same way? If you learned it after a one-hour demo, why do you think others will require a full day of training?

Will: Hmmm. I never thought of it that way.

Bob: Do you have people who are proficient enough at the tool that they could teach or coach others?

Will: Yes. I think so.

Bob: What other support would you like to provide the employees besides the online training?

Will: I had not really thought about that yet.

Bob: Are there free resources, like videos or articles that we could leverage?

Will: Oh yeah. Erin is already compiling a spreadsheet of useful videos and articles.

Even in this condensed transcription of the initial response, you see that the consultant is taking his time, building trust by processing the request professionally while collecting clues and looking for an opportunity to gracefully shift the conversation.

Shift the Conversation

> *Telling your clients to focus first on outcomes can cause a massive disconnect when your title has "education" or "training" in it.*
>
> —Bob's Axiom No. 7

Lead the conversation to focus on outcomes or results at the appropriate juncture.

> *Bob: Okay. Based on what I am hearing, I suggest we look at a plan that provides the programmers with the virtual training in the same time period that they are getting access to Bunky.*
>
> *Will: That makes sense.*
>
> *Bob: So I was wondering. How did you guys come to select Bunky anyway?*

If I had started the meeting with this question, Will would have kicked me out of his office: "I asked you in here to talk about getting training. I did not bring you here to tell you everything about my business!" Now that I have sown some goodwill, I am hoping (and expecting) that Will will lay out the business case for Bunky. And he does.

> *Will: For years we have been having a problem of connecting applications from different platforms efficiently and reliably. I have two whole teams, 22 employees, who do nothing but deal with integration code. Most of that code is bug-ridden crap, and my guys are ready to kill themselves. Well, Bunky is a cloud-based PAAS that connects applications using an integration platform as a programming interface. This makes it so that there does not have to be as much integration code written.*
>
> *Bob: That sounds excellent. I can only imagine how things would improve if you did not have to spend as much effort writing and maintaining the integration code.*

Note here that I am starting to get to a point in the conversation where not only do I not know what the heck he is talking about, but I do not even really know what the heck *I* am talking about.[8] Platforms? Integration code? It is gibberish, but I can work through it. Do your homework, be curious, and you can be conversant in any topic. People who are good at their jobs love talking about their work, and Will is no exception. If it is at all possible to have an interesting conversation about integration platforms, Will is about the best chance I am ever going to get. He is smart, he is an expert, he is an executive at a big company, and right now, to me, he is sooooooo interesting!

> *Bob: So let me get this straight. Is the big thing that you want to reduce the overhead of creating the integration code? Or are you looking for greater system stability? Does Bunky create efficiencies with other tools that are being used? Or something else?*
>
> *Will: The short answer is we want our engineers to spend less time on creating and maintaining the integration code. The backstory is interesting. Let me tell you all about it . . .*

Now we have Will on a roll. He sparks up, feeding me chapter and verse on the business case. Knowing all of that new context, I can move back into the training conversation with a better understanding. As we talk it through, Will shares more relevant facts. The programmers need to be highly proficient with the tool, but testers and others do not. The testers do not need the same training; they need less. They just need awareness. Actually, they might not even need the formal training. Some of the people who learned Bunky earlier learned it by spending a half hour with someone who knew it and then figured it out by playing with it.[9]

---

[8]Years ago, I was an instructional designer at a large bank. The subject-matter expert started talking about things I didn't understand. I said, "Well, I'm not sure I understand everything you are saying. I'm new to banking." In response, the expert gave me some great advice. "I've been doing this for ten years, and I still feel new to banking. You won't get very far with that as an excuse."

[9]The inspiration for that paragraph was my experience talking to agilists at the ScrumAlliance Global Scrum Gathering in 2014. Real engineers in the field have great learning agility. They constantly have to learn new tools in order to remain relevant and, frankly, they do not want to spend days, or even hours, going to training every time a new tool is introduced. This is a key source of resistance (or worse) that I hear from engineers with respect to training. If one person gets trained on a new tool, that person can go back and tutor the entire team very quickly. Who has time to wait around for a training class to materialize, and then go to a class? Makes sense to me. The days of engineers going to training to learn which buttons to press on an application are quickly heading into the rear view mirror. If you need to go to an 8-hour class to learn how to use an application, it must not be a very well-designed application.

So this is how you reframe a training request. What started off as an order-taking situation has turned into a consulting opportunity. I am building a relationship with this manager. I am talking about the outcomes of the initiative. I am starting to look at the most expedient way to enable engineers to use the new tool. Even though this manager is sharp and well accomplished, I still need to guide him through the thinking on this matter. Because our partnership will mature as we go along, the consulting will go faster next time.

Holding a successful reframing conversation with a client requires significant practice and involves many nuances. When successful, the reframing conversation, such as the one I had with Will about Bunky training, sets the stage for the *gap analysis* to follow.

Identifying the Performance Gap

> *Defer identifying a solution until the performance problem is identified.*
>
> —Bob's Axiom No. 8

Performance consulting is not just about the consultative conversation, but the analysis that supports the recommendations.[10] There are many analytical methods used to determine the need before undertaking a project or to measure worth of a new product feature. You will see expanded treatment of several of those techniques in Chapter 7. Here we review the concept of gap analysis with a brief example.

Figure 3-1 shows the formula for determining the need, also known as the performance gap. The performance gap is the difference between current and desired performance.

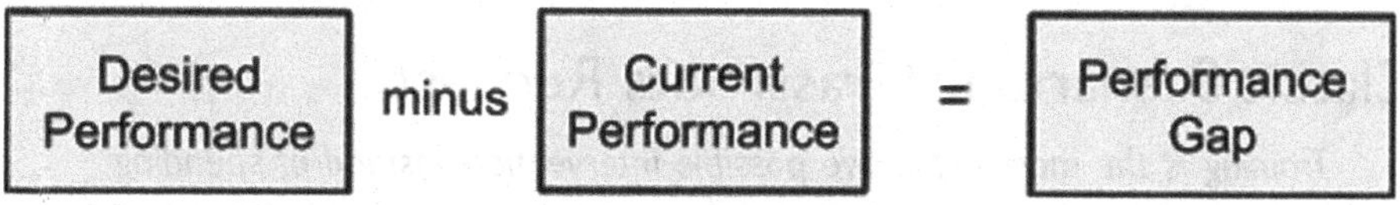

Figure 3-1. The formula for determining a performance gap

Desired performance describes the performance that the management wants to see. Current performance describes what is going on now. The difference between the two is called the performance gap. The work done to determine the performance gap is called gap analysis.

[10]In ISPI language, this is called *determining the need or opportunity.*

Again we must mind the distinction between measures of behavior and performance. Behavior is measured by observation of a worker doing something. Performance is measured by quantifiable work output by an individual or a team. Table 3-1 shows the distinction.

Table 3-1. The difference between behavioral and performance gap. Behavior is an observation. Performance is quantified

	Behavior	Performance
Success measures	Supervisor or trainer observation of an employee properly preparing a fried egg over easy.	Time from when a waitress takes a breakfast order until it is served to the customer
Current	Cook cannot prepare a fried egg over easy if his life depended on it	14 minutes
Desired	Prepare a fried egg over easy, such that the albumin is solidified but the yolk is liquid and unbroken.	10 minutes
Gap	The ability to cook the fried egg	4 minutes

In the example here, the performance is related to the efficacy of the entire system. The ability of a cook to prepare a fried egg is only one factor among many behavioral and other systemic ones that contribute to delivering the egg to a patron within a specified standard of time.

Let's look a second classic scenario, this time in the form of a grassroots request. In response, the consultant demonstrates how to transition the conversation from talking about a vendor training class to identifying a holistic, outcomes-focused approach.

Classic Scenario II: Grassroots Request

Training is the most expensive possible intervention. Instead of spending tons of money making everyone take some pointless and aggravating training, how about we throw a big party?

—Bob's Axiom No. 9

From: Rhonda Zizzle

To: Bob Winter

Subject: Training on Testing Best Practices

Hi Bob—

The support organization needs to communicate the best practices of using our development mainframe systems to our internal developers. Your name was given to me as someone who might be able to assist. We would like to release a one-hour LMS-style course[11] *to our internal developers. We have drafted some of the content, but I want to make sure it is in the right format for a course.*

Are you able to assist with creating a class, and is there a formal process we should follow?

Rhonda

I find myself in the familiar position of not being sure what this person is talking about. That's okay. I can do some rudimentary research on the one sentence she gives me about the topic area. As with Will, Rhonda is coming to me with a solution in mind, a training course, and she wants help developing the course with a specific delivery method. My job as the performance consultant is to reframe the conversation, setting aside the focus on the solution long enough to talk about the problem at hand. I have no idea what the problem is here. All I read is that they need to "communicate the best practices."

Name the Problem

Identify the actual business problem, not just the so-called training need.

—Bob's Axiom No. 10

[11]With all due respect to the (unnamed) requester here, "LMS-style course" is not a curious way to describe a learning intervention. For readers who do not know, LMS stands for *learning management system*. An LMS is the gigantic application that houses and delivers training courses and maintains records of all of the classes that everyone has taken. A charitable description of a typical LMS would be an inelegant monstrosity that causes many headaches. Sometimes when I'm browsing the Internet, the browser will serve up ads that ask "Do you hate your LMS?" In some environments people equate LMS with e-learning. So in the case of Rhonda Zizzle, she meant that she wanted an e-learning. But to think of a training course as being created in the "LMS style" is to picture Frank Lloyd Wright designing a house in the "cinderblock style."

Along with good learning agility, curiosity is a key characteristic of someone who is cut out to be a performance consultant. Curiosity (and a little research) is fuel for redirecting the conversation. Before responding to Rhonda, I reach out to a few of my engineering friends to get an idea of what is going on. Apparently, there are two mainframe systems on which QA engineers test new code. These systems crash from time to time. When one of the systems crashes, there is a disruption. A typical disruption affects 50 testers, who cannot do their work for one hour. Maybe this is what is happening on those occasions when I see 20 engineers playing human Pac-Man in the aisles of the cubicle farm?

The implication here is that if people don't follow the "best practices," then the testing can overwhelm the system and cause it to crash. This is potentially a training person's dream. If the absence of a certain behavior (the testing best practices) causes systems to crash, causing a performance problem (a quantifiable loss in productivity), which we can quantify, then *voilà*, we can align training directly with a productivity gain. That's the beginning of my idea around measurement, anyway. I want to find a way to quantify the impact of the problem.

Quantify the Problem

> *Attempt to use existing measures before inventing new ones*
>
> —Bob's Axiom No. 11

Let's try a little math to calculate the cost of the problem.

Productivity loss for one crash

= 50 engineers x 1 hour x $150/hour (cost of an engineer)

= $7,500 in lost productivity per crash

Total productivity loss for the duration of this problem

= $7,500 x number of crashes

Wow—this is a real, live hypothesis! If we can reduce these crashes through changed engineer behavior, we could really be saving a quantifiable (and potentially huge) amount of lost productivity.

I write back to Rhonda. While I've done some research and thinking, I am not going to mention it in my email reply. I will save it for our in-person discussion. Remember the Agile principle: "The most efficient and effective method of conveying information to and within a development team is face-to-face conversation."[12]

> *From: Bob Winter*
>
> *To: Rhonda Zizzle*
>
> *Subject: RE: Training on Testing Best Practices*
>
> *Hi Rhonda—*
>
> *Yes, I can help you. I'll set up a short call for next week to go through everything?*
>
> *Bob*

Later that week, Rhonda and I meet. I am eager to see if my hypothesis is correct. I lead her through the reframing conversation much as I did with Will in Classic Scenario I. I'm delighted when Rhonda reveals an extensive spreadsheet that contains a comprehensive log of all of the crashes that have occurred over the past year.[13] The log details which system went down, for how long, and how many engineers had to delay their tests as a result. On another tab, she has a list of 20 best practices that she would like to include in the training.

> *Bob: So, let me see if I have this straight. If you could just get the engineers to follow these 20 best practices*[14] *for testing, then there would not be any more crashes?*
>
> *Rhonda: Well, not exactly.*
>
> *Bob: Okay.*

[12]From the Principles behind the Agile Manifesto. Read more about them in Chapter 4. `http://agilemanifesto.org/principles.html`.
[13]I won't digress too much on the format of the log itself, but let's just say that this was about the most bad-assed spreadsheet in the history of spreadsheets. She had formulas, feeds, charts, and pivot tables. I'm not easily impressed, but I dig pivot tables.
[14]Rhonda calls them *best practices*, but essentially they are rules. In the interest of developing rapport and not sounding like a smarty pants, I choose not to split hairs on this point.

Rhonda: We have done some root cause analysis in our investigations, and we found that there are some instability and capacity factors in the systems themselves that cause some of the crashes. We now have a plan to install three additional systems. The new systems are more stable, and each one will only need to carry a portion of the testing load that the original two did.

Bob: Okay. How often do these crashes happen now?

Rhonda: We have had 72 outages in the past year, including one big one yesterday.

Bob: So can you tell me how many of the crashes are caused by these system issues and how many are caused by engineers not following the best practices?

Rhonda: Well, of the 72 crashes, we estimate that 6 were caused by bad engineering behavior.

Further discussion reveals that for the six crashes caused by engineers behaving badly, they collectively involved a failure to follow just 3 of the 20 engineering behaviors.

Monetize the Value of Consulting

Consider what will happen if nothing is done.

—Bob's Axiom No. 12

Fast forward to the implementation. We ended up creating training on the three "best practices" that were causing the outages. The course turned out to be only 15 minutes long. Additionally, we found that only QA people, not all engineers, needed to take the training.

Here is where we see the value of consulting in and of itself. Table 3-2 shows the difference in training expense as requested and as we delivered it.

Table 3-2. Total Cost of Training. Every time you put out new training, there are variable expenses of creating the training and of taking people away from work to take the training. (Note: This calculation does not include the fixed costs of having a training department.)

	As Requested	As Delivered
Number of employees trained	800	400
Time to take training	1 hour	0.25 hour
Value of an engineer's time	$150/hr	$150/hr
Cost of time for employees to take training x $150/hour	1 hour x 800 employees x $150/hr = $120,000	0.25 hour x 400 employees x $150/hour = $15,000
Cost to develop the training at $90/hour*	100 hours labor x $90/hour = $9,000	25 hours labor x $90/hour = $2,250
(100 hours of labor per 1 hour of training)		
TOTAL COST OF TRAINING	**$129,000**	**$17,250**

**These cost/hour averages refer to full-time employees with benefits, and they are rough blend.*

A word about repurposed labor Although the key number here is the total cost of training in the "As Delivered" column ($17,250), the difference between the cost of training as delivered versus as requested is also a benefit to the business, in the form of repurposed labor. The repurposed labor is the value of engineers' time *not* spent taking the longer version of the training, and the value of the instructional designer's time *not* used developing the longer version of the training.

In this scenario, we are in a position to calculate the return on investment (ROI).

> ROI = (Benefit of solution) minus (total cost of developing and implementing solution)

The benefit of the solution (avoidance of outages caused by bad engineering behavior) = avoidance of 6 outages/year x $7,500 lost productivity/outage = $45,000.

> This gives us a nifty ROI calculation.
>
> = $45,000 – $17,250
>
> = $27,750

So, we see that there is benefit to doing the training. If we had pursued the suggested course of action (one hour of training for all 800 engineers), we would have spent more money in creating and delivering the training ($129,000) than we would have gained in the avoidance of engineering-caused outages ($45,000).

These calculations are rough estimates for illustrative purposes. Realistically, being able to make even this good of a calculation is rare, but it is good enough to make the business case for training. My goal is to always identify business outcomes, quantifying it if possible. Any metric of this sort is preferable to having a goal of "everyone needs to take the training."

A giant caveat accompanies this whole scenario. The provision of training alone will not prevent the outages. Based on my observations, most managers at all levels miss this point or choose not to deal with it. This is a **major** problem, which I mention repeatedly through this book and in my work life. Along with the training recommendation, I suggested that some other activities will need to be undertaken by the business. For the behavior change to stick, and for the training to translate into a performance improvement, the business will need to:

- Communicate the expectations for following the best practices
- Encourage managers to reinforce the message at the team level
- Install a procedure for following up with engineers who have caused outages or who violate the best practices
- Provide transparency with the people about the scope of the problem, what is being done about it, and progress that is being made

It is the consultant's duty to help the manager look at problems in a systemic way and define holistic solutions. The ability to do so is an existential one for us learning people. I repeat: If we can't establish some sense of value beyond learning metrics such as usage (cheeks in seats) and favorable reaction (smile sheets), then when it's time to make business decisions during a recession, it becomes really easy to make the case that the learning function adds no value.

Determining the Cause

Address the cause of the problem.

—Bob's Axiom No. 13

In *Classic Scenario II*, the cause of the system outages fell into our laps, because of the data gathering that Rhonda and her team did. In other cases, the causes will be revealed through your emergent analysis, by way of structured and proactive data gathering.

As we learned in Chapter 2, cause analysis is a cornerstone analytical practice for performance consultants and many other professionals.

There are a number of methods out there that will guide you through cause analysis. Process improvement systems, such as Total Quality Management (TQM) and Six Sigma provide thorough treatment of root cause analysis practices. These concepts and methods can and do get complicated. This book is not about complicated. This book is about making it simple and letting the practitioner do further research or improvise to make it work. That is Agile.

I think of causes analysis as three steps. (Other processes get much more complex.)

1. Identify the problem (I have blisters on my heels, and they keep getting worse.)
2. Determine the cause (My new leather shoes are rubbing on my heels.)
3. Propose a solution to remediate the cause (Stop the new leather shoes from rubbing on the heels. A simple solution would be to wear familiar shoes until the blisters heal.)

Treatment of the blisters with salve and bandages will help the wounds heal, but it will not prevent blisters from forming again. An action to treat the cause, such as intermittently wearing familiar shoes, will help my feet get used to the new shoes. After a while, I won't get blisters.

With that in mind, let's look at *Classic Scenario III*, where I perform emergent analysis in real time. It all started as I embarked on a business trip.

Classic Scenario III: Emergent Analysis

The default assumption should be that everyone is trying to do the best job they can.

—Bob's Axiom No. 14

This is the true story of a comically poor customer service experience with a major car rental company in Boston (Figure 3-2). Let's call them the Difficult Car Rental company. The ordeal demonstrates how failure to perform cause analysis leaves performance problems reflexively linked to "training."

Figure 3-2. Classic Scenario III took place at a car rental center in Boston. Here I drive into a case study in the potential power of cause analysis.

I have heard the refrains all too often through the years, from customers and managers: "The service sucks because they aren't trained." "This person doesn't know what they're doing. Send them to training." "My team is not on board with the new program. They need more training."

In my 23-minute experience at the airport with Difficult, I have a series of touch points with employees, each encounter pointing to a major service quality problem. To the lay observer, most seem like "training" problems, but even cursory speculation points to other issues in the workplace.

Sunday night: I need a different rental car

I pick up a rental car the evening before I am to leave on a business trip. As I drive back to my house, I notice that the windshield wiper fluid squirter isn't working, and the wiper blades are worn out. This will not work for a drive through New England in December. I call Difficult, and I arrange to swap this car for another car the next morning.

7:00 a.m., at the entrance

At the entrance to the garage, Francesca checks in the car and seemingly does everything correctly, checking mileage and so forth. I explained that I needed to exchange this car for another. She asks, "Are you a Garnet Club Rewards Member?" "No." "Go up to counter on the second floor." Including the people I dealt with in renting the car the evening before, this makes four consecutive employees who have asked me if I was a Garnet Club Rewards Member. I'm already weary of typing the full name; let's just call it Garnet Member for short.

> **Problem:** Everyone asks me if I'm a Garnet Member, but no one invites me to become one. Being reminded over and over again that I am not a Garnet Member plants a mental seed that I am not getting the best or most efficient service.
>
> **Possible cause:** Process issue. The performance is consistent, but the process is flawed. It's clear that every employee has it drilled into their head to greet every customer warmly and, before providing any service whatsoever, ask if he or she is a Garnet Member. The process itself is causing the pain point for me.
>
> **Possible solution:** The service process could be redesigned in such a way as to not ostracize non-Garnet Members. They should also examine why they ask this question and what affect it has on customers. If they want more people to become Garnet Members, then the process should include an invitation to become one.

7:05 a.m., in line at the rental counter

I get to the counter on the second floor, first in line. There is one agent behind the counter, Janet, serving another customer. Another employee, a young man named Ted, enthusiastically greets me at the front of the line.

> *Ted: Good morning! Welcome to Difficult! How may I help you?*
>
> *Bob: Good morning. I need to exchange my rental car for another. The windshield wipers and squirter don't work. I called last night.*
>
> *Ted: Are you a Garnet Member?*
>
> *Bob: No.*

Ted: Well, even though you are not a Garnet Member, you can probably go to the Garnet desk in the garage, and they can take care of you!

Bob (in my head): Oh, you mean that place right next where I dropped off the old car?

Bob: (out loud): Well, there's only one person ahead of me, so I might as well just wait for him to be done.

Ted: Okay. You have a great day!!!

Ted, like Francesca, is very nice. He tries to help me out by giving me an inside tip, but I don't find his tip helpful at all.

> **Problem:** If I had known that I could get a new car via the desk in the garage, I would not have had to walk about 150 yards to the main rental counter.
>
> **Possible cause:** Policy and communications. Two employees have two different conceptions of the policy for exchanging a car. Francesca sent me upstairs because I'm not a Garnet Member, but apparently, based on Ted's advice, there are exceptions.
>
> **Possible solution:** The company needs to set proper expectations with employees about the policy. It needs to be clear, and everyone needs to know the policy. If there is leeway for exceptions, for example, when it's not busy, employees should know that and be consistent when explaining it to customers.

7:11 a.m., still at the rental counter

Minutes seem like hours. Janet is still with the same customer. Finally Ted waves me over, "I'll help you over here! Let me just sign into this terminal." He goes around the desk, and after trying two stations, finally gets logged in to a terminal. As he is trying to log in, Janet comes over and bitterly asks Ted why there isn't anyone else working the counter besides her. "Because there isn't," Ted replies sharply. It makes me wonder if Ted is a supervisor or in another role just trying to pitch in and help out.

Problem: Even though there are only two customers present, the man that Janet is helping and me, service is dreadfully slow, and the employees are stressed out.

Possible cause: Supervision (staffing and scheduling), system performance, and training. Based on the amount of time that Janet has spent with one customer, either she doesn't know what she is doing or the system terminals are not working. Based on Ted's performance, I do not think that he knows how to sign in and perform this transaction. Janet is overwhelmed, and Ted is trying to help.

Possible solution: If Ted is supposed to perform transactions, he needs to be trained to do so. The company also needs to look at the systems. Both Ted and Janet are struggling to get customers processed.

7:14 a.m., supervisor to the rescue

As I wait for Ted to sign in, Suzy approaches and warmly greets me. I explain my situation, and her first question is, of course: "Are you a Garnet Member?" "No." She assures me, very nicely, that Ted can help. Time passes. I wonder if I should have bought more ice melt for the house in case it snows again. Then I wonder if I am missing a haircut appointment while I'm away this week. Difficult makes it easy to worry about the life you are leaving behind while driving one of their rental cars.

Ted gets logged in, and starts the transaction. "Did you put the old car into the spot where you found it?" I respond, "No, I brought it to Returns, like the person on the phone told me to." I'm not enjoying this experience. At all.

As Ted is trying to assign me a new car in the system, he gets stuck. He calls Suzy over to help. Suzy nudges him out of the way and completes the transaction. Apparently Ted pressed an incorrect button along the way. As Suzy helps me, Ted steps out from behind the counter and begins answering questions for other customers now waiting in line. Suzy completes the transaction. "Thank you for your patience today, Mr. Winter!" It feels like she delivers this line often.

Problem: Suzy thinks that Ted knows what he is doing, but apparently he does not.

Possible cause: Supervision. Suzy needs to schedule and assign employees based on their capabilities. It wasn't busy at the rental counter, but the employees were still overwhelmed.

Possible solution: Suzy needs to get a handle on her employees' capabilities and not put them in situations where they look incompetent. Also, as a side note, if Suzy does want to help Ted learn how to do a transaction, she should help him to do the transaction, rather than hip-checking him out of the way to do it herself.

7:21 a.m., leaving the parking lot

I get to the new car, and I check the wipers. All set. Leaving the parking lot, I need to speak with Tasha, who looks over my paperwork. After warmly greeting me, she asks, "Full tank of gas?" "Yes." "Have a great trip!" As with the other employees, she could not have been nicer. At 7:23 a.m., I leave the parking lot and immediately head toward the nearby Ted Williams tunnel, which requires drivers to pay a toll. Oh no! This car has no E-ZPass transponder, and I have no cash! Fifteen seconds later I brazenly drive through the E-ZPass lane with no E-ZPass, cursing Difficult to high heaven. Ironically, when I checked out the original car, the employee checking me out of the parking lot asked me if I had my E-ZPass transponder, which I did, but she did not ask me if the gas tank was full, which it was not.

Problem: Inconsistency. If the primary purpose of them stopping me on the way out (other than ensuring that I am taking the correct car) is to make sure that I'm all set, then the questions that the employees ask of the customers should be consistent.

Possible causes: Process design and supervision. Based on the two times I went through the check-out process, different employees look at different things. Apparently, the people who prepare the cars to be rented make a variety of small mistakes, at least one per car!

Possible solution. These interactions should be designed to focus on common problem areas as well as creating peace of mind with the customer. Systems should be put in place to minimize these annoying problems, as well as create a consistent customer experience.

The Power of Observation This scenario uses an analysis technique that has fallen out of favor: direct observation. So often as consultants we rely so much on data and executive perspective that we rarely observe the performance of the people within the system. In large companies in particular, observation is considered too expensive, intrusive, or prone to error. This is a loss. What is more persuasive or valid—a big spreadsheet with awesome pivot tables or seeing something with your own two eyes?

What to make of this?

Here is what my observations yielded: five touch points; five annoying interactions. Let's tally the possible root causes of the problems:

- Supervision: 3
- Process: 2
- System: 1
- Policy: 1
- Communications: 1
- Training: 1

Difficult has myriad problems with customer service, but training is not the primary concern here. Training could be part of the solution (e.g., teaching Ted how to use the system for transactions), but training alone will not fix any of Difficult's issues.

This anecdote shows my on-the-fly proactive analysis of the situation at that car rental company on that particular day. If I worked at Difficult, I would process this analysis into a recommendation for the executive responsible for customer service.

Recommending Solutions

> *These executives we deal with are very smart and savvy. That's why they are where they are.*
>
> —Bob's Axiom No. 15

Six months later, I'm starting my second full week working as an internal consultant at Difficult Rental Car.[15] A few days after an introductory visit with Val Oberst, the head of operations, he reaches out to me for my first directive.

Classic Scenario IV illustrates how I would conduct analysis, and then develop and present a recommendation for this executive.

---

[15]Not really. I'd like to say that Difficult brought me in after one of the higher-ups read my accounting of comically bad customer service on my blog. But really, I'm just dreaming about what I could have done for them.

Classic Scenario IV: Executive Request

From: Val Oberst
To: Bob Winter
Cc: Julius Krall; Desdemona MacPhail
Subject: Customer Service Scores for July

Hi Bob—

I was just briefed on our customer service scores for the month of May, and I'm quite disappointed at the trends I see. On the 100-point scale, our score is 67, down from 78 last May. The industry benchmark is 81. I need these numbers to start moving in the right direction.
Julius from the Customer Love Group (CLG) will send his full report over to you. I told Julius to expect a call from you so that you two can discuss the situation.
I need a recommendation from you about how to put some better customer service training in place, so that we can improve this result in the coming months. I'll have Desdemona schedule a meeting next month to hear your proposal.

Thank you,
Val

Happy Monday. Let's start the week with an executive request!

Provide Analysis of the Current Situation

> *Most of the time, the number one problem is failure of management to set expectations for the employees.*
>
> —Bob's Axiom No. 16

In the intervening four weeks, I apply the skills in the performance consultant's toolkit to get a better picture of the situation.[16] One might assume that Val has a good grip on the situation, but he does not. He only knows what he sees in reports and hears from his management team. Sure, he might mingle with employees or even rent a car once in a while, but he will never see what I saw as an anonymous shopper.

[16] I will not provide a full description of the analytical methods used here. They are covered elsewhere.

Four weeks of analysis? That doesn't sound very agile One of the key differences between traditional project management and the Agile methods is the amount of up-front analysis and planning that is done. Traditional project management calls for comprehensive planning and strict adherence to the plan; Agile calls for just enough planning, followed by responsiveness to change. The same applies for analysis. It's nice to do comprehensive and scientifically valid analysis, but how much time do you want to spend in analysis to plan a work item that will be completed in two weeks? We explore this issue further as we introduce the history and practices of Agile. For now, let's say that the amount and level of rigor in our analysis should be just enough to make the case for starting the work.

Let's provide Val with an executive-level, systemically focused picture.[17] Based on my analysis, here are the problems that lead to dissatisfaction for customers:

1. **Check-out procedures:** Everyone has been to training, but the recently updated check-out procedure is being inconsistently applied. The new procedure calls for the employees to explain three points about E-ZPass, yet we have an uptick in feedback about E-ZPass instructions. I observed 50 checkouts by three different people and there were 10 instances when the employee did not explain the three points.
2. **Service system availability:** POS terminals are down too often, particularly during high-demand periods, leading to slow service. System availability is 0.9971. The month before the last update package was installed, the availability was 0.9992.
3. **Staffing levels:** The branches have incorrect staffing levels at certain times. For example, the lowest-rated service happens on the Monday morning shift, which also has the longest average queue time. The staff are overwhelmed, and this is reflected in the queue times.
4. **The Garnet Member solicitation**: Customer satisfaction data shows that being asked to join Garnet Club every time they talk to an employee is a dissatisfier.

[17]*Executive-level* is the key here. I'm surprised how many people fail to keep things simple for busy executives. We want to give them information that is relevant, thought out, and easily consumable. There may be copious backup data for each of your assertions, but keep that in the background. You can make it available to them. They know how to read.

The cause analysis leads us to examine all aspects of the customer service situation. The executive asked for more training, but it is obvious that there are other systemic issues leading to the poor service scores.

Define Outcomes

Focus on the stuff you can do, not the stuff you cannot do.

—Bob's Axiom No. 17

Key metrics that will reflect improvement in customer service include:

- E-ZPass confusion.
- Baseline = No. 1 dissatisfier in the recent customer satisfaction assessment
- Oversolicitation of Garnet Club.
- Baseline = No. 2 dissatisfier
- Service system availability.
- Baseline = 0.9971
- Total wait time (time spent waiting in line plus the time to complete the transaction).
- Baseline = 10.7 minutes for the Monday morning shift. 8.3 minutes overall.

Many consultants and others will suggest that you also provide a goal for each metric. I usually don't articulate business goals for individual projects, unless the client does. In this case, Val specifically noted only that the customer service number declined and that he wanted to see it "moving in the right direction." In my experience as an internal consultant, a promise of improvement is enough. In Agile, any improvement is good, and lack of improvement is not good.

Align Solutions with Causes

Training alone will, only in rarest of circumstances, address a performance problem.

—Bob's Axiom No. 18

Present the performance outcomes in a simple form, such as we see in Table 3-3, with detail available elsewhere. By focusing on only a few items, we can agree with the executive that we are pursuing only those solutions that we think will contribute to improving the customer satisfaction scores. There is plenty else we could do, but these are most important right now.

Table 3-3. Solutions aligned with causes and recommended solutions. The consultant presents a manageable selection of recommendations, derived from causes.

Problem	Cause	Recommended Solutions
Check-out procedures	Supervision	Memo to all employees about key areas of check-out procedure Instruct supervisors to discuss at staff meetings Heightened profile of current dissatisfiers
Service system availability	The POS terminals go down during busy times	Systems team needs to add server capacity
Staffing levels	Supervisors are inconsistent about adjusting staffing levels based on demand patterns	Increased transparency about service level metrics by shift Create guidelines for staffing based on historical demand Management team discussion
The Garnet Club member solicitation	Service procedures call for every customer interaction to begin with an inquiry or solicitation about Garnet Club	Modify the procedure, so that each customer gets asked only once about the Garnet Club Communicate via email Modify new-hire training materials Reinforcement in staff meetings

From these causes, we were able to fashion a set of recommendations that address the root causes and conformed to the key elements that we knew we wanted to see in the solution.

Create Product Backlog Items

Put it in the backlog!

—Bob's Axiom No. 19

The recommendations are the basis of product backlog items (sometimes referred to as work items or stories). Typically, the work items will expand to areas beyond just training. There are two ways to proceed.

1. Put all items in one backlog and form a cross-functional scrum team to work on them.
2. Take the pertinent items (in my case, ones related to education) back to the functional scrum team, and leave the other areas to deal with their own items in their own way.

One challenge in trying to do Agile is that even if your team is practicing Agile, you will collaborate with others who are not. If this is the case, you will probably confuse, confound, and generally frustrate the Vals of the world. In any case, a prioritized list of actions can be agreed to by the executive. However, you have more recommendations than can be worked on at one time, and some that depend on others. The discussion is about which things to do first. You do not have to be Agile to understand that concept.

Table 3-4 shows how the articulation changes as you put the items into the Agile story form, and align the recommendations with them.

Table 3-4. Looking at a backlog. Here we articulate the work items in the story format

Original Work Items	Work Item in Story form
Consistent delivery of check-out procedures	As a customer, I need to know how to use the E-ZPass in the rental car, so that I don't become stressed out about getting tickets or having to fumble with cash at toll booths.
Remediate system availability issue Staffing levels aligned with forecasted business	As a customer, I need to be able to rely on a somewhat consistent and efficient experience at the rental counter, so that I can plan my travel.
Change procedure to make Garnet Club solicitation fewer times	As customer, I need employees to be friendly and focused on getting me through the car rental and return process in a timely manner, so that I can have a pleasant experience.

Our natural inclination is to articulate objectives from the point of view of worker ("The associates at Difficult need to take more customer service training"). Converting the work items into this format puts focus on the beneficiary of the work, the user of the system. In places like rental car companies, we work off of the user persona of the customer.

Ask for Permission to Go Forward

> *The game becomes teaching/coaching the executives to teach/coach their people.*
>
> —Bob's Axiom No. 20

At various points during the consulting engagement, you will want to ask permission to go forward. Indeed, if many of the actions are considered out of scope for what the client expects from a training person, you will want to use asking permission as a technique.

Here are some powerful consulting questions that help move things forward.

- I agree that we need all of the VPs to be on the same page about this customer service situation. I'd love the opportunity to come to your staff meeting to share my findings and hear their perspective. Would that be okay?
- I'm not really sure why people aren't consistently delivering the talking points about E-ZPass, but I do have some ideas about how to find out. Would it be all right if I reached out to some supervisors and garage people to find out more?
- I wonder what the procedures people think about how well the new check-out process is working. Who in the procedures area should I contact to find out more?

This line of questioning helps remove barriers to getting inside the organization. Only by getting this sort of access will I be able to move from a reactive to a proactive consulting stance. As I hear about problems earlier from executives and employees, I can supply recommendations based on emergent analysis.

These types of questions serve another purpose. Here I am setting up opportunities for me to model the behaviors that I need the executive to demonstrate. If Val gives me permission, he will witness me teaching and coaching the VPs, the line supervisors, and the procedures people on what needs to be done to remediate this customer service situation. I will look for opportunities to remind the executive that he is accountable for the result, and that his participation and support is critical to any success.

Insist on Executive Support

Nobody takes training just because the training guy jumps up and down.

—Bob's Axiom No. 21

Too often, an executive agrees to a plan (training or otherwise) but stops short of providing visible and meaningful support. As part of the proposal, delineate what is expected from them. Here are some examples:

- Management needs to take responsibility for delivering any messaging about expectations, including any requirement to take training.
- Executive teams should articulate how they plan to reinforce any new policies or requirements.
- Accountability for improved performance or completion of training should fall on the management team, not the supporting function.

Insist on it. Without real, live, walking, talking executive support, you have little hope of success.

The Lament of the Performance Consultant

Some days I think my profession is all about smoke and mirrors.

—Bob's Axiom No. 22

The performance consultant's job is to help our business partners provide employees with support that will help them improve their performance. As we see, training has a role, but more often environmental factors make the difference. We focus on outcomes rather than just providing training. It seems so simple.

We are in an uphill battle here. I would like to say that we only need to reeducate business executives on how training can help them be more successful. But I also see that many in my profession remain in the "order-taking" mode. The way they articulate their accomplishments supports that idea.

Flipping through online profiles of chief learning officers, training directors, and the like, here are the types of accomplishments that you often see:

- Managed a $9 million budget.
- Built a $20 million training center.
- Delivered training to 8,000 people.
- Implemented a new standardized onboarding program.

- Expanded the annual management training program from 100 participants to 200 participants.
- 100% of the employees completed their compliance training.

What is common about all these accomplishments? They are learning metrics with no standalone customer value. They reinforce the notion that training is a cost center, not a driver of business outcomes.

There are two types of metrics in the training world: Those that training people care about and those that the business people care about. While there is goodness in the former, the latter should be our focus.

Epilogue

It ain't training.

—Bob's Axiom No. 23

Three days after enduring Classic Scenario III, I return the vehicle to the Difficult Car Rental company. Jesse, who checks in the car, doesn't greet me warmly, doesn't smile, and doesn't ask me if I'm a Garnet Club Member. Through our interaction he says four words: "Hello . . . yeah . . . all set." Now I've lost it. This guy needs some damn training!

As I start the lonely walk across the cold parking garage at the end of a week-long business trip, wondering at 10 p.m. if I can find a cab anywhere nearby, a man yells at me from the next aisle over.

"Hey! Hey!!! You all set?!?!?!"

I wonder what is going on. Why is this guy yelling at me? Oh, he's wearing a Difficult uniform. "Yeah," I reply, waving my receipt. "The other guy took care of me."

He walks closer. "Where you going? You catching a flight?"

"No. I'm going home."

"You need a ride to the taxi stand?"

"Actually, yes."

Thus begins a brief but delightful experience with Manny. He drives me, in the rental car I just returned, to the taxi stand at Terminal A. Manny doesn't follow a script. He doesn't ask me if I'm a Garnet Member. He doesn't even really smile, but he is affable and helpful. We converse easily about the weather, the construction at the airport, and the consequences of driving through a toll booth without an E-ZPass. I don't think about whether Manny is following a procedure, what his role is, or even if he needs more training. He's just Manny, a guy who makes sure that I'm all taken care of.

CHAPTER

4

The Basics of Agile

The Scrum Team consists of a Product Owner, the Development Team, and a Scrum Master. Scrum Teams are self-organizing and cross-functional. Self-organizing teams choose how best to accomplish their work, rather than being directed by others outside the team. Cross-functional teams have all competencies needed to accomplish the work without depending on others not part of the team. The team model in Scrum is designed to optimize flexibility, creativity, and productivity.

—Ken Schwaber and Jeff Sullivan, *The Scrum Guide*[1]

When I presented my topic at ISPI's *THE Performance Improvement Conference* in 2014, I was prepared to share my ideas with colleagues about the nuances of Agile to buttress comparisons with the standards and principles of human performance technology (HPT). What my audience that day wanted was the basics of Agile. They asked me, in a dozen different ways, "What the heck is Agile?" This chapter provides an introduction to Agile software development and direction for those who want to explore further. If you are already well into your Agile journey, I have a few tidbits for you as well.

We begin with the seminal event in the history of the Agile movement.

[1]`http://www.scrumguides.org/docs/scrumguide/v1/scrum-guide-us.pdf`, page 4. This work is licensed under the Creative Commons Attribution-ShareAlike 4.0 International License. To view a copy of this license, visit `http://creativecommons.org/licenses/by-sa/4.0/` or send a letter to Creative Commons, PO Box 1866, Mountain View, CA 94042, USA.

The Creation of the Agile Manifesto

In February 2001, seventeen software engineering types gathered at The Lodge at the Snowbird ski resort in Utah. Three days of discussion (and apparently eating and skiing) yielded the *Manifesto for Agile Software Development*, which, in 68 carefully chosen words, articulates the values of Agile.[2] The men who authored the manifesto are known as the "original signatories."[3] Any person can now electronically sign at agilemanifesto.org, with comments, and thousands have done so.

This get together was not the beginning of the Agile movement, as this group, along with other like-minded people, had already been turning the software world upside down for a decade with "lightweight" techniques and practices. These methods included Extreme Programming (XP), Scrum, Dynamic Systems Development Method (DSDM), Adaptive Software Development, Crystal, Feature-Driven Development, and Pragmatic Programming.[4] Lightweight approaches were distinguished by providing an alternative to the waterfall approaches that had become *de rigueur* for the profession. After many years of poor results, the industry was starved for an alternative to heavyweight, documentation-driven, large project plan–encumbered, innovation-crushing, rigid (non-Agile) methods.

About the word about the word *Agile* At the Snowbird meeting, the group decided on "Agile" as the blanket term to describe these values and principles. The manifesto authors concluded that "lightweight," although descriptive, wasn't a strong enough word. Jim Highsmith notes, "The only concern with the term agile came from Martin Fowler (a Brit for those who don't know him) who allowed that most Americans didn't know how to pronounce the word agile."[5]

The rest is history. We will learn more about that history in the coming pages. First let's pause to examine the entire text of the Agile Manifesto.

[2]*Manifesto for Agile Software Development* is the official name. Most people just call it the *Agile Manifesto.*

[3]No women were among the original signatories. Walk through any cubicle farm of a software development function, and you will see that there are very few women in the field. Estimates vary, but a safe one would be that women make up no more than 25 percent of software engineers. Visit `http://womeninagile.com` to hear what some of the leading female voices have to say about Agile and women's role in it.

[4]I will describe XP and Scrum in some detail later in this book. The remainder on this list, while important in their own ways, are among dozens of frameworks, methods, and practices that I won't bother to define.

[5]See: `http://agilemanifesto.org/history.html`

MANIFESTO FOR AGILE SOFTWARE DEVELOPMENT

We are uncovering better ways of developing software by doing it and helping others do it.

Through this work we have come to value:

Individuals and interactions over processes and tools

Working software over comprehensive documentation

Customer collaboration over contract negotiation

Responding to change over following a plan

That is, while there is value in the items on the right, we value the items on the left more.

Kent Beck	James Grenning	Robert C. Martin
Mike Beedle	Jim Highsmith	Steve Mellor
Arie van Bennekum	Andrew Hunt	Ken Schwaber
Alistair Cockburn	Ron Jeffries	Jeff Sutherland
Ward Cunningham	Jon Kern	Dave Thomas
Martin Fowler	Brian Marick	

Breaking Down the Agile Manifesto

The words of the Agile Manifesto are often quoted and misquoted. They are the subject of divagations, both enlightening and nauseating. But the text itself is beautiful and should be considered carefully. Let's do a line-by-line breakdown so I can share what exactly these 68 words mean to me.

> *We are uncovering better ways of developing software . . .*

"Uncovering" is an interesting word. It implies that the better ways already exist, they just need to be discovered. Finding those better ways is something that independent-minded, creative developers and top performers strive to do. Right away you can see that the values of Agile are going to run afoul of traditional business structures, particularly in large companies, where the ways are told to you by management. Because of this, managers can struggle finding their role in Agile, which we will see a little later.

In retrospect, I suspect that the authors would like to use a different word than "software," since we find that Agile and agility have vast applications beyond software. But the authors are all software people, and they were trying to fix problems in their industry.

> *... by doing it and helping others do it.*

Make no mistake: the original signatories are engineers. Inventors of the wiki, test-driven development, Scrum, and many other innovations were at that meeting. Although many of them have consulting businesses now, they are and have been "doing it." In addition, notice that "helping others do it" speaks to the communities of practice that have formed under the banner of Agile and to the refreshing collegiality and openness that you see among its practitioners.

> *Through this work we have come to value:*

Following this line are the four values of Agile. This is the value that emerged as the signatories conducted their work with an open mind.

> *Individuals and interactions over processes and tools*

I have observed an inherent mindset in many engineers: everything can be automated through technology and process. This viewpoint, so useful to software development, manifests all of the time in my internal education consulting. The thinking goes like this: If we can just create a big system with a comprehensive set of learning resources, then we will not have to take any responsibility for the development of our employees. I agree that some things can be streamlined and automated, but effective managers will never be off the hook for paying attention to their employees' development.

Although it is true that many repetitive work processes can be made more efficient, the best agilists realize that ultimately the creation of new things is about people. In any work situation, people will work better if they interact and collaborate.

Agilist vs. agilista An *agilist* is a practitioner of Agile methods. An *agilista* is fanatical devotee of Agile. The latter term is sometimes used in a jocularly pejorative sense.

Like software engineering, corporate learning is a field of creation. Yet we see the forces of mechanization taking hold in learning functions just as they are breaking down in engineering. I increasingly hear of the training assembly line, templates and formulas designed to commoditize learning. The emphasis on having an efficient and scalable production factory outweighs the emphasis on performance improvement. In fact, the factory and consulting folks are in conflict with one another, the former wanting to produce as many training courses as possible, the latter only as many as absolutely necessary.

Working software over comprehensive documentation

Working software is the measure of progress. Documentation should be minimally viable (articles about how the software works, help files, and the like) so that people can continue to develop and use the application. Do you remember user guides, popular in the 1990s? Did you have a shelf of those three-inch-thick books that would tell you, in excruciatingly detailed step action tables, how to use accounting, spreadsheet, or word processing programs? How useful were they? Think about how much time they spent creating those books, when they could have used the time to make the application better, more intuitive to use, or released earlier?

For example, take a new feature that is part of iOS 8, the operating system for the iPhone. If you double-click on the button, you not only get access to your open apps, you also see at the top of the screen *Favorites* and *Recents*. Two good things happen here. First, you can quickly navigate to the people you most likely want to call or text. Second, the beautiful design of the feature makes documentation unnecessary. It's intuitive!

I see this value come to life in my work. Well-intentioned internal clients push for a comprehensive set of training resources covering every possible topic under the sun. While the sentiment is admirable, providing these assets as a standalone piece will not create people who can perform better in their jobs.

Like comprehensive training, comprehensive documentation has limited utility. If software is good, you do not need a lot of documentation to use it. If the environment is good, people can learn to perform well in their jobs without comprehensive training.

Customer collaboration over contract negotiation

Here the agilists introduce the idea of working with customers instead of against them. Sure, if you're an outside party or a project manager, you want to contract certain things. But the idea of a contract negotiation is inherently adversarial (and inefficient). Negotiating dates, hours, and change requests risks pitting customer and development team against one another and distracts from the work at hand. That's one reason so many Agile people have disdain for project managers.

Recall the ISPI Performance Standard 4, *Work in Partnership with Clients and Stakeholders*. Performance improvement is seldom the one-time affair that contracting implies. When it works right, performance improvement is agile, an iterative and cooperative activity.

> *Responding to change over following a plan*

To be agile is to be responsive to change. You can make an elaborate plan on day 1, but on day 2, you already know more about the situation than you did when you wrote the plan. Be flexible. Change the plan as needed. Avoid comprehensive project planning documentation, while keeping your eye on the desired outcome.

There is a common misconception that Agile is a free-for-all where people do not plan anything. Nothing could be further from the truth. In Agile, you are planning all of the time, with formal planning sessions occurring every two to four weeks.

Absent exceptional circumstances, you follow the plan for the duration of a sprint, and then you are never more than two to four weeks away from another scheduled opportunity to "respond to change" with the next sprint planning meeting.

> *That is, while there is value in the items on the right, we value the items on the left more.*

Notice that here "value" is used in the sense of things that mean something, not just a system of beliefs. Compare this to HPT's use of "worth"—a rough equivalent to *"value" (Chapter 2)*. In both HPT and Agile, the words ask the practitioner to monetize or quantify the contribution of human performance or the creative output of a team.

This is a key point. The Agile values do not say we should never do documentation or follow a plan. They say that we need to keep focus on the things that are important:

- Individuals and interactions
- Working software
- Customer collaboration
- Responding to change

Those four ideas, the items on the left, are what's most important to remember from the *Agile Manifesto*, and they are its most cited words.

Principles behind the Agile Manifesto

Several months after the meeting in Utah, the "12 Principles behind the Agile Manifesto" were added to the site. They read, in their entirety[6]:

> *We follow these principles:*
>
> *Our highest priority is to satisfy the customer through early and continuous delivery of valuable software.*
>
> *Welcome changing requirements, even late in development. Agile processes harness change for the customer's competitive advantage.*
>
> *Deliver working software frequently, from a couple of weeks to a couple of months, with a preference to the shorter timescale.*
>
> *Business people and developers must work together daily throughout the project.*
>
> *Build projects around motivated individuals. Give them the environment and support they need, and trust them to get the job done.*
>
> *The most efficient and effective method of conveying information to and within a development team is face-to-face conversation.*
>
> *Working software is the primary measure of progress.*
>
> *Agile processes promote sustainable development. The sponsors, developers, and users should be able to maintain a constant pace indefinitely.*
>
> *Continuous attention to technical excellence and good design enhances agility.*
>
> *Simplicity—the art of maximizing the amount of work not done—is essential.*
>
> *The best architectures, requirements, and designs emerge from self-organizing teams.*
>
> *At regular intervals, the team reflects on how to become more effective, then tunes and adjusts its behavior accordingly.*

These principles are worthy of discussion with colleagues. They clarify a belief system that describes the agile mindset. You will hear these aphorisms cited often if you work in an Agile shop. There is a place for them in any profession where something of value is produced. Just swap out the word *software*

---

[6]See `http://agilemanifesto.org/principles.html`. © 2001.

for a word describing what you produce. As you first saw in Chapter 1, the HPT principles and the Agile principles are compatible and complementary. We will encounter more examples as we proceed.

We have seen how Agile came about over the past two decades. Now let's ask: Does it work?

The Promise of Agile

At its worst, typical software development projects involve missed deadlines and low-quality (buggy) output. This is accompanied by team acrimony, burned-out individuals, and overworked teams in a perennial death march.[7] I've seen it, and it's sad and depressing, even from afar.

The Agile Manifesto provides a common lexicon that represents a guiding light for new teams and hope for discouraged teams. For some teams, to be guided by the Agile Manifesto is to be driven by a shared faith in the goodness and possibility that the words represent. For others, the prospect of fixing the pain of modern software development is enough.

Whatever the motivations, we see in recent years that adoption of Agile in the software industry is accelerating.

Adoption in the Software Industry

Since 2006, VersionOne, an Agile support application vendor, has conducted its annual *State of Agile* survey to show the penetration of Agile and the reasons that companies adopt it. Here are some of the results from 2013.[8]

Ubiquity

- 88 percent of respondents said their organizations were practicing Agile.
- 88 percent of respondents had at least one year of personal experience with Agile development practices.

[7]"Death march" is a wonderfully macabre term used in project management and software development to describe a team's shared feelings of hopelessness and despair on the road to what appears to be certain project failure.

[8]All metrics presented in this section come from VersionOne (2014), 8th Annual State of Agile Development Survey, available at the Library of White Papers of the VersionOne website, `http://www.versionone.com/pdf/2013-state-of-agile-survey.pdf`.

- 31 percent have more than five years of experience with Agile.
- 73 percent said that they felt that Agile helps them complete projects faster.

In the software industry, Agile is ubiquitous and growing, and its image has evolved with it. Ten or fifteen years ago, Agile (and its predecessor, lightweight) was perceived as a radical approach, practiced only by rebels, hippies, and cowboy coders. Now it is accepted by most Fortune 500 companies.

How things have changed in that period of time. It used to be that software would be updated in release periods of months or years, with massive changes. In the 1990s, a new release of Microsoft Word was a newsworthy event, touting scores of new features with hundreds of bugs fixed. The public hungered for these things ("of course I'll buy an upgrade!"), but the program became increasingly bloated, slow, and difficult to use and contained many features that few, if any, people used. In addition, the release cadence was glacial, as we are only on version 15 after 25 years.

If you want to see the ubiquity of Agile in action, take a look at the available application updates on your smart phone.

Releases are frequent, each containing small feature enhancements and quality improvements (bug fixes).

Top Reasons for Adopting Agile

Respondents were able to cite multiple reasons.

- Accelerate time to market (32 percent)
- Manage changing priorities (27 percent)
- Better align IT/business (23 percent)
- Increase productivity (19 percent)
- Enhance software quality (18 percent)

Agile encourages creativity and flexibility, taking into account that every company or work group is in a different situation with different challenges. The top five reasons here are all sensible, and they are all consistent with the values and principles of Agile.

Top Benefits of Adopting Agile

- Ability to manage changing priorities (92 percent)
- Increased productivity (87 percent)
- Improved project visibility (86 percent)
- Improved team morale (86 percent)
- Enhanced software quality (82 percent)

These top benefits are ones that any non–control freak manager or reasonable worker could rally behind.

Looking back at earlier VersionOne studies, almost all of those percentages cited above are on an upward trend. Clearly, more and more software organizations are practicing Agile. At 88 percent, you could round up and simply say that *everyone* in the software industry is doing it. Outside of software, there is limited penetration, and there is still time to be cutting edge and radical.

However, believing in Agile is one thing. Evidence of business results is another.

Evidence of the Efficacy of Agile

All of that optimism is great for individuals and teams. Before businesses commit to Agile development, they need research-based proof that it actually works. After all, in other respected fields such as medicine, psychology, and the physical sciences, a long-standing research basis and protocol establishes what works and what does not. Why is software development so different?

Research is under way, but the business case for Agile is largely anecdotal and experience-based. The dearth of empirical evidence supporting Agile is obscured by its thoughtful, smart and charismatic thought leaders. Fortunately, in recent years, some research has emerged that advances the case.

Much of the evidence is geared toward determining if software projects are "successful." In terms of traditional project management, that would mean that the project was completed on time, on budget, with few defects. Here are some studies that support the efficacy case.

More Successful Projects

Figure 4-1 shows that Agile projects, compared with their waterfall counterparts, succeed more often and fail less often.

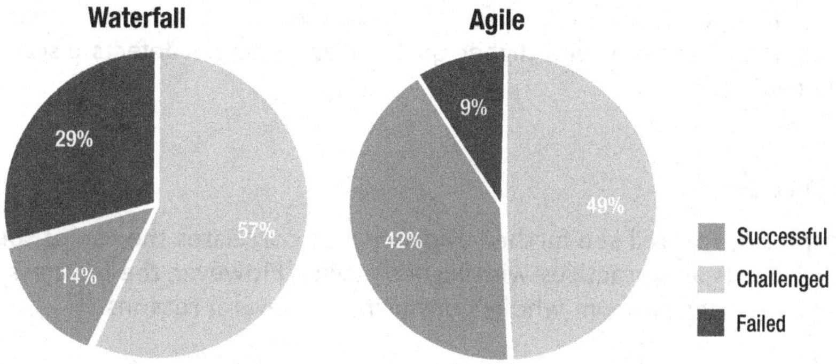

Figure 4-1. Agile projects succeed more often and fail less often. Source: The CHAOS Manifesto, Standish Group, 2012.

Cheaper, Faster, Higher Quality

Tables 4-1 and 4-2 show research from the Cutter Consortium, which demonstrates how projects using XP and Scrum, respectively, produced better project results.

Table 4-1. Follett Software Colocated XP versus Industry Average (using an average project size of 500,000 lines of new and modified code)

	Industry Average	Current Performance	Delta
Project cost	$3.5 million	$2.2 million	-$1.3 million
Schedule	12.6 months	7.8 months	-4.8 months
Defects during QA	242	121	-50%
Staffing	35	35	N/A

Source: Michael Mah, "How Agile Projects Measure Up, and What This Means to You," Cutter Consortium Agile Product & Project Management Executive Report 9 (9) (2008), `http://www.cohaa.org/content/sites/default/files/How%20Agile%20Projects%20Measure%20Up,%20and%20What%20This%20Means%20to%20You.pdf`.

Table 4-2. BMC Software Distributed Scrum versus Industry Average (using average project size of 700,000 lines of new and modified code)

	Industry Average	Current Performance	Delta
Project cost	$5.5 million	$5.2 million	-$0.3 million
Schedule	15 months	6.3 months	-8.7 months
Defects during QA	713	635	-11%
Staffing	40	92	+52

Source: Ibid.

Note that in each example, the projects came in at a lower cost, in a shorter period of time, with higher quality (that is, fewer defects discovered during testing).

Is That All?

In Chapter 5, you will see further evidence that correlates the use of specific Agile methods and practices with higher quality. However, the business case for Agile remains far from wholly convincing for several reasons.

Research Is a Work in Progress

The research does not yet provide overwhelming, irrefutable evidence that teams who use Agile methods succeed more often than those who do not. When you go to your next Agile class or conference, you will hear trainers and presenters struggle to convincingly explain the business case for Agile (if they even try). There is nothing wrong with these experts. They simply believe in Agile! They'll work tirelessly to help you understand and practice the methods more effectively—but the belief is stronger than the evidence.

Bad Actors

Voices of dissent, both loud and subversive, are not going away. Try searching for "Agile doesn't work," "I hate Agile," or "Agile sucks," and you'll get a taste of the cynicism that Agile has engendered. Even within companies that have visionary executives, employees at every level resist Agile in the same ways that some will resist any kind of change. Change management and transformation management are an absolute necessity for any organization moving to Agile.

No Causal Relationship

I am skeptical that a causal relationship will ever be established between practicing Agile generally and success. There is a push and pull between the hard skills of Agile (the engineering practices and techniques) and the soft skills of agility (individuals and interaction, collaboration). Leaders can devise beautiful strategies for enabling letter-of-the-law practices of XP or Scrum, but they will not succeed until the culture is addressed. As Peter Drucker famously said, "Culture eats strategy for breakfast."

That's why this book is here. Let's get the engineers past the idea that everything can be automated, essentially eliminating the need for people. Let's get the executives to stop thinking only about execution and deadlines and milestones, and have them start thinking about how to engage and empower employees. Only by doing these things will we unlock the potential of our teams through Agile—unleashing the creativity, innovation, and sense of pride that is within everyone.

Scrum

Many methodologies, practices, and frameworks apply the values and principles of Agile. Scrum is by far the most popular, so much so that many novices think of Scrum and Agile as synonymous.[9] They are not, but Scrum is good vehicle to elaborate on the concepts associated with Agile.

In this section, I provide a description of Scrum and its lexicon. There are many sources of this type of information. Our goal here is to describe Scrum concisely so that the reader can begin to become conversant with its terminology and concepts. This knowledge will pay dividends as the reader consumes the remainder of this book, discusses the ideas with colleagues, and begins to practice Scrum.

Getting started with Scrum If you are thinking about practicing Scrum, you should start doing so as soon as you can. There is enough information in this chapter to get started. There are several outstanding books describing Scrum in detail. You might consider *Succeeding with Agile: Software Development Using Scrum*, by Mike Cohn.

It is a long book, but it is very accessible, and it focuses on the finer points of transforming an organization to Agile. Later in this chapter I present highlights of the *Scrum Guide*, by Ken Schwaber and Jeff Sutherland, a pithy yet authoritative book. But no matter how much you read and talk about Scrum, you will stink at it when you first start. So finish this chapter and just start doing it!

Defining Scrum

Scrum is an iterative and incremental Agile development framework that can be applied to the development of any product output that is valuable for the customer. By *iterative*, I mean that there are specifically defined work periods within which product is produced. A work period is called a *sprint* (also known as an *iteration*), and it is usually two or four weeks in duration.

---

[9]By "popular," I mean it has become a full-fledged cottage industry. The ScrumAlliance, which provides a range of certification programs, has 350,000 active (dues-paying) members. Being an Agile consultant specializing in Scrum can be a nice way to make a living. The marketing success of Scrum has bred some cynicism by some of the Agile purists. They may have a point in some cases, but overall, the popularity of Scrum is largely responsible for the rise in popularity of Agile in general, as well as its expansion beyond the software business, both of which are good things.

Figure 4-2 is simple representation of the Scrum framework.[10] Here is **the one-minute description of the basic Scrum workflow:**

> A **story** is added to the **product backlog**. Through backlog **refinement**, the product owner decides on rank-order priority among the stories and adds detail to the ones that are likely to be done in the foreseeable future. The product owner presents the **sprint backlog,** the list of stories that are designated for the impending sprint, to the team during the **sprint planning** meeting. The development team commits to as many of the highest-ranked stories as its capacity will allow. Through the course of the **sprint**, the team meets daily for a **daily scrum**. At the end of the sprint they look back at how they worked together through a **retrospective** meeting. At the end of the sprint, the team demonstrates each story that is **done** to the customer. Feedback shared during the **sprint review** will be fodder for new stories in the product backlog.

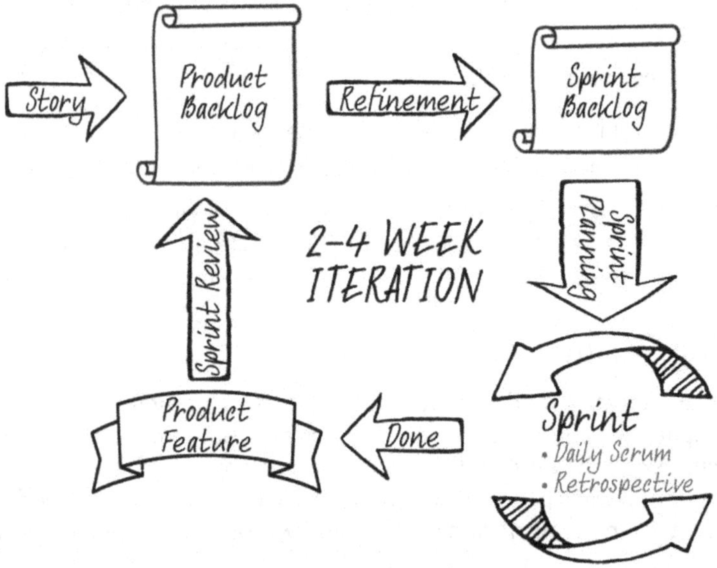

Figure 4-2. Basic Scrum Workflow. The sprint cycle continues on a cadence of two to four weeks. This diagram shows how the artifacts and events of Scrum interact.

---

[10]In Chapter 6, I introduce agile performance improvement, which focuses on how the people involved in the process interact, not just the flow of work.

Now that you have the high-level description of Scrum, let's go into more detail. There are the artifacts, the roles for the team members, and a set of events (sometimes called ceremonies). The rules and terminology around these things define Scrum.

The Artifacts of Scrum

All of the work that is to be completed is kept in a *product backlog* (sometimes just called a *backlog*), which is the big list of possible items to work on in the future.

Each item in the backlog is known as a *product backlog item (PBI)*, *work item*, *user story*, or simply *story*. In the language of software, *stories* are where you put the requirements.

The list of stories that are designated to be completed within a sprint is called a *sprint backlog*.

About Stories

A story is articulated through description of these three components:

- Persona (user of the product)
- Function
- Purpose

Thinking of stories this way ensures that you articulate the value that will be added by enabling the function. So, a story may be written in this form:

> As a <user>, I need <function>, so that I can <achieve a purpose>.
>
> "As a dog owner, I need an easy way to carry and dispense doggie waste bags, so that I'm not fumbling around when I go to pick up the dog's mess."

Along with this definition, each story will have *acceptance criteria*, which describe what the work output will look like when the story is finished. For example, "the device will be attached to the dog leash, and the user will be able to pull out, detach, and open a dog waste bag easily with one hand." The value for the user is the mitigation of inconvenience, frustration, and the possible dog poop on the hands of the user.

A story that is too big to be completed within one sprint is sometimes called an *epic*, and a big epic is sometimes called a *theme*. An epic or theme might be to reinvent the dog leash altogether. The epic will be composed of many stories, each representing features of the new leash as defined by the *product vision*. It is unlikely that the team can design and build all of the features within one sprint. So the team tackles them one at a time, starting with the most important one.

The Events

There are four events (sometimes called ceremonies). With the exception of the *sprint review*, where the team interacts with the customer, the events are by, of, and for the development team. Others may attend, but they are not allowed to participate.

The Tale of the Chicken and the Pig

A chicken and a pig are walking together.

Chicken: We should open a diner together.

Pig: Should we? What would we serve?"

Chicken: Eggs and bacon.

Pig: No way, man. You'd only be involved, but I'd be committed.

You will not be practicing Scrum long before you hear this joke, or see a comic strip version of it. Know that people on the scrum team are pigs; everyone else is a chicken. If chickens come to a daily standup or sprint planning as a guest, they don't talk during the meeting. Period.

Sprint Planning

The *sprint planning* meeting occurs at the beginning of the sprint, and lasts between two and eight hours, depending on the length of the sprint and the will of the team.[11] The meeting is planned and facilitated by the scrum master,

[11]As a general guideline, a four-week sprint calls for an eight-hour planning meeting; two-weeks a four-hour meeting; one week a two-hour meeting. The team can make the decision to make the meeting longer or shorter. My team usually does four hours of planning for a four-week sprint. Thorough preparation by the product owner is the key to efficient and acrimony-free sprint planning meetings.

but it revolves around the interaction between the product owner and the scrum team. The product owner introduces stories from the sprint backlog one at a time, starting with the highest-priority item. Once the team has gained an understanding of the particulars of the story, including the acceptance criteria, they discuss how to tackle the story. They talk through the story in just enough detail to estimate the effort to complete it. Estimation is usually done using *story points*, which have no direct relation to time, although some teams estimate in hours or days.

Once the team agrees on the work to be done and the story point estimation, they commit to completing the story during the sprint. The product owner introduces the next highest priority, and the cycle continues until the team has exhausted their capacity. Team capacity is called *velocity*, and it is the estimated number of story points (or a time-based unit) that the team has proven it can finish within an *iteration* (or *sprint*). Velocity is estimated by looking at team's *historic velocity*, that is, actual productivity in previous sprints. At the end of the sprint planning meeting, the development team has a set of stories to which it is committed. This set of stories is called the *sprint backlog*.

A taste of planning and estimation Creating a plan and sizing the work are difficult jobs to do well, especially in collaboration, and teams get better at it with practice. For a full treatment, I recommend the book *Agile Estimating and Planning*, by Mike Cohn, one of the recognized classics of the Agile genre, or Cohn's online video course of the same name.

Daily Standup

Every work day, the scrum master facilitates a 15-minute *daily standup* meeting, also known as the *daily scrum*. Each development team member provides answers to three questions:

1. What I did I accomplish yesterday?
2. What am I working on today?
3. Do I have any impediments that are preventing me from working on or completing a story?

The scrum master notes all *impediments* and actively works to remove them. There are no updates, status reports, or presentations. The team can ask questions, but if the meeting gets off track, the scrum master reserves the tangent as a topic for a meeting with the correct combination of people.

The daily standup has a particular agenda and peculiar format, which takes some getting used to. But it is an amazingly efficient and impactful event when practiced well by teammates who trust one another.

On my team, our daily standups usually last 5–10 minutes. This is time well spent. These meetings provide transparency within the team—everyone knows what everyone is working on. Issues (impediments) are addressed immediately, instead of festering indefinitely. The quick updates within the meeting engender organic collaboration outside of the meeting.

Of course, you don't have to have standups daily; you just can't call it Scrum if you don't.

Sprint Review

At the conclusion of the sprint, the scrum team invites customers, who may be internal or external, to the *sprint review*. During the sprint review, hosted by the product owner, the team recaps the sprint and demonstrates stories that that have been completed—that is, that satisfy the team's *definition of done (DoD)*. The customer provides feedback to the team on what has been done. As the team hears the feedback, it considers how to inspect and adapt their work accordingly. If the story meets the established acceptance criteria, the customer accepts the work and plans to implement it. Any new work or suggestions are captured as stories in the *product backlog*.

DoD* versus *acceptance criteria Novice agilists sometimes confuse these two terms. *DoD* is a general set of standards, defined by the development team, that are applied to every story. DoD is different from the *acceptance criteria*, which is unique for every story.

The sprint review event is critical to building the relationship between the development team and the customer. How often in traditional product development do we ever connect with the consumer of what we develop?

Things go wrong on projects. Due to the frequent iterations of Scrum, we fail quickly so that we can adjust as we go. In waterfall we sometimes don't discover we were totally wrong until the product hits the market!

Sprint Retrospective

During the *sprint retrospective* (often called simply the *retrospective*), the team reflects on how things went during the just-finished sprint. Each person on the team gets time to share what they thought went well and what could have been improved—without interruption or reaction from the rest of the team. After everyone has spoken, the team discusses the feedback and decides on an action to focus on in the upcoming sprint. The retrospective keeps the team focused on *continuous improvement*, a guiding light as they improve their agility over time.

Inspecting and Adapting

All of the Scrum events revolve around the idea of inspecting and adapting how the Scrum is working. Look at what is happening (inspect), often, and make adjustments to improve (adapt).

- **Sprint planning** *inspects and adapts* what is going to happen in the next iteration.
- The **daily standup** *inspects and adapts* what has happened in the last day.
- The **sprint review** *inspects and adapts* the work product and the ways the team interacts with the customer.
- The **sprint retrospective** *inspects and adapts* how the team collaborates.

Teams doing Scrum have ample opportunity to consider what they can do to promote continuous improvement. I learn from Scrum: If you are getting better each time, that is all you can really hope for.

The Roles

A group of people working together in Scrum is called a *scrum team*, also known as *development team* or, simply, *team*. Typically a scrum team consists of five to nine people, and the team collectively has the skills to do the work of the team.

Where did we get the word *scrum*? The term "scrum" comes from the game of rugby. A rugby union scrum consists of two teams' sets of eight forwards, each set crouching and binding shoulder to shoulder in three rows and interlocking with the other set head on. Into the tunnel formed between the teams as they drive against each other, a back called the "scrum-half" introduces the ball, which both sets of forwards try to hook backwards with their feet to their waiting scrum-halves.

There are just three roles on a scrum team: product owner, scrum master, and scrum team member.

According to the rules of Scrum, the team members are to be allocated 100 percent to the team. Composing teams that way is challenging for large organizations with heavy inertia toward status quo and against people working together toward common, not individualized goals. Without dedicated team members, you miss out on the benefits of swarming stories, applying diversity of thought, and unity of purpose.

Of course, you don't have to have dedicated team members; you just can't call it Scrum if you don't.

Product Owner

The *product owner* is the primary liaison between the scrum team and the world outside of the team (customers, upper management, product management, finance, and the like).

The product owner has these distinct responsibilities:

Write the stories. The highest-priority stories, those that have a realistic chance of being done in the next sprint, need to have sufficient detail so that the team understands exactly what the output of the story will be. The performance of these duties is called *backlog refinement* or grooming. The product owner describes the output of a story through acceptance criteria, which details what the customer will need to see to receive the work with a smile.

Prioritize the product backlog (that is, decide which stories get done first). The stories will be listed in rank order based on what will add the most value to customers immediately. The product owner works closely with the customer to make decisions about the prioritization and details of the stories. The product owner also works closely with product management and architects, leveraging their strategic input.

Ensure readiness. For a story to take a high position in the sprint backlog, it needs to be ready to be worked on in such a way that it can be completed within one sprint. If a story has associated dependencies out of the team's control, it is not ready. If a story is too big to be completed with a single sprint, it will not be ready until it is decomposed into two or more smaller stories. Teams will often establish a *definition of ready* to help with the decision to work on a story.

In addition to these specific responsibilities, the product owner participates in all scrum team ceremonies.[12]

During sprint planning, the product owner presents the sprint backlog. Stories are introduced to the team in ranked priority order. As the team commits to each story, it assigns *story points* (or a time-based estimate) and decides who will work on it.

---

[12]As you learn about Agile, you might hear that the product owner is not supposed to or does not have to attend the daily scrum. I disagree. The product owner is part of the scrum team. Bad things happen when the product owner gets disconnected from the team.

Throughout the sprint, the product owner works closely with the team to ensure that they understand and are executing toward the team's DoD and the customer-centric acceptance criteria.

The product owner facilitates the sprint review, where the team demonstrates completed stories to customers.

Scrum Master

The *scrum master* is a servant-leader to the team and keeper of the scrum process. She helps the product owner manage the artifacts. She coordinates and facilitates all team events. During the daily standup, she helps the scrum team by fielding impediments and barriers that slow or distract them. Between standups, she drives resolution of impediments. The scrum master uses the retrospective process to facilitate continuous improvement. She keeps the sprint planning meetings moving along, and she is the emcee for the sprint reviews. The scrum master job is many things, depending on the day. She is project manager, coach, bulldozer, mediator, Scrum guru, and den mother.

The Scrum Team

The *scrum team* is the cross-functional group of people who do the work. During sprint planning, they learn the details of each story, so they can estimating the relative effort needed to complete it. Only after the team understands everything involved in completing the story will they commit to working on it. Then the team figures out how they will get the story done.

This Agile idea of the team committing to stories is different from traditional project management methods, where the employees are told what to do and how to do it.

For the scrum team, short iterations place an impetus on finding ways, as a team, to move faster with higher quality. The obvious way (easier said than done) is to decompose the stories into smaller chunks. Certainly, flawless adherence to the rules and ceremonies of Scrum helps improve team performance. Ultimately, however, adoption of better, more integrated, engineering practices (see Chapter 5) is the key to improving velocity and quality of work.

Other Roles

That is it. Everyone on the scrum team has one of those three roles, period. Outside of the scrum team, there is the rest of the organization, which could be 50 percent or more of the employees at a large software company. Books have been written, bales of cash have been forked over to consultants, and incalculable blood, sweat, and tears have been spilled trying to sort out how to scale Agile to the enterprise. Look up "scaled Agile" or "enterprise Agile" and prepare for a headache. Not that the role of the overall organization in supporting Agile is trivial. On the contrary, trying to practice Agile within a company of any size that is steadfastly not Agile in its culture, thinking, or practice is crippling. Nonetheless I leave the topic alone and declare it out of scope for this work, with the two following exceptions.

Agile Coaches

As teams figure out Agile, some are supported by a designated Agile coach, intended to accelerate improvement of the teams' performance through the practice of Agile. Some companies employ internal coaches, and some hire external ones. Agile coaching is a cottage industry, and these consultants typically provide a high level of expertise that helps companies get a jump start when they are transitioning to Agile. As companies develop expertise, an internal coaching capability is a make-or-break commitment they are wise to make.

The topic of Agile coaching is vast, and there are many excellent books, websites, and consultancies dedicated to the topic.[13]

The Manager

The front-line manager is not part of the scrum team but has a vital role in making sure that the teams to which his employees are deployed can focus on the work at hand. This will involve helping remove organizational barriers to success.

Here are a few of the key responsibilities of a manager in an Agile environment:

- Providing the employees with the tools and support they need to work efficiently
- Assembling teams of individuals who collectively have the capabilities to do the required work
- Supporting skill development or refining team composition as the demands of the work change
- Shielding the teams from disruptions that take their attention away from the stories to which they are committed

[13]One highly regarded book on this topic is Lyssa Adkins' *Coaching Agile Teams* (Addison-Wesley, 2010).

One can envision the role of the manager by metaphor in a gadget factory. The teams focus on making the gadget. The managers stay out of the gadget-making and instead make sure everything is good in the factory. The workers have the proper equipment, technology, and training to do their jobs. The working conditions are good and safe. Problems that arise are resolved in a way that does not slow the work down.

The teams are self-directed and self-organizing. They figure out how to make the gadgets according to the DoD, and they figure out who does what.

The role of a manager overseeing teams practicing Agile is considerably different from the "traditional" people manager, who is often the most proficient and skilled craftsperson. Many managers have a difficult time letting go of the gadget-making and embracing the running of the factory. Be wary of promoting your best craftsperson to be a manager or coach. Gadget-maker and manager are totally different skill sets, especially in Scrum.

If you follow team sports, you see this idea at work. Coaching and managing are totally different skills sets than playing. Most of the greatest coaches or general managers were not great players (Vince Lombardi of the Green Bay Packers, Greg Popovich of the San Antonio Spurs), and most the greatest players made lousy coaches (Magic Johnson of the Los Angeles Lakers, Wayne Gretzky of the Phoenix Coyotes). Other greats were never given a chance, even though they wanted to coach. Babe Ruth and Kareem Abdul-Jabbar are famous examples.

Cross-Functional Teams

The elimination (or de-emphasizing) of functional roles in favor of Scrum roles[14] is a powerful impetus for individual development. The Scrum roles break down barriers that highly differentiated role descriptions buttress. Code writers, UX designers, QA people and tech writers are all simply scrum team members now. Depending on the priority of the day, code writers will design and run tests. QA people will need to write, not just test, code. This necessity drives everyone to develop a more well-rounded skill set as all team members work to develop whatever skills are needed to meet the sprint goal. You still have your specialty, but you also become competent at all of the nearby disciplines. Kenny Rubin calls this T-shaped skills,[15] where each person's capabilities run narrow and deep, enabling a more flexible team.

---

[14]Some companies have gone so far as to make the Scrum titles their employees' official job titles.

[15]Rubin, Kenny. (2012). *T-shaped Skills and Swarming Make for Flexible Scrum and Agile Teams*. Retrieved March 20, 2015 from Scrum Expert: `http://www.scrumexpert.com/knowledge/t-shaped-skills-and-swarming-make-for-flexible-scrum-and-agile-teams/`

With a mature and highly-functioning scrum team, an employee will spearhead a story in the wheelhouse of his skill set, often leading others in completing the work. Other times, the same employee leaves his comfort zone to work on a story in someone else's wheelhouse. This all happens without regard for rank or tenure. As the team commits to stories in sprint planning, they need to work together to work out the who, what, and how.

Good things happen. Emergent leadership is revealed. Team members teach one another. If a team member is unexpectedly absent, someone else is able to do the work.

For example, as product owner, I introduced a story that required the team to design and facilitate employee focus groups. As far as I knew, nobody on this team had experience with this type of work. During sprint planning, I was pleasantly surprised to learn that someone had expertise in that area. Other times you will be delighted when someone takes the initiative to put themselves through a crash course in designing and/or facilitating focus groups. Go ahead! This is the way the team builds their communal knowledge. They support each other to complete the work to which they have committed.

Part of the manager's role is to ensure that the skills needed to do the job reside (or can be learned) within the team as a collective. Team composition or skill development needs to be addressed accordingly.

The manager can help, but overall the team needs to figure it out. Necessity is the mother of invention, and doing Scrum forces you to be inventive. That applies to any team pursuit.

Now that you've heard my explanation of how Scrum works, let's check in with the inventors of Scrum.

Test Your Knowledge of the Scrum Guide

Scrum Guide, the Definitive Guide to Scrum: The Rules of the Game, developed and sustained by Ken Schwaber and Jeff Sutherland (whose portraits from the *Scrum Guide* are reproduced in Figure 4-3) is an authoritative reference.[16]

[16]The 16-page pamphlet is available for free at `http://www.scrumguides.org/docs/scrumguide/v1/scrum-guide-us.pdf`.

Figure 4-3. Inventors of Scrum. Ken Schwaber (L) and Jeff Sutherland are the authors of the *Scrum Guide*.

I advise anyone trying to practice Scrum to look at the *Scrum Guide* from time to time. I write this section after reading the guide for probably the third time in two years, and I cannot believe the misconceptions, some nuanced and some major, to which I have fallen victim. Not that the *Scrum Guide* is the final or only word on Scrum (much less Agile), but this book does a wonderful job of defining those certain things about Scrum that are immutable. Plus, it's written by the guys who invented Scrum, so it is (obviously) very credible. You will find clarification about issues where you or your team have decisions to make. Arguments about rules and definitions are readily mediated. Aside from the rules of the game, there is wisdom and experience in the words of the authors, as this book has been revised and rereleased many times since 1991. On that basis alone, it is worth a look as your practice of Agile matures with the book.

How Many of These Questions Can You Answer Correctly?

1. *How many times does the Scrum Guide mention "software"?*
2. *How many pages does the Scrum Guide dedicate to the topic of the Scrum ceremonies?*
3. *How many diagrams does the Scrum Guide use to explain Scrum?*
4. *According to the Scrum Guide, when is a Sprint Goal formulated?*
5. *How much time does the Scrum Guide suggest that the development team dedicate to backlog refinement?*
6. *How many times does the Scrum Guide mention "release planning"?*

Answers

Q1: How many times does the Scrum Guide mention "software"?

Answer: 0.

This is interesting because it glosses over one of the oft-quoted principles behind the Agile Manifesto: "Working *software* is the primary measure of progress." As you read through, you can see that the rules of Scrum have been wordsmithed so that they can apply to any group of people making a "product" that is "released." In place of working software, you will see references to "working product" (p. 4). Scrum may have been invented by software people, but its inventors know that it can be applied to pretty much any work that involves an creative output of any kind.

Q2: How many pages does the Scrum Guide dedicate to the topic of the Scrum ceremonies?

Answer: 0.

The document doesn't use the term "scrum ceremony" at all, but it does dedicate 5 of the 16 pages to "Scrum events" (same thing, different name).

Q3: How many diagrams does the Scrum Guide use to explain Scrum?

Answer: 0.

I found this amazing. There is no single standard diagram that depicts how the artifacts, events, and roles of Scrum fit together. For all of the talk about how Scrum is easy to understand, I've never seen anyone adequately explain it in one diagram. Even this book, which aims to explain only what is essential, needs two diagrams to explain Scrum (the one in this chapter concerning the workflow, and the one in Chapter 6 explaining the interactions). Nonetheless, the *Scrum Guide* is still the most concise source for credible information about Scrum.

Q4: According to the Scrum Guide, when is a Sprint Goal formulated?

Answer: It is created by the team during sprint planning. "After the development team forecasts the PBIs it will deliver in the Sprint, the Scrum Team crafts a Sprint Goal" (p. 8).

I did not know that until this recent reread! In the past few months, I've spoken with several people about the idea of sprint goals, and I always assumed (as I think did some of my conversation partners) that the product owner created a sprint goal as part of backlog refinement. The *Scrum Guide* document is full of little gems like this one.

Q5: How much time does the Scrum Guide suggest that the development team dedicate to backlog refinement?

Answer: "No more than 10% of the capacity of the Development Team" (p. 13).

I cannot argue with that number, but my development team spends considerably less than that amount of time. Agree or disagree, this nugget is a worthy team discussion point.

Q6: How many times does the Scrum Guide mention "release planning"?

Answer: 0.

I first decided to reread the *Scrum Guide* in search of an answer to a question about release planning: How does Scrum help product owners to take a long view of product development? After all, the demands of executives, bean counters, and the market require product owners to articulate longer-term (more-than-one-sprint) planning.

The *Scrum Guide* offers three references to releasing product, but none to release planning. The document mentions "strategy" zero times as well. It does mention "sprint plan" or "sprint planning" fifteen times.

About that term, *release planning.* Traditionally, software development teams use the term release planning to cover everything that they develop between releases, the culmination of work over multiple sprints. A common Agile success metric is "accelerated release cadence," such that teams would try to put out a new release, say, every 2-3 months instead of every 12-18 months. Mike Cohn suggests that the term is obsolete in a world where many companies release features more than once per sprint, as often as several times per day. "It may be time to retire the phrase 'release planning' from the Scrum or agile vocabulary," Cohn blogs.[17] "Don't get me wrong: Being able to predict what will be delivered three, six or twelve months into the future is still essential for many teams and ScrumMasters. But the term is no longer correct. We need a new term." You will now hear Agile thought leaders more often say 'longer-term planning' in lieu of the term release planning.

The *Scrum Guide* does not address my question about release planning. Happily, Rubin's excellent book, *Essential Scrum: A Practical Guide to the Most Popular Agile Process*, published in 2013, does.[18] In a chapter called "*Release Planning (Longer-Term Planning)*", Rubin explains how to manage the prospect of fixed-scope *or* fixed-date (but hopefully not fixed time and date or fixed everything) planning, looking ahead months or years without losing the flexibility that characterizes Agile.

[17] Mike Cohn, "*Release Planning: Retiring the Term but not the Technique*" *blog*, August 19, 2012. Mountain Goat Software: `http://www.mountaingoatsoftware.com/blog/release-planning-retiring-term-not-technique`.

[18] *Kenneth S. Rubin, Essential Scrum: A Practical Guide to the Most Popular Agile Process*, Addison-Wesley, 2012.

Conclusions

I don't need to tell you what getting two out of six correct or all six correct says about you. You know.

The global industry that is Scrum continues to grow. That the *Scrum Guide* has been purged of every direct reference to software shows that the Scrum model is looking to grow into other fields.[19]

Like most great reference pieces, you can turn to it in times of confusion and find clarity and inspiration. Take a look at the *Scrum Guide*, even if you have read it before.

The Honey-Do Scrum

For virtually any non-summer weekend when we are home without visitors, my lovely wife makes a list of things that need to be done around the house. Like many households, we call it the "honey-do list." Some jobs are home improvement; some are maintenance; some are just housekeeping.

Wait, isn't this chapter about software engineering? Translating honey-do terms into software engineering terms: maintenance is fixing defects, home improvement equates to new features, and housekeeping is akin to refactoring.[20]

In this section, I show how the guidelines and rules of Scrum can be applied in a setting far removed from software, the home. Here is a real honey-do list of mine from October 2012.

Bob's Honey-Do List for This Weekend

- Caulk (silicone) floors next to all tubs.
- Remove air conditioner units from windows and store them in the basement.
- Touch up chipped and scuffed paint all around the house.

[19]The same cannot quite be said for Scrum.org, the publisher of the Scrum Guide, whose tagline remains, as of this writing, "Improving the Profession of *Software* Development."
[20]See Chapter 5 for more about refactoring.

- Steam clean all the carpets, including the stairs.
- Dump run—old lamp, cardboard boxes.
- Hang towel racks and TP holder in new bathroom.
- Install extra storm window in the dining room window that doesn't have one (the one on side of house).
- Clean paint specks off of the freshly painted bathroom floor.
- Sweep ashes out of two fireplaces.
- Organize bathroom closet.

There is nothing unreasonable with this list. Any self-respecting homeowner would like to rid his life of any of these gaps. The problem is that it is nearly impossible for one person, especially one with a full-time job and kids, to finish all of these jobs in one weekend. Well, it's possible, but it would require working like a dog for two straight days, not to mention missing whatever kids' activities are happening. That's not a sustainable pace. However, failure to complete the list could lead to domestic discord. What to do?

This is the situation in which work teams of all varieties, software engineering and otherwise, often find themselves. The company, and in particular the manager, have an endless list of specific "critical" things that "must" be done "right away." Fixed scope and time duration and quality requirements: that's what the Agile Manifesto was rebelling against.

After a while, efforts to keep up with the endless and impossible task list, like the honey-do list, will lead to slapdash work, missed deadlines, unhappy customers, and worker burnout.

Scrum for Your Life

Scrum as applied to domestic responsibilities was a revelation for me. Very simple—see Table 4-3.

Table 4-3. Team Honey Doo Doo Scrum

Scrum	Team Honey Doo Doo
Product	The Winter family home
Iteration length	2 days: Saturday and Sunday, every non-summer weekend when we're at home without visitors
Backlog	The honey-do list. List of things need to be done around the house.
Customer	My lovely wife
Product Owner	My lovely wife
Scrum Master	My lovely wife
Scrum Team	Adoring husband
Chickens	2 children, 2 cats, and a dog

Honey-Do Backlog Refinement

The first order of business is to look at the large list and ask what is most important to get done right away? By completing it immediately and in a high-quality way, what will add the most value? The following is the list in prioritized order, with each item ranked.

Ranked Backlog

Theme: Finish the Bathroom

1. Hang towel racks in new bathroom.
2. TP holder in new bathroom.
3. Caulk (silicone) floor next to the tub in the new bathroom.
4. Clean paint specks off of the floor of freshly painted bathroom.

Theme: Winterize the House

5. Remove air conditioner units from windows and store them in the basement.
6. Install extra storm window in the dining room window that doesn't have one (the one on side of house).

Other

7. Dump run—old lamp, cardboard boxes
8. Touch up paint: kids' play room.
9. Touch up paint: second-floor hallway.
10. Steam-clean all the carpets, including the stairs.
11. Caulk (silicone) the floor next to shower in kids' bathroom.
12. Touch up paint: stairs.
13. Sweep ashes out of two fireplaces.
14. Organize bathroom closet.

Look at what happened here. During our backlog refinement discussions, we achieved a more clear idea of what is important. Two important things drove this prioritization, and we started to think of this work in themes.

Theme: Finish the Bathroom. The bathroom had just been remodeled by a contractor, but several things remained to be done. Completing those finishing touches is the most important theme right now. These stories will add the most value, because they will make my product owner (wife) happy. The first four items on the list are related to getting the bathroom in good shape and completely ready to use. We broke the story about "caulk (silicone) floors next to all tubs" into two smaller stories, one to do this task for the new bathroom (very important) and one to do same for the kids' bathroom (not quite as important)

Theme: Winterize the House. It is October in the Boston area, the weather is cooling off, and the heat will soon start running. We need to take the air conditioners out, pull the storm windows down, and install a storm window where there wasn't one. We will add other weatherproofing stories to the backlog once it gets colder, but for now, these two will do.

If we can get the bathroom in good shape, that would be a good accomplishment for the weekend. If we can start to get the house ready for winter, that would be nice, too. But, it's only October, and we won't see extravagant heat bills for another month or two.

The items that do not fit into those two themes go into a catch-all category called "other." Realistically, it doesn't look like we'll get to those items this weekend. By then there might be other items added to the backlog—stories that are more important than what is currently there. So we do not worry too much about the other stories yet.

Meanwhile, even going through this prioritization exercise has given me hope that I can make some good progress with the list and still have some time to enjoy the weekend. By working at a sustainable pace, my morale remains high and I do not dread upcoming weekends.

Honey-Do Sprint Planning

The sprint will be Saturday and Sunday. Based on the non–sprint-related commitments that we have, including two youth hockey games, a trip to the farmer's market, and hopes for a short boat ride, I declare that I have a capacity of five hours total to dedicate to the honey-do list. We will go through the sprint backlog in order (Table 4-4), estimating and committing to each story until we reach five hours.

Table 4-4. The Honey-Do sprint backlog. The work items are listed in prioritized (rank) order, determined by the product owner. The estimated effort is provided by the team. Estimation can be done in story points or hours.

Work Item*	Rank	Estimate	Owner
Hang towel racks in new bathroom	1	1 hour	Bob
TP holder in new bathroom	2	1 hour	Bob
Caulk (silicone) floor next to the tub in the new bathroom	3	0.5 hour	Bob
Remove air conditioner units from windows and store them in the basement	4	2 hours	Bob
Install extra storm window in the dining room window that doesn't have one (the one on side of house)	5	0.5 hour	Bob

**Work item is also variously known as product backlog item (PBI), item, user story, or story. Some agilists will split hairs about the distinctions among these terms. In practice, they are essentially the same thing, and I often hear them used interchangeably.*

The Honey-Do Sprint: Doing the Work

Saturday arrives. I have my sprint backlog, consisting of five work items, to which I have committed. When I have time throughout Saturday and Sunday, I work on completing the items, in the sequence specified by the rank.

With a finite list and reasonable time estimates, I actually take my time on the work items. I do the work neatly and completely. There are no unfamiliar tasks here, so my estimates turn out to be rather accurate. The one exception is the removal of the air conditioning units, which only takes me one hour instead of two. Since the whole list took me one hour less than I had planned, I decide to do the next item on the list, which was to take the old lamp and the cardboard boxes to the dump. This takes me an hour, including the customary socializing that always takes place at the town dump.

Honey-Do Sprint Review: Inspecting and Adapting the Work

Early Sunday afternoon, I show my work output to the customer and product owner (my lovely wife). I am happy to report that I completed six items: all five of the highest ranked items in the sprint backlog, plus one (the dump run).

We talk about the quality of the work and ideas for other related stories. It turns out to be a celebratory moment. I'm proud of the work I've done. She is happy to finally have the bathroom in good shape and the air conditioners in the basement. Furthermore, she is delighted that I ended up having time to make the dump run. It is important for us to go through the sprint backlog, so that she can see what I've done, and I can get her feedback.

The feeling at the end of the sprint is a much different feeling from the old system. In the old system, I would have worked harder, with no hope of completing the entire list. Household acrimony likely would have ensued.

Honey-Do Sprint Retrospective: Focus on Continuous Improvement of the Team

Sunday afternoon brings magnificent weather, and we do have time for a short boat ride. While on the water, my lovely wife and I conduct our sprint retrospective, discussing how it went (see Figure 4-4). We take turns stating what was positive. Then we each talked about what could be done better. All of this is done without interruption.

Figure 4-4. My lovely wife, Monica, and her adoring husband conduct a pleasant sprint retrospective during a short boat ride.

On the positive side, I discuss how I liked having an achievable list of things to do, instead of an impossible one. My wife talks about how happy she is with the bathroom. She would have been less happy if I had done the same total amount of work but didn't complete all of the bathroom tasks. We were elated that the weekend of chores ended on a happy note.

Then we discussed areas of improvement. We talked about how if, when painting the bathroom the previous weekend, I had covered the floor with a tarp, I would not have had to clean up the paint specks.[21] We talked about how next spring I might need some help with the air conditioners, as moving them around by myself is not very back-friendly.

Unlike some past discussions of home maintenance, the conversation is pleasant, focusing on what went well and what we can do better in the future. The focus is on continuous improvement.

By finishing those items that were of the highest importance, I made a noticeable and satisfying upgrade to the condition of the house. I added value! The half dozen or so undone items from the original list now compose the current product backlog. More items will be added along the way, and prioritization will take place again before the next work weekend.

[21]The specks of paint on the floor represent *technical debt*, discussed in Chapter 5.

Using the household as an application for Scrum may be an imperfect metaphor, but it does highlight how the frameworks of Agile can be applied in other areas, even outside of work.

At times I worry that I'm becoming an agilista, blindly evangelizing for Agile in all areas of life. Then things happen that bring me back to Earth.

Are There Any Drawbacks to Agile?

As I was leading the session at the 2014 ISPI Conference, I was taken aback by my response to a perfectly reasonable question. Are there any drawbacks to Agile?

A binary question, to which I responded, appropriately. "Well, yes there are." Then I paused. The audience was not satisfied, and my head was swelling with the conversations I have on a daily basis about the strategic challenges of Agile. So, I went for a divergent and long-winded (for me) answer:

> The software development community is divided on the efficacy of Agile. Some research shows that Agile development projects improve speed and quality. But there has not been enough research over a long period of time to convince everyone.
>
> The popularity of Scrum, which has become a cottage industry for charismatic, book-writing consultants, has inculcated some misconceptions which have undermined, ironically, the case for Agile. People focus so much on Scrum, which is basically a set of rules for the planning game, that they tend to ignore the enabling engineering practices that ultimately fuel effective software teams.
>
> With the possible exception of one mention of 'business people' in one of the principles, the Agile Manifesto is notably silent about the role of the manager and leadership, so important to any transformational effort. There is some emergent thought leadership in this space, but there is more work to do. I have seen managers at all levels underestimate the cultural component of such an effort, depowering any transformative oomph that such an initiative might have. I hear executives proceed as if Agile is just a training thing. 'Get the people trained on Agile, and we will be agile,' they say.

> Top-down governance, a necessary evil in big, publicly traded companies, is usually highly disruptive to Agile teams, unless all of the operational functions understand Agile and adopt an agile mindset. The same can be said of the support functions, which would include the lawyers, the bean counters, and yes, the people people (HR).
>
> Other than that, it's just great.

The person who asked the question had more questions for me after the session. "What are you saying? Are you a champion of Agile or a critic?"

Sigh.

I believe in Agile. Following its values and principles can lead to work output that is more focused on outcomes. I love that so many smart people, the authors of the Agile Manifesto and the Scrum Guide, other thought leaders like Mike Cohn and Kenny Rubin, and many people with whom I work, are so invested in making Agile work, just because they think it's the right thing to do. Not only is it the right thing to do, agile ways of thinking and doing can transform the world of work and beyond.

CHAPTER

5

The Agile Software Engineer's Toolkit

We're tired of writing crap. We are tired of embarrassing ourselves and our employers by delivering lousy software. We have had enough of telling our customers to reboot at midnight. We don't want bug lists that are a thousand pages long. We don't want code that grows more tangled and corrupt with every passing day. We're tired of doing a bad job. We want to start doing a good job.

—Uncle Bob Martin[1]

When you hear about Agile software development, the talk is dominated by the planning game. Scrum, Kanban, and other popular frameworks define how to plan what will be produced and when. The focus is on how to choose the stories that will produce the most value for the customer. The stories are

[1]Uncle Bob Martin, "Software Craftsmanship: What it's all about," Clean Coder Blog, January 17, 2011, `http://thecleancoder.blogspot.com/2011/01/software-craftsmanship-what-it-all.html?_sm_au_=iVVWTj7qJf1MvHz7`.

broken into small enough pieces that they can be completed within one iteration. The benefit is in working on the correct things and completing them in a somewhat predictable manner. Once the planning game is in place, attention is turned to how the work will be completed. Often we find that how the work is done is a limiting factor. That's where the Agile engineering practices come in.

Over the past two decades, thought leaders in the Agile software development world have codified a series of enabling engineering practices fueled by agile principles that help produce higher-quality software faster.

Most of the practices are easily explained by way of metaphor or whimsical sayings. For the former, one might liken refactoring to maintaining the cleanliness of a kitchen. For example, if you take a few minutes to clean up every time you eat, you won't have to spend many minutes washing a big pile of dishes in the sink. For the latter, the practice of pair programming can be summed up by an old saw: two heads are better than one. Of course, simplistic metaphors and aphorisms can only take us so far. For us to learn the lessons of modern software development and ways to apply them to other professions, we need to dig deeper. Fortunately, there is a level of depth in the thought leadership and history that invites more detailed consideration.

Many of the concepts present as inaccessible to the lay (nonengineer) practitioner. The terminology itself is unfamiliar and in many cases unintuitive. Common explanations, supported by an avalanche of hefty books, blogs, websites, and conference keynote presentations, are shrouded in engineering speak and code examples. The iconic figures of the Agile engineering practices are super smart but seem to have little regard for communicating in terms that the rest of us can understand.

The prospect of exploring these practices is daunting. As a consequence, few outside of the software engineering field dare to step into that world. Nonetheless, the work of demystifying these concepts will be a worthwhile investment, providing an abundance of ideas for how to work better in your profession.

In this chapter, I explain some of the most well-known practices from the Agile software engineer's toolkit. The goal is to elucidate how they can be applied to the development of nonsoftware assets, such as training courses, human resources systems, and other creative outputs.

XP: The Origins of the Practices

In 1999 I had no idea what the engineering practices were, and I didn't work in the software industry. Now as I look back, it's like peering into the origins of history. Before the Agile Manifesto and before the explosion in popularity of Scrum, there was *extreme programming* (XP). In 1999, Kent Beck, one of the original Agile Manifesto signatories, released a book called *Extreme Programming Explained: Embrace Change*.[2] In it, he lays out the "Extreme Programming practices," which focus on improving software quality and responding to change:

- **Fine-scale feedback**
  - Pair programming
  - Planning game
  - Test-driven development
  - Whole team
- **Continuous process**
  - Continuous integration
  - Refactoring or design improvement
  - Small releases
- **Shared understanding**
  - Coding standards
  - Collective code ownership
  - Simple design
  - System metaphor
- **Programmer welfare**
  - Sustainable pace

This list is a general reference. I present detailed commentary on roughly half of them in this chapter, and I discuss others that are not listed here.

Fin de siècle XP and Scrum developed during roughly the same time period. Beck's book came out in 1999. Scrum was invented some time in the early 1990s, and it was codified in 2001 with the release of *Agile Software Development with Scrum*, by Ken Schwaber and Mike Beedle. Today the ScrumAlliance, the most popular association of Scrum practitioners, has approximately 350,000 members.

---

[2]Kent Beck, *Extreme Programming Explained: Embrace Change* (Addison-Wesley Professional, 1999).

The success of XP relied on a need for team authority for determining how they will work. Whether that means a flat organizational structure or something else, teams need to be largely insulated from the day-to-day, minute-to-minute distraction of management oversight. Many individual contributors will gladly explain how management, in traditional constructs, gets in the way of getting a job done. You will see that these practices are really examples of how professionals are, the Agile Manifesto says, "uncovering better ways of developing software by doing it and helping others do it."

Automated Testing and Beyond

Automated testing (also called *test automation* or *Agile testing*) is among the most discussed of the Agile engineering practices.

Automated testing is a process where code is inspected for *defects* (bugs) as it is checked in to the *code repository*.[3] Instead of quality assurance engineers manually inspecting and testing code, they use testing software to automatically perform the job. Automated testing, like automated anything, saves a tremendous amount of labor, which can be repurposed[4] for other things. It also yields higher quality software by more accurately and more quickly finding defects in the code.

Note Quality assurance engineers are also referred to as *testers, developers-in-test*, or *QA*. I use these terms interchangeably.

If you have automated testing, the next thing you will want is continuous automated testing. This is where the code being checked into the code repository triggers the automated execution of a test suite.[5]

Then as you bring the productivity gains of automation and focus on quality to higher levels, *continuous integration* is introduced, which is having all developers continuously integrate their changes with every other developer working on the same system. Beyond integration is the actual delivery of the

[3]A *code repository* is a place where the current version of the binaries (also known as *source code*) is stored. Think of it like a shared drive where people check in and check out the code as they work on it. Code repositories are connected to other functions and tools that are needed to make the code actually work. For example, dependency tools hold code for other applications that are needed to run the software.

[4]See Chapter 7 for a discussion of repurposed labor as a monetizable success metric.

[5]To a writer, that's the same thing as spell check instantaneously pointing out misspelled words.

new feature. Automation of this function is called *continuous delivery*. Then, *continuous deployment* is the approach that continuously integrates clean code into production.

The bar continues to be raised. Today, the ultimate state of automation and integration is called DevOps, one of the hottest topics in the software business today. This is a bringing together of the development (code writing and testing) and operations (and systems administration) functions. Finally here we see the automation of processes that bring new code from the source code repository directly to the market.

Figure 5-1 shows the typical path of a new feature or function, from the writing of the code to delivery to the customer.

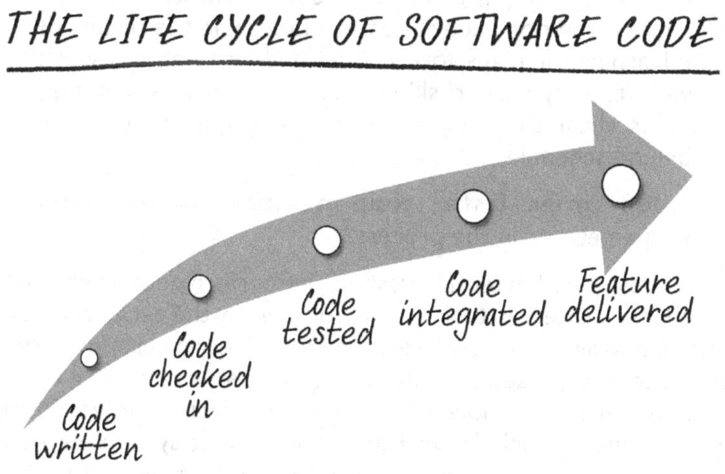

Figure 5-1. The life cycle of software code. When done manually, this all takes a long time. Code writing is still done manually by humans, but when the testing, integration, and delivery are automated, the whole sequence is completed in a much shorter time.

Picture it: an engineer writes a line of code, or a few lines, that introduces a new functionality. As he quits for the day or goes to lunch, he checks his code back into the source code repository, where it is tested, integrated, and delivered in a short time. This defect-free code is possible due to the early detection of defects through automated testing.

The practices of continuous integration and continuous delivery make it possible for applications to be updated all the time with new features, with no distraction to the user. For example, you might notice as you log in to cloud-based applications such as Facebook, Amazon, or eBay, new features and functions that weren't there yesterday seem to magically appear and work perfectly. Contrast this with versioned software that we are all accustomed to seeing, such as Microsoft Office or iOS, where you need to load new versions to your hardware before you can enjoy the new features.

There is copious research that has shown the benefits of test automation. David Rico reports that agile testing is:

- **10 times more efficient than code inspections.** Code inspection, also known as *manual debugging*, is where quality engineers pore over code to find known bugs.
- **100 times more efficient than traditional testing.** Traditional testing is when a quality engineer runs the application manually, clicking every button and trying out every function to make sure it all works. This technique is the one I see almost exclusively in the testing of e-learnings. It takes forever, and it doesn't always work well. It's very easy to skip a test, and humans will sometimes cheat the process, especially if they are tired or behind schedule.
- **1,000 times faster than manual testing.** Tests happen earlier in the process.[6]

Frankly, this topic is of limited interest to the performance consultant, but it should be of great interest to readers working on the technical side of the production of anything. The key to improved engineering productivity is these practices, which are focused on automating processes that bring the product features to the customer more often with no defects. The world of learning technology (which includes learning management system administration and production of electronic resources such as e-learning and performance support tools) is rapidly moving in this direction. In fact, the eLearning Guild hosts a conference annual now called DevLearn, which focuses on learning as well as workplace technology.

An Agile shop, one that is committed to producing higher quality software faster cannot be without these innovations. Customers today have little tolerance for defects, and they certainly do not want to wait 18 months for a release, particularly when a more agile company is delivering value every two weeks through iterative development.

---

[6]D. F. Rico, *The Cost of Quality (CoQ) for Agile vs. Traditional Project Management* (Fairfax, VA: Gantthead.com, 2012).

Test-Driven Development

Figure 5-2 shows a very basic view of *test-driven development* (TDD), one of the most powerful practices. With TDD, the test is written and run (and fails) before the code is written. The goal of writing the code is to pass the test and nothing more.

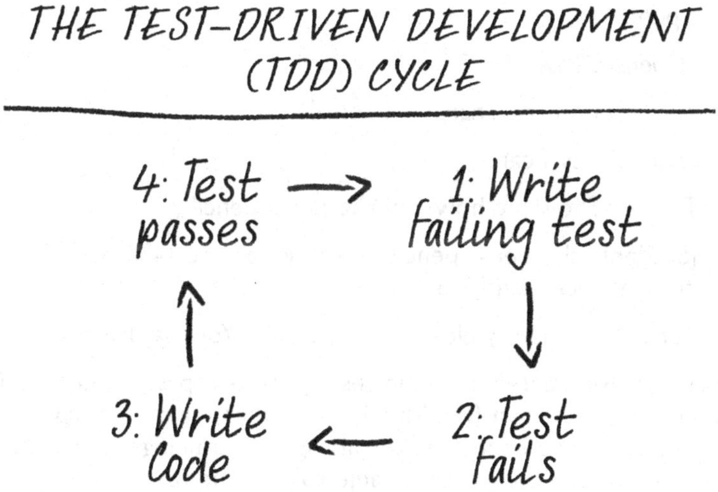

Figure 5-2. The test-driven development (TDD) cycle. A test fails before the code is written.

Uncle Bob Martin expands on his definition with "The Three Rules of TDD"[7]:

1. You are not allowed to write any production code unless it is to make a failing unit test pass.
2. You are not allowed to write any more of a unit test than is sufficient to fail; and compilation failures are failures.
3. You are not allowed to write any more production code than is sufficient to pass the one failing unit test.

Writing a failing test first does powerful things. Writing the test first ensures that the objective is examined first. Having a test fail before writing code that makes it pass ensures that something has changed.

[7]See `http://butunclebob.com/ArticleS.UncleBob.TheThreeRulesOfTdd`.

Application of TDD to Teaching

Years ago I designed a training activity that elucidated the importance of verifying the application of learning, which in this case involved observing the desired workplace behavior. Let's say we're in a situation in which we're asked to teach someone to sharpen a pencil. It goes something like this:

> *Teacher:* Today I am here to teach you how to sharpen a pencil.
>
> *Student:* Okay.
>
> *Teacher:* Can you sharpen a pencil?
>
> *Student:* Yes, I can.
>
> *Teacher:* Show me how you sharpen a pencil.
>
> [Student sharpens pencil, meeting the established performance standards.]
>
> *Teacher:* Okay, very nice. Training is over. You may leave.

In this example, we started with the test. If the test passes, then no further action is required. If the test fails (that is, the student cannot sharpen the pencil), then we know the student needs training. The training we provide should be just enough for the person to be able to pass the test, and nothing more. By administering the test first, we potentially save a lot of time.

TDD as Performance Improvement Practice

From a human performance improvement standpoint, an awareness of TDD can bolster our practice of front-end analysis. Let's look a typical request to develop a training course. As a performance consultant, I am often (at least weekly) presented with a request to create learning assets with no reference to the business problem being solved. "Yeah, I need a one-day training class on basket weaving." This is related to the classic scenarios presented in Chapter 3.

When encountering an "order-taking"[8] situation such as this, there are simple yet powerful questions we ask to reframe the request. They include:

- What is the desired outcome?
- What will change as a result of us implementing something?
- What will be different after the solution is delivered?

[8] *Order-taking*: a situation where the consultant is recast as a diner waitress.

- What will happen if we do nothing?
- What is the root cause of the performance problem?

Do not be surprised if a frustrating, circular, rhetorical conversation ensues with your client, where everyone needs to acknowledge that only rarely is the answer to these questions related to training. After all, if it was a pure training need, as the original request assumed, we could have remediated the employee capability gap with training only. No surprises here, since in the vast majority of cases (some say 85% of the time),[9] training alone is not the solution to problems of human performance. Our client requestors will see this state of affairs as unfortunate. They were hoping that we could help them tick the box by developing and rolling out a training "solution."

If we can start with designing the outcome—that is, if we can write the test before we design the intervention—we significantly improve the odds that our solution will contribute to solving the business problem. Or at a minimum, we know whether the solution answers the test question.

Continuing this line of discussion, I often find myself as the bearer of bad news: "Mr. Client, I agree that you have a problem, and I'm not yet sure what the answer is, but it ain't training."[10] Maybe your people don't understand your expectations? Maybe the process is broken? Maybe the interface on your application is not intuitive? Maybe people are not motivated to do what you want them to do? In these cases, training is not the answer. If you look at the possible causes of issues that inspire training requests, it is really difficult to imagine a case where training alone is the answer. We saw this in Chapter 2, during our discussion of Thomas F. Gilbert's behavior engineering model.

What to Do?

Do not let the client walk away; we can still help them! Yes, even the education people can help with business problems.

If we responded to every training request with diligent and dutiful fulfillment, as I did for many years, we would be very busy creating things that add no real business value. On the other hand, if we restricted our efforts to projects that met some sort of academic definition of training/education, we would be doing almost nothing. Both of those situations are bad places to be. The sweet spot is doing things to help our clients succeed, regardless of whether solution meets our definition of training.

---

[9]In Chapter 2, I explained how I was unable to verify the 85 percent rule as a research-based assertion. Anecdotally through my own experience as a performance consultant, that number sounds perfectly reasonable, if not conservative.
[10]Speaking of which, be sure to check out my blog, *It Ain't Training*.

Almost any work we do in response to this type of analysis is okay as long as it's adding value. To add value is to correlate a business benefit after the thing is implemented. If you can get your client to express their acceptance criteria ahead of the work, there's a better probability that you'll be able to deliver a worthy outcome. That is, if what we do works, what test will be satisfied?

In my profession (and hopefully yours as well), we are in the business of adding value, rather than the business of creating useless products. We have to think differently about how we create tests. Many of us in the learning business are familiar with how to create training tests in the realm of the classic Kirkpatrick model. This would include knowledge reviews, behavioral observations, and even games. But by applying TDD to education, we will need to invent different types of tests to answer different types of questions. How do you measure awareness? Buy-in? Teamwork? Innovation? Strategic thinking? These questions might be out of our comfort zone, and indeed, out of scope for what we think of when we think of corporate learning, but that doesn't mean we shouldn't attempt to work with our clients to write tests for them. It will take persistence, creativity, and innovation, because every business problem is unique. Certainly our clients are often out of their comfort zone with these questions as well. That is why they called us in the first place.

Refactoring

We build on the concept of TDD with refactoring. Martin Fowler (Figure 5-3) provides what we will consider, for the purposes of this discussion, the official definition of this term. *Refactoring* is "a disciplined technique for restructuring an existing body of code, altering its internal structure without changing its external behavior."[11]

[11]Fowler wrote the book, with some coauthors, *Refactoring: Improving the Design of Existing Code* (Addison-Wesley, 1999). In Fowler, we are introduced to another of the original Agile Manifesto signatories. When you search for Martin Fowler, "refactoring" prefills after his name, leading me to the conclusion that he is best known as the refactoring guy. When you look up refactoring, the first prefill option is "refactoring Fowler." I call this *bidirectional prefill authority*, or BPA. This is how you invent an esoteric engineering term.

Figure 5-3. Martin Fowler. He literally wrote the book on refactoring. (Photo courtesy of © Ade Oshineye)

He continues, "Its heart is a series of small behavior preserving transformations. Each transformation (called a 'refactoring') does little, but a sequence of transformations can produce a significant restructuring. Since each refactoring is small, it's less likely to go wrong. The tests written via practicing TDD provide the confidence that the system's behavior hasn't changed. The system is kept fully working after each small refactoring, reducing the chances that a system can get seriously broken during the restructuring."[12]

Refactoring is occasionally referred to as *design improvement*. We will see that it is an apt alias, but nonetheless you will hear the term refactoring far more often.

Refactoring Your House

Refactoring can be explained by way of analogy. You may hear it described as being analogous to maintaining and improving the condition of your house (Table 5-1). The house is the product or application. If you install a home theater or add a dimmer switch to an existing light switch, that is adding a new feature or functionality. If you reorganize the linen closet or change the filter in a vacuum cleaner, you are refactoring, making internal or structural improvements without changing the function.

[12]This explanation comes from `refactoring.com`, which is a section of `martinfowler.com`

Table 5-1. New Feature versus Refactoring in a Household Maintenance Examples

Term	Definition	House Analogy
New feature	A functionality that did not exist before	Install home theater; add a dimmer switch
Refactoring	Changing the internal structure without changing the external functionality	Reorganize the linen closet; change the filter in a vacuum cleaner

The homeowner analogy is further explored later in this chapter. But first a word about technical debt. You can't understand refactoring without understanding technical debt.

Technical Debt

One of the precepts of Agile is to create defect-free software in small increments. *Technical debt* is a wonderful term that engineers use to describe code that causes the system to be less extensible and more expensive to maintain. Usually people associate defects (bugs) with technical debt, but more common is the presence of duplicate code (the same lines of code unnecessarily appearing in multiple places).

Every time a piece of software is released with a technical debt in it, it is like borrowing money. Eventually you have to pay it back, with interest. The more debt you have, the greater portion of your money is spent paying the interest.

Later in this chapter, I introduce the concept of clean code. One of the goals of Agile is to produce *clean code*, free of defects and code smells. If the code is clean, there is no technical debt.

If you clean up your mess as you go along, there will be no accumulated mess. Spend a little time cleaning up your dishes right after dinner, and you will never face a sink full of dirty dishes. The time that will be required to clean the dishes later is dish debt. There is also laundry debt, workbench debt, belly fat debt, appreciation for the people who love you debt, and many others.

Technical debt will still build, even if the features start off with no defects. Technology changes, compatibility issues arise, functionality becomes obsolete. Proactive refactoring can slow the accumulation of technical debt.

Over time the problem of technical debt can become crippling, and software engineering functions grapple with how to manage—as Uncle Bob said—"bug lists that are a thousand pages long." In most large companies I have seen and heard about, there are *sustaining teams*, whose jobs are only to fix bugs and pay back technical debt. I have witnessed as much as 50 percent of a function's personnel and resources dedicated to addressing technical debt. Imagine the uphill climb that a company faces if they only have half of their engineering team working on forward-looking development, innovation, new features, and bringing new products to market. Technical debt, if left uncontrolled, is a gigantic competitive disadvantage. Most large software companies (and large companies with substantial technology functions) grapple with it. Recent stock price history for large IT companies should tell you what you need to know about how that is working out.

Startups and nimble smaller companies tend to have fewer problems with technical debt. They can't afford it.

Code Smells

In Fowler's book *Refactoring*, he and Kent Beck discuss the idea of code smells, defining and briefly explaining 16 of them.

Code smells are "structures in the code that suggest (sometimes they scream for) the possibility of refactoring"[13].

The number one code smell is duplicate code. It's not hard to understand. If you duplicate code, then a change in one place will have to be repeated in every place where the duplicated code appears. Chances are good that you'll miss one of these changes, causing incorrectness in the programming.

The opacity of the engineering world Many of the books, blogs, and speeches are off-putting because of the incomprehensible code examples and oblique terminology. Code smells is such a subject. Here are some of the labels for code smells that Fowler and Beck throw at us, which I will not describe in detail: *long parameter list*, *divergent change*, and *parallel inheritance hierarchies*. It's worth persevering through the terminology to get to the concepts.

Going back to our house maintenance metaphor, a wobbly handrail on your stairs is a code smell. The wobbliness suggests refactoring. After noticing this condition, you can, with a relatively small effort, tighten the loose screws so that the rail holds firm. You have not changed the function of the rail, which is to provide something to grasp when using the stairs, but you have improved the structure of that rail by making it more stable. If you defer tightening or replacing those screws, eventually the railing will get ripped off of the wall, robbing you of the functionality of the handrail, and exposing you to a much larger home improvement project. By waiting, you also introduce risk that with a loose or missing handrail, a stair climber or descender has a greater chance of falling down the stairs and breaking his neck.

[13]Fowler, *Refactoring*, 3

With refactoring, you might eventually conclude that more significant structural changes are in order. If, after tightening the screws, the railing becomes loose again after a few weeks, you might decide to change how the railing is attached to the wall. You might introduce anchor screws. You might change the position of the mounting brackets so that the screws holding the railing to the wall can be driven into wall studs. In either case, you have not changed the functionality of the railing. There was a slightly bigger effort here, but you have made it so that the railing is less likely to require maintenance in the future. Although simply tightening the screws might have seemed like the lazy way out, it did represent the minimum potentially viable effort to stabilize the railing. If that minor repair held fast, then you did not waste the time on the more involved repair.

Back in the Learning Department

We accumulate debt in the learning department. While continually focusing on the production of new learning assets (e-learnings, job aids, classroom training materials, quizzes), the need to provide care and feeding of existing courses builds up in the background. Every waterfall method has a word or phrase to describe this need for maintenance. Sometimes it's called sustainment; sometimes it's called control. Whatever you call it, it rarely gets sufficient attention, because there is always a new thing[14] to work on. As soon as we finish creating one thing, the next thing in the queue is right behind it, waiting to be created. If you calculate what it would take to maintain or overhaul all of your courses, you might find that there is no time for anything else.

What to do? How does refactoring help? From a strict definitional approach, refactoring is changing the internal structure without changing the external functionality. Take an e-learning as an example. As content inevitably evolves, words, diagrams, statistics, and other pieces of the content need to be updated, but the e-learning will function just the same, delivering content aligned with the same objectives.

We can calculate how long it would take to perform maintenance, say, every six months. At this juncture, ask these questions:

Does it need to be maintained at all?

---

[14]The word *thing* may seem a bit colloquial, even by the standards of this book. However, there is a bit of a back story. Years ago, before I knew about Agile stories, our team was searching for an all-encompassing word to describe all of the different types of learning assets that we developed. We settled on *thing*. In engineer-speak, we might call these *objects* (as in, object-oriented design or the administration of learning management systems, which we will not discuss in this work)—but, to an English major, an object is a thing, and calling a job aid an object sounds just plain weird.

If we are talking about a course that is adding little continued value, then the answer is probably no. If nobody is taking the course, or the objectives are no longer aligned with a critical strategy, then there is no good justification for performing the maintenance. If on the other hand you have a course that is gangbusters—with lots of usage and tons of relevance—it will be more important to keep the course in tip-top shape.

Should maintenance be a scheduled story, or can refactoring be done outside of the backlog?

This is a thorny question, one the team needs to decide how to handle. Overall, if the refactoring is going to be related to the impending release of new functionality, then the new functionality itself should be a story, and the refactoring can happen as a matter of course.

Typically clients are far more interested in new functionality than maintenance, so it's hard for them to regard refactoring as a story unto itself. Clients are not often persuaded by promises of a clean code base.

Heroic team members may take on maintenance or refactoring outside of the scheduled work. Or courageous scrum masters may lobby for a fixed portion of team capacity to be dedicated to such activities on an ongoing basis. No good deed goes unpunished.

How much time should be set aside for refactoring, or is it something that is just done "in one's spare time"?

If your product catalog or code base is in good shape, refactoring can be done as a matter of course through spare time, or as opportunities arise. I think of the idea of fixing a hole in the wall. The official story might be to fix the hole with a new piece of drywall and some plaster. But as long as the wall is open, we might choose to tidy up some other things. We might put some additional insulation in there. The impromptu installation of insulation is refactoring.

Make It Work and Then Make It Clean

Martin Fowler[15] makes a distinction between two distinct modes of work in programming.

---

[15] I have never met Martin Fowler or seen him present in person, but I have spent many hours watching his presentations on YouTube. Self-styled on his website bio as a "loud-mouthed pundit," Fowler's stage persona sets him apart from many other Agile luminaries. First, he's British, so his accent provides instant credibility. (As a friend of mine says, "the British accent adds ten IQ points in the mind of an American.") Striking a professorial demeanor, he is tremendously articulate and engaging as a presenter. Once I start watching videos of him, I have a hard time stopping. In that respect, my impression of him resides in the same area of my brain as skateboard crashes, Sidney Crosby's stick handling, and music videos from pop diva Ke$ha.

1. *Make it work:* The first phase takes place in the basic cycle of TDD. This is about making the code work in the simplest and most straightforward way possible. You don't necessarily think about systemic issues beyond passing the test.
2. *Make it clean:* The second phase is refactoring. This is where you look to improve the internal structure without changing the external behavior.[16]

You see in Figure 5-4 where refactoring fits in with our earlier cycle of TDD. After the test passes, you refactor to improve the code and then move on to the creation of your next failing test.

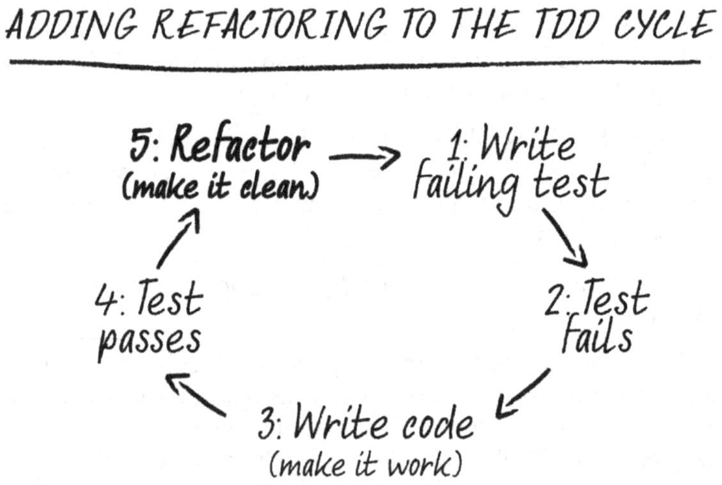

Figure 5-4. Adding refactoring to the TDD cycle. When the code is first written, the goal is to make the test pass. After the test passes, focus on refactoring, that is, improving the code.

The make-it-work-and-then-make-it-clean approach is applicable to the development of any product. You may have heard the expression, "perfect is the enemy of good." Too often we (in collaboration with our client and subject matter expert) get carried away in trying to make a training course the best it can possibly be, at the expense of time. Something "good enough" can be released now. As we let some people take the course or review the course, we can use feedback and observation to guide us as we make it clean.

[16]Martin Fowler at OOP2014, "Workflows of Refactoring," `https://www.youtube.com/watch?v=vqEg37e4Mkw`.

Think of the expense of doing both modes at once. What if the output of "make it work" is good enough? What if it takes four more weeks to go from making it work to making it clean, but the consumer never saw the "make it work" version? What if the product is destined to never see the light of day, and you worked on it for four more weeks than you had to before finding out?

From the Water Cooler We once delayed an online course on interviewing skills for months because the customer insisted that the avatars' lips had to move. This was *after* we tested the content with users and found it to be effective.

Pair Programming

Scrum and other related frameworks are only an elaborate take on what is referred to in XP as "the planning game." The rest of the game is about how to improve the way the work is done to deliver on the promise of Agile—that is, higher quality products with more value delivered.

One of the most talked about and controversial of the practices is *pair programming*. It works like this: Two engineers sit at one workstation as they write code together. One person writes the code (the driver), and the other reasons about the code (the observer, pointer, or navigator). They switch roles regularly. Sometimes there will be structure to how the roles are switched, and sometimes it's just, "I'm tired of driving; you take it," as the keyboard is passed.

In software engineering, pair programming unites the processes of code writing and code review. In a traditional model, the programmer writes the code, and when he is done, tosses it over the wall to a tester.[17] By working together, pairs can enjoy the synergies between the two workers, who presumably, have different skill sets and different ideas of how to solve a problem. QA's time is best used in doing exploratory testing in the solution for corner/edge cases. QA engineers are usually not as facile with code as developers are and will not perform a code review at the same level as a developer would. With the QA person sitting alongside the programmer, bugs, defects, and faulty logic can be spotted and improved as the code is written.

[17] *Tosses it over the wall* is a term of art used to describe this non-agile practice, with varying levels of sincerity, irony, or cynicism. The traditional lament of the quality engineer goes something like this: "I wait around for months until the code writing is done, then the programmer *tosses it over the wall* to me, two days before the deadline. They're out drinking beers because their part is done, and I'm still here in the office. I'm pulling all-nighters trying to make sense of their crappy code, fix the bugs, and make their damn feature work. I'm so unappreciated."

Pair programming provides numerous benefits, many of which have been verified by empirical studies.

- **Quality:** Pair programming results in a 15 percent improvement in quality (number of defects/line of code).[18]
- **Camaraderie:** 95 percent of programmers report that they enjoy programming as a pair more than programming alone.[19]
- **Learning:** Any time you work closely with another person, learning is bound to happen. In the case of pair programming, you will often match a code writer with a tester, or you might match a novice with an expert. The two different roles will look at things in different ways. Studies have shown that greater productivity gains happen when people work in pairs as opposed to working alone.[20] An interesting technique that causes rapid knowledge and expertise sharing is known as *promiscuous pairing*, where the pairs rotate often.

There are also a number of downstream benefits to pair programming, such as improved design quality, shorter code, strengthened teamwork, and less time spent testing.

The Downside of Pair Programming

Pair programming sounds like a no-brainer, doesn't it? Not for everyone. Only about 30 percent of survey respondents reported that they use the technique.[21] I can verify that in my eight years supporting technology groups at two large companies, I have not seen or heard of pair programming taking hold in any way, be it structured or grassroots. I have heard of it happening in small shops. Go to any Agile conference, and you will hear all sorts of proselytizers touting the impact and beauty of pair programming. Then you go home to your large company and subsequently see almost nobody doing it.

[18]Laura Williams and Robert Kessler, *Pair Programming Illuminated* (Addison-Wesley, 2003), pp. 27–28.

[19]Laurie Williams, Robert R. Kessler, Ward Cunningham, and Ron Jeffries, "Strengthening the Case for Pair Programming," *IEEE Software*, July–August 2000.

[20]Kim Man Lui, "Pair Programming Productivity: Novice–Novice vs. Expert–Expert," *International Journal of Human–Computer Studies* 64 (9): 915–925. doi: 10.1016/j.ijhcs.2006.04.010.

[21]VersionOne, 2013 State of Agile Survey, `http://www.versionone.com/pdf/2013-state-of-agile-survey.pdf`.

The main drawback is the default perception that pair programming will lead to a huge drop in productivity. Intuitively, this makes sense. The manager thinking would be: Two people working on one thing together, instead of two things separately, means that it will take at least twice as many person-hours to complete each thing.

Less Productivity

Research has shown that pair programming is slower for code development. In terms of line of code produced over time, pairs programming is 15 percent slower than individual programming.[22] You could picture it: As the driver writes a line of code, the observer can point out that something is wrong or misguided. They take a little more time to correct the issue. Presumably, the result will be better code. A little slower but a little better seems like a break-even scenario to me. Considering the cost of fixing defects or of having defects make it into production, most engineering managers would trade off a little time for a significant improvement in quality.

Resistance

The second most common objection comes in the form of resistance from engineers themselves, some of whom just like working in solitude, with ear buds in place.[23] I have a hard time knowing what to do with that. The stereotypical software engineer is long on smarts and short of social skills. But recall that moving to Agile is first and foremost a cultural initiative.

Let's say that a team decides to commit to pair programming for a while, and everyone but one person is willing to participate. That last person just "isn't into it" and, by the way, has been working this way for 20 years. There are two ways to approach the last holdout. On one hand, the team itself could take accountability for getting that last person to take the ear buds out and

---

[22]Alistair Cockburn and Laurie Williams, "The Costs and Benefits of Pair Programming," *Proceedings of the First International Conference on Extreme Programming and Flexible Processes in Software Engineering* (XP2000), 2000.

[23]Technical Editor Joe Richer adds: "I think with some engineers there is a creative pride component to this as well. Paired oil painting is probably not very popular because the artist craves personal recognition. I've no doubt paired oil paintings would often be superior... but that would be a product of the relationship."

play along. Or the manager could intervene and "force" the last person to conform. I think the former is a better approach. The manager intervention[24] in the problem would undermine the empowerment and self-organization of the team.

An extreme interpretation of pair programming is called *mob programming*, which calls for "all the brilliant people working at the same time, in the same space, at the same computer, on the same thing."[25] The peer pressure is ratcheted up so there is no place for resisters to hide.

Shared Screen Technology Anyone who has shared their screen in a meeting has unwittingly practiced pair programming. Both look at the same screen. One drives. The control can be passed around at will. Today's screen sharing technology flattens the problem of geographically distributed teams. People who are not colocated can participate in pair programming. If you add audio and video to the shared screen, it's (almost) as good as being there.

The Peer Programming Experiment

Our education team experienced a typical scenario where we found each person on the team working on separate, unrelated efforts most of the time. Although we keep in touch through the daily stand-up, after a while it feels like six tiny little scrum teams of one, instead of one team of six.

We lived with this situation until we finished a four-week Sprint with a velocity of zero. Everyone on the team worked hard on their stories, but we finished not one thing. Gulp.

We had a lively retrospective discussion about this situation. One of the things we decided to do was an experiment with pair programming. Our variation on it, which we dubbed *peer programming*, was to have each story assigned to two people.

The results were encouraging. When we discussed it at the end of the next iteration, it was clear that we enjoyed the benefits that this method promises. We learned from one another by collaborating on stories. Review time was reduced. Better ideas were generated. Mutual accountability happened.

---

[24]The thought of encouraging managers not to meddle in team business came easily to me, but people without much exposure to Agile might be surprised. Clearly there are situations in which the manager should intervene. But overall the team should be left to figure out how to collaborate, how to do the work, and how to continuously improve. The role of the manager in an Agile environment is a topic unto itself, something that I address in more detail in Chapter 4.

[25]See `http://mobprogramming.org`.

One of the most interesting things was how collaboration on stories democratized the interpersonal dynamic on the team. All of a sudden we had junior people working with more senior people, instructional designers working with project managers, and analytical people working with creative types. The team had more meaningful planning discussions about which two people could create the best outcome for each story. (Note that the *team* decided; the manager had nothing to do with it.)

As a result of the peer programming and some other modifications to how we worked, we got our velocity back. We were able to commit to fewer stories, while completing more. In the ensuing three months, our *batting average* (completed story points divided by committed story points) shot up from .000 to .863. This means we completed 86 percent of the story points to which we committed in sprint planning.[26]

Craftsmanship over Crap

In a keynote speech at the Agile 2008 conference in Toronto, Uncle Bob Martin (Figure 5-5) proposed a fifth value to append to the four presented in the Agile Manifesto. He called it "craftsmanship over crap."[27] As usual for Uncle Bob, the chosen terminology points precisely to the idea that software engineering is above all a professional discipline.

Figure 5-5. Robert C. "Uncle Bob" Martin. He is an original signatory of the Agile Manifesto and a distinguished author. He also spearheaded the creation of the Manifesto for Software Craftsmanship. (Photo courtesy of Robert C. Martin)

[26]This batting average metric around story points is not one that I've seen used in Agile. Mostly you hear the Agile gurus talk about velocity, which is simply how many story points were completed. But I think it's important to consider how that velocity fits in with committed story points. Any story that is started but not completed involves some wasted capacity, even if that incomplete story is carried over to the next iteration. I provide a full discussion of batting average in Chapter 8.

[27]Following a little backlash and further consideration, Uncle Bob redacted this value to say "craftsmanship over execution." I like the original wording myself.

Uncle Bob's books *Clean Code: A Handbook of Agile Software Craftsmanship* (2008) and *The Clean Coder: A Code of Conduct for Professional Programmers* (2011) are dedicated to demonstrating the rigor, professionalism, and discipline that goes into creating good (that is, useful and defect-free) software code. In addition he spearheaded the creation of the Manifesto for Software Craftsmanship, which states, in its entirety[28]:

MANIFESTO FOR SOFTWARE CRAFTSMANSHIP

Raising the bar.

As aspiring Software Craftsmen we are raising the bar of professional software development by practicing it and helping others learn the craft. Through this work we have come to value:

Not only working software,

but also well-crafted software

Not only responding to change,

but also steadily adding value

Not only individuals and interactions,

but also a community of professionals

Not only customer collaboration,

but also productive partnerships

That is, in pursuit of the items on the left we have found the items on the right to be indispensable.

Software craftsmanship parallels the spirit of artisanship. Traditionally, the idea of an artisan was of a master of a practical craft. Usually we think of using hands to make something useful or decorative. Woodworking, jewelry making, and handmade furniture come to mind. With the phrase "practicing it and helping others learn the craft," Uncle Bob and his signatories bring artisanship from the physical to the electronic. Software engineers and dressmakers both strive to make useful things that are well made. Over time, the artisan

[28]See `http://manifesto.softwarecraftsmanship.org/`.

develops partnerships with customers as he learns how to better add value for users. At the same time a community of apprenticeship and knowledge develops, which enables sharing about the nuances and practices of the craft.

If you want to hear a mind-blowing presentation around this idea, take a look at the video of his talk called "The Land That Scrum Forgot," which was delivered during the 2011 Norwegian Developers Conference.[29] In it, he tells the story of the famous meeting at Snowbird that led to the creation of the Agile Manifesto and the explosion in popularity of Scrum. Then watch him share the truth about how otherwise able Scrum practitioners continue to fail because they have not incorporated the technical disciplines, such as the ones discussed in this chapter, into their work.

The manifesto trend has found its way to the field of instructional design in the past few years.[30] I have heard two different conference presentations that talked about running an e-learning factory using Agile methods. The idea really gained steam with the 2013 release of the Serious eLearning Manifesto.[31] Similar to the Software Craftsmanship Manifesto, it outlines a belief system and related principles aimed at a higher level of professional focus, quality, and usefulness, specifically as it relates to the production of e-learnings. One of the instigators of the Serious eLearning Manifesto is Michael Allen,[32] a prominent figure in my field who wrote *Leaving ADDIE for SAM* (ASTD Press, 2012), a popular book that introduces an Agile-fueled process for the design and production of training courses. Although I'd like to take credit for being the first to bridge the gap from Agile to the learning and development field, Allen beat me to it.[33]

So Many Manifestos

Like the Agile Manifesto and the Software Craftsmanship Manifesto, any like-minded person can sign the Serious eLearning Manifesto. Table 5-2 compares the some manifestoes by popularity.

---

[29]See `http://bit.ly/1AbbWOo`.

[30]You are reading the words of a man who has signed all three: the Agile, Software Craftsmanship, and Serious eLearning Manifestos. Yeah, I know: with that and $2.50, I can buy a medium coffee.

[31]See `http://elearningmanifesto.org/`.

[32]The other instigators are Julie Dirkson, Clark Quinn, and Will Thalheimer.

[33]While I freely admit that Allen was the first (that I know of) to connect Agile to learning, there are some important differences between his idea and the premise of this book. Allen's excellent book is focused on the practice of instructional design (thus the easy connection to Uncle Bob's craftsmanship and clean code movement). This book is about connecting Agile to the practice of performance consulting.

Table 5-2. Signatories of Various Manifestos (as of October 2014)

Name	Year Created	Total Signatories
Agile Manifesto	2001	15,680*
Manifesto for Software Craftsmanship	2009	14,649
Serious eLearning Manifesto	2014	687
U.S. Declaration of Independence	1776	56

**Author's estimate*

Kids at Play

I have two school-aged kids, a 10-year-old daughter and a 9-year-old son. They like to play video games, particularly Minecraft. Minecraft is classified as a "sandbox construction" game. Sandbox games (also referred to as "open world") allow the player great latitude in travelling through a virtual world, deciding what to focus on.

In the game, players are plopped into an orthogonal three-dimensional world (one built with blocks but without circles), that might remind one of the Wild West. Players can travel around and build an environment wherever there is open space. They can build a house of any layout; they can furnish the house; they can build a corral around land; they can add domestic animals inside the house; they can add farm animals to the outside of the house. Based on available resources, they can build just about anything imaginable. There are two primary modes of play: survival, which is about building structures to protect against nocturnal creatures, and creative, which avails the players of additional building materials without worrying about survival against predators or hazards.

I have seen the kids play Minecraft separately and together. When they play together, particularly in creative mode, I observe many of the practices discussed in this chapter come to life. When the kids play Minecraft on the computer, they are being agile and doing Agile at once.

As they start playing, they will decide on an objective, such as building furniture for the living room of their house. The sizing and prioritization comes naturally to them. They make their stories small enough to complete in one sitting. If they want they move onto another story, they do. Sometimes instead of starting a new story, they return to other features and improve them through refactoring. As soon as the game stops being fun, they stop playing.

They prioritize by discussing what they want to work on first. They develop a common goal, and they work toward that goal. They work on one thing at a time. It doesn't matter who contributed what. They say it was created by them together.

Once in a while they have a problem, but they know that they have to resolve it if they want to continue the partnership. They continue because they have a common goal of incrementally improving the Minecraft environment they are creating. Playing the game is more important than letting discord end the game.

They do pair programming (Figure 5-6). One person will drive, and the other will observe. When the driver creates something, the observer will provide immediate feedback, like a coder and tester working together.

Figure 5-6. Kids playing Minecraft together in the creative mode. They display great agility and exemplify the benefits of pair programming.

When the observer comes up with an idea or the driver gets weary, the driver can cede control of the keyboard. They don't define roles. They never talk about who is older or more proficient at the game. They just play.

The result of their collaboration appears to be greater than what would have been possible alone. The combination of my daughter's creativity and my son's industriousness makes for an easy partnership.

The game displays how my kids innately demonstrate all of the engineering practices. They have fun. They maintain a sustainable pace. They continuously improve how they work together and the thing they are working on. That's Agile.

My children are not unique in this respect. They will enter the workforce with an innate agile mindset. Their generation is into video games, which are mostly immersive and cooperative. The schools at all levels are reforming to have children do more schoolwork this way. Corporate education is becoming gamified.

What Next?

The generation of people joining the workforce since 2000 is known as the *Millennials*. The Millennials have their own statement of values, which is expressed in the Holstee Manifesto, written by David Radparvar, Michael Radparvar, and Fabian Pfortmüller and designed by Rachel Beresh as reproduced in Figure 5-7.

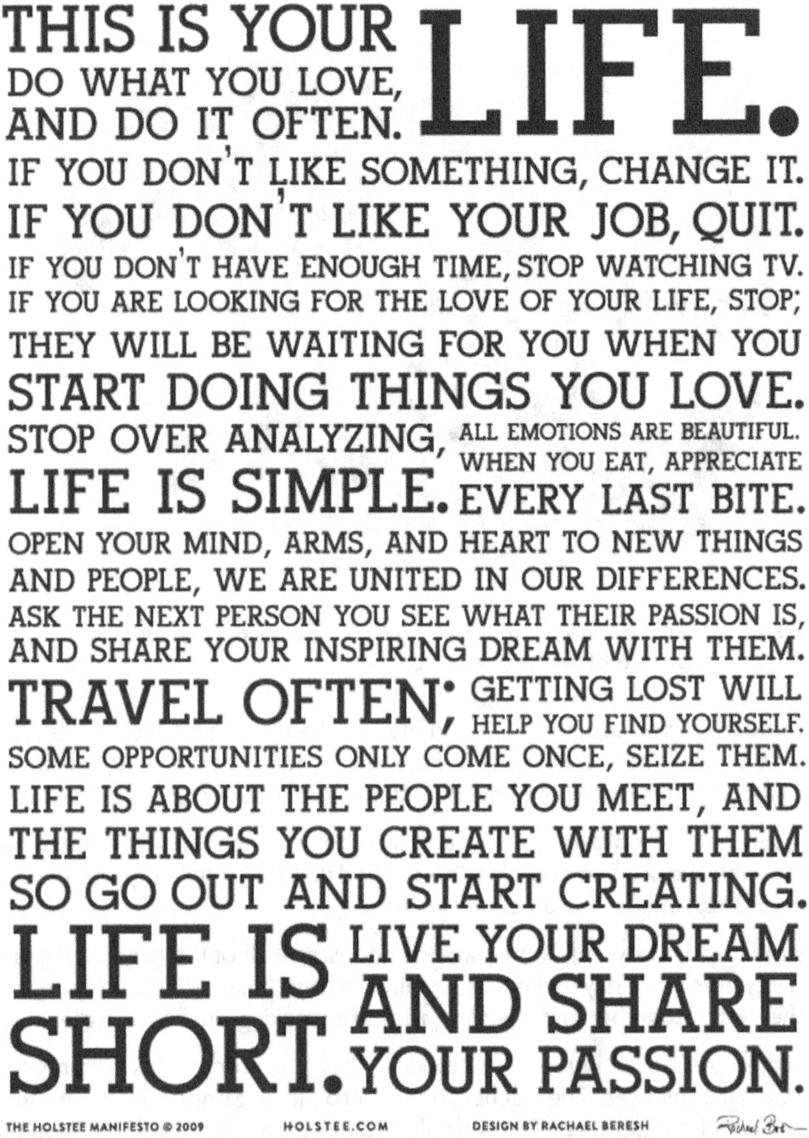
THIS IS YOUR LIFE.
DO WHAT YOU LOVE, AND DO IT OFTEN.
IF YOU DON'T LIKE SOMETHING, CHANGE IT.
IF YOU DON'T LIKE YOUR JOB, QUIT.
IF YOU DON'T HAVE ENOUGH TIME, STOP WATCHING TV.
IF YOU ARE LOOKING FOR THE LOVE OF YOUR LIFE, STOP;
THEY WILL BE WAITING FOR YOU WHEN YOU
START DOING THINGS YOU LOVE.
STOP OVER ANALYZING,
LIFE IS SIMPLE.
ALL EMOTIONS ARE BEAUTIFUL.
WHEN YOU EAT, APPRECIATE EVERY LAST BITE.
OPEN YOUR MIND, ARMS, AND HEART TO NEW THINGS
AND PEOPLE, WE ARE UNITED IN OUR DIFFERENCES.
ASK THE NEXT PERSON YOU SEE WHAT THEIR PASSION IS,
AND SHARE YOUR INSPIRING DREAM WITH THEM.
TRAVEL OFTEN;
GETTING LOST WILL HELP YOU FIND YOURSELF.
SOME OPPORTUNITIES ONLY COME ONCE, SEIZE THEM.
LIFE IS ABOUT THE PEOPLE YOU MEET, AND
THE THINGS YOU CREATE WITH THEM
SO GO OUT AND START CREATING.
LIFE IS SHORT.
LIVE YOUR DREAM AND SHARE YOUR PASSION.
THE HOLSTEE MANIFESTO © 2009
HOLSTEE.COM
DESIGN BY RACHAEL BERESH

Figure 5-7. The Holstee Manifesto. It is the Agile Manifesto for the Millenial generation.

This value system for this new generation is consistent with how we describe Agile. To wit, "Life is about the people you meet and the things you create with them, so go out and start creating."

The Agile engineering practices represent ways for people to start creating. Smart people have written whole books on each of the practices I discuss in this chapter. Blogs, websites, and conferences are dedicated to them. There are countless other Agile practices worthy of consideration.[34] You don't have to adopt all of them at once. You don't have to adopt all of them period. You don't have to use any of them. You can make up your own. These are all examples of "uncovering better ways of developing software by doing it and helping others do it." There are no "best" practices—just practices that work for you and your team.

[34]The AgileAlliance.org website offers an online *Guide to Agile Practices* that includes 59 practices, with an accompanying timeline that takes us back to 1968.

CHAPTER

6

Agile Performance Improvement

There is a pleasure in philosophy, and a lure even in the mirages of metaphysics, which every student feels until the coarse necessities of physical existence drag him from the heights of thought into the mart of economic strife and gain.

—Will Durant[1]

Agile performance improvement is a way of thinking and a work approach that blends the best of human performance technology (HPT) and Agile. As a way of thinking, agile performance improvement finds ample common ground within the two principles-based approaches. As a work approach, agile performance improvement leverages methods and practices that ensure a focus on delivering a continuous stream of customer value while optimizing collaboration and performance among the product owner, the development team, and the customer.

Is *agile performance improvement* an agile approach to the practice of performance improvement? Or is it about improving the performance of Agile practices?

[1]Will Durant, *The Story of Philosophy* (New York: Washington Square Press, 1961).

Happily, it's both.

Here is what agile performance improvement is not. It is not a box set of templates and forms and processes. You will not be able to plug-and-play your way to becoming Agile. Neither will you be able to follow steps 1, 2, and 3 to improve human performance. This is not that book.

Readers who have gotten this far have seen what the practitioners of Agile and HPT can learn from one another (Figure 6-1). We learn from Agile the benefits of breaking work into small pieces, delivering product more frequently, and continuously improving. From HPT, we learn the art of reframing requests and the science of front-end and cause analyses. In addition to these distinctions, we recognize the common ground. Terminology may be a little different, but within each discipline is a focus on outcomes and delivery of value through working collaboratively with clients/customers.

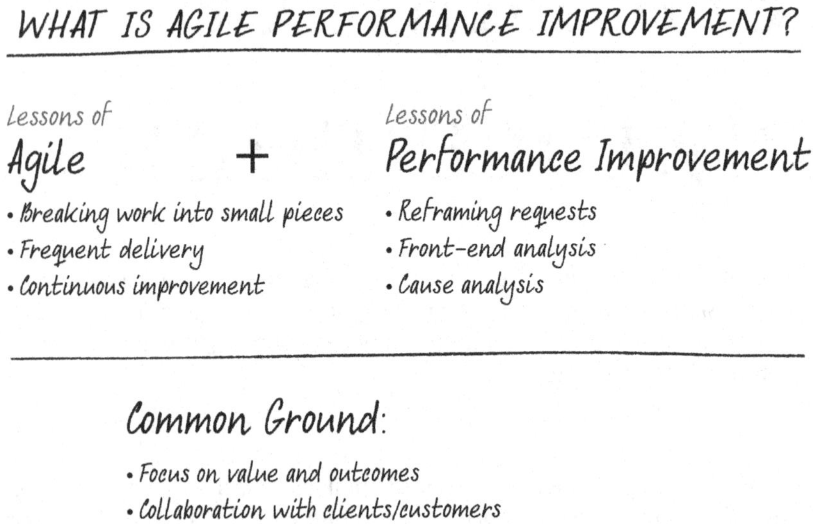
WHAT IS AGILE PERFORMANCE IMPROVEMENT?
Lessons of
Agile
+
• Breaking work into small pieces
• Frequent delivery
• Continuous improvement
Lessons of
Performance Improvement
• Reframing requests
• Front-end analysis
• Cause analysis
Common Ground:
• Focus on value and outcomes
• Collaboration with clients/customers

Figure 6-1. What is agile performance improvement? It is about the Agile people and the performance improvement people learning from one another, recognizing that they share common ground.

Will Durant's quote in the epigraph refers to the difficulty of taking a philosophy and applying it. Agile performance improvement is a philosophy of sorts, but it is meaningless until it can be applied to the "mart of economic gain and strife."

This chapter is a reflection about the philosophy. Later in the book, we look at specific methods to apply it. What makes these techniques and ways of thinking work in practice? What is there when it works, and what is missing when it doesn't work? Agile performance improvement relies on fluidity of work driven by effective collaboration. At the same time, the work is done within a larger ecosystem, which includes the team, plus everyone outside of the team who is connected to the work. The team needs to interact with outside forces that threaten to disrupt the carefully calibrated work and relationships within the Agile framework. They need to be responsive to disruptive forces, as well as the normal churn of change, in ways that optimize team performance.

After introducing the players, we will look at the how success relies on the flow of work through the system and collaboration among those involved. All of this is only done well when the team responds well to change and disruption. Team will measure the quality of collaboration and responsiveness through a set of six success measures, which I will introduce throughout this chapter.

A brief glossary of interchangeable terms In explaining the concepts of Agile and HPT throughout this book, the reader encounters different terms to describe (roughly) the same thing. Now that we explicitly describe the two disciplines as one, I need to choose one term at a time to refer to both. Here are a few interchangeable terms:

Product Owner ←→ Performance Consultant

Customer ←→ Client

Team ←→ Development Team ←→ Scrum Team ←→ Work Team

Item ←→ Work Item ←→ Story ←→ Backlog Item ←→ Project

Output ←→ Product ←→ Solution ←→ Software ←→ Program ←→ Feature ←→ Thing

Value ←→ Outcome ←→ Result

Code ←→ Design

If you don't like the term I choose, see if replacing it with one of these synonyms helps.

The agile performance improvement system includes three *players*—the customer, the product owner, and the development team. These players are all part of a cycle of delivering value to the customer's business in a sustainable and repeatable way. Figure 6-2 shows the role of each player in term of ownership and authority within the system.

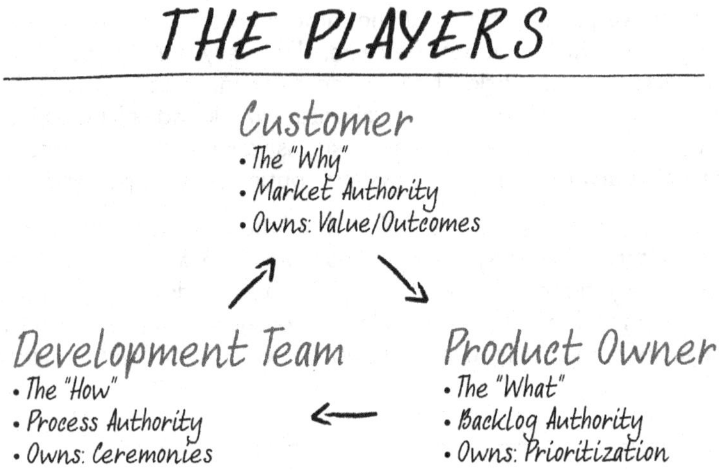
THE PLAYERS
Customer
• The "Why"
• Market Authority
• Owns: Value/Outcomes
Development Team
• The "How"
• Process Authority
• Owns: Ceremonies
Product Owner
• The "What"
• Backlog Authority
• Owns: Prioritization

Figure 6-2. The players. This model shows ownership and authority of the three players in the agile performance improvement system.

The customer owns the "why" by way of market authority. As a representative of the product's end-user, the customer knows what is valuable in the marketplace. He has authority to define desired outcomes of any output.

The product owner owns the "what," and defines it through authority to build the backlog. The product owner has a consultative relationship with the customer, and she constructs the backlog. The vision for the product, along with the wishes of the customer, drives her decisions around prioritization.

The development team owns the "how," and as such has process authority. They implement work processes as well as structured interactions (the Agile ceremonies) to move work items toward completion.

Human performance is the goal for everyone in the agile performance improvement system. If any of the players fail to execute the core responsibilities of their role well, or if the collaboration is not productive, then flow will be broken, and things of value will not be delivered to those who need them.

Early days will usually involve ample broken flow and lousy collaboration. The game becomes one of incremental continuous improvement of all aspects of the environment. As we look at efficacy in the system, the product owner (or the performance consultant as product owner) is the lynchpin of the team. The product owner is the one person in the system who, by definition of the role, has a view of the entire system. She possesses both the analytical and interpersonal skills to make this whole thing work.

Each player has a role in improving responsiveness, flow, and collaboration.

Responsiveness is agility defined, and there are two types.

- **"Responding to change over following a plan"[2] responsiveness,** which is a prerequisite for collaborating with customers. Customers have a right to change their mind as they learn more, and we have a duty to adapt to that change.
- **Responsiveness to outside forces** but within the larger ecosystem of a company. Later in this chapter we discuss how to respond to the actions of various levels of management trying to do their jobs, sometimes with agility, sometimes without.

Efficacy is the product of *flow* and *collaboration*. The *product owner* skill set supports continuous improvement by facilitating effective collaboration. To be successful, the product owner needs to also apply the *performance consultant's* consultative and analytical approach that enables the flow of work through the system.

Product owner → Collaboration

Performance consultant → Flow

Flow

Life is a series of natural and spontaneous changes. Don't resist them—that only creates sorrow. Let reality be reality. Let things flow naturally forward in whatever way they like.

—Lao Tzu

Lean is a manufacturing process that is often associated with Agile software engineering. Its principles include maintaining flow. Waste of time and resources slows the value stream to the customer and puts the team's viability at risk. Agile performance improvement invites us to consider how the collaboration among the three players helps maintain flow. Each player has accountability in a particular area. That is, one player's efficacy is influenced by and dependent on productive collaborative working relationships with the other two.

[2]"Responding to change over following a plan" is one of the four values of the *Agile Manifesto*.

About the flow diagrams to follow In this section, I present diagrams to show three aspects of flow in the agile performance improvement system: work flow, information flow, and articulation flow. Flow moves in one direction (otherwise we would call it turbulence!), so you will see arrows to represent that movement. Keep in mind that the flow is the product of interactions. For example, the customer is responsible for articulation of the value, but he will only arrive there after consultation from the product owner. Later in this chapter, I describe the two-way collaboration between each pair of players.

Work (Iteration) Flow

Work or iteration flow is the journey of backlog items. It begins with the product owner and continues as the team commits to the work. Then once the work meets its acceptance criteria, the customer provides acceptance. (Figure 6-3).

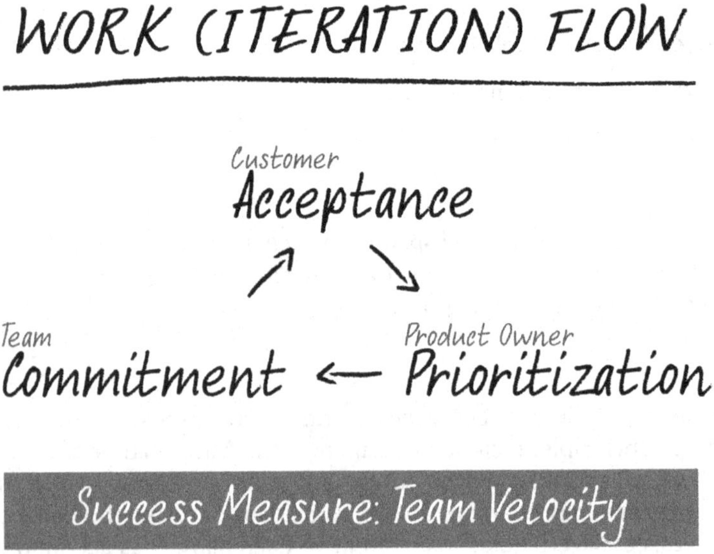

Figure 6-3. Work (iteration) flow. The product owner initiates the iteration flow with the prioritization of the backlog. The team commits to the work. Once the work is delivered, the customer accepts the work. These contributions in flow lead to team velocity.

From all of the possible work items in the backlog, the product owner creates a prioritized list for work to be done within the next iteration. The scrum team is responsible for committing to the highest-priority stories from the top down until it reaches its available capacity, based on historic velocity. At the conclusion of each iteration, the customer provides acceptance of the work output during the sprint review.

Success measure: *team velocity.* If the work flows well, the team should complete more stories, which is greater velocity.

Information Flow

As work makes its way through the system, there is a parallel stream of *information flow* (Figure 6-4), which is the movement of shared data required to complete the work. From one iteration to the next, the staging of Scrum events (ceremonies) facilitates communication and collaboration among the customer, the product owner, and the scrum team. The team's *scrum master* is responsible for making sure that the events happen. He addresses impediments and obstacles to keep the process moving. All of this work serves to enable continuous improvement. Once the stream of work is established—an ongoing relationship between customer and service provider—there is no defined end.

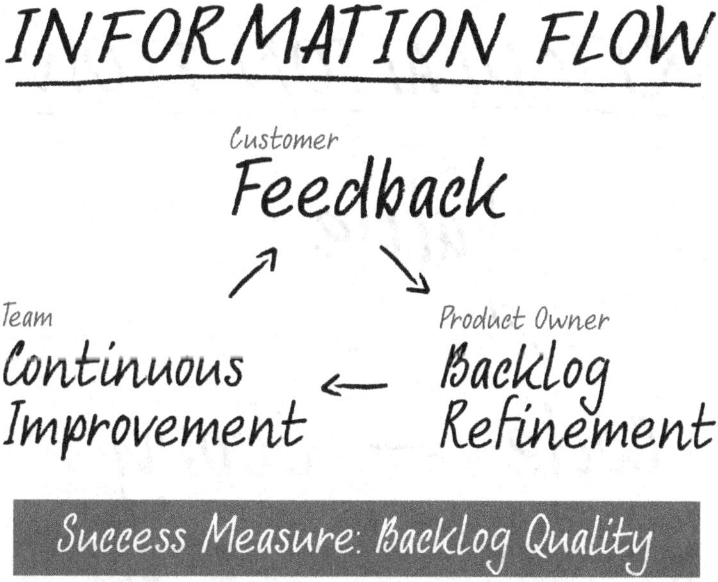

Figure 6-4. Information flow. The team drives continuous improvement through the information that is shared during the Agile ceremonies. The result is a high-quality backlog.

The Scrum ceremonies drive the flow of information within the agile performance improvement system. The sprint review in particular provides a forum for the customer to provide feedback to the team. The product owner processes the feedback through backlog refinement. The team addresses team productivity issues through other formal ceremonies and by adapting their work approach.

Success measure: *backlog quality*. If the information flow is good, then the product owner should improve her ability to refine a backlog that reflects ongoing feedback from customers. A team can choose to define high-quality backlog using a variety of metrics, such as *cumulative flow*,[3] length of sprint planning meetings, or propensity for the team to get annoyed with the product owner.

Articulation Flow

Everyone in the cycle is responsible for articulating an aspect of the work. *Articulation flow* (Figure 6-5) is the movement of ideas and expertise from one player to another. The customer is responsible for articulating the desired business value (or outcome). The product owner is responsible for articulating the story (including solution parameters), which is derived from the value. The development team is responsible for articulating the code (a.k.a. design), leading to an output that satisfies the requirements of the story.

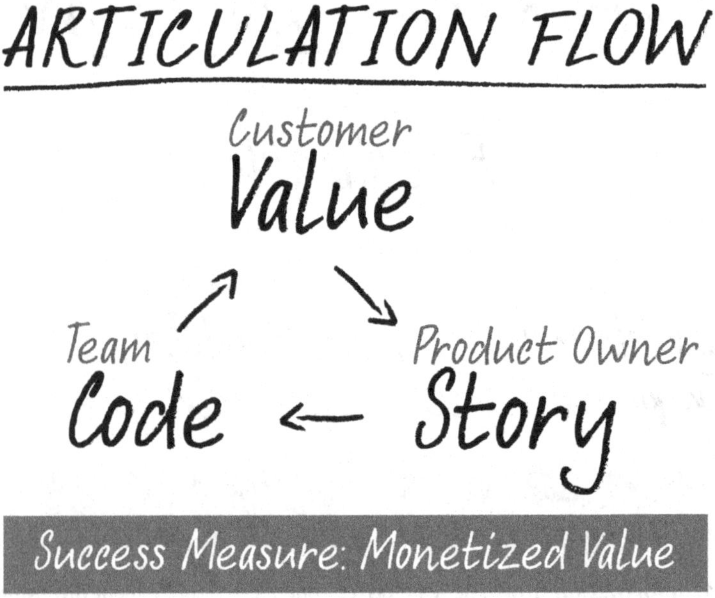

Figure 6-5. Articulation flow. Customer articulates potential value. Product owner interprets the customer's value statement and articulates the output of the team by way of a story. Development team articulates the code (design), which is used to create the product.

[3]*Cumulative flow* is a set of time-based metrics that look at how long it takes work items to proceed through the development cycle. It also counts how many work items sit in each phase of the cycle. The term is commonly used in software engineering and lean product development. Additionally, Cumulative Flow will be my rap name if I ever return to the mic.

What do we mean by code? In terms of software engineering, source code (or just code) refers to the instructions written in a programming language that make the software work. Some say that the code is the design. Referring back to the *Agile Manifesto*, the working software is favored over comprehensive documentation. The software working is result of articulation through the code. By extension, code could mean the design of a training class or other product output.

To create a product that delivers value, this cycle of articulation must continue. If the articulation flow stalls, so does productivity.

Success measure: *monetized value*. If the articulation flows well, starting with the customer, then what is created should add value that is quantifiable in terms of money. Being able to monetize the contribution of your efforts is also known as the *holy grail*. Chapter 7 will outline a variety of methods for monetizing the value of team outputs.

Improving Flow

Fluency improves through repetition, but the product owner can influence the improvement of flow, particularly with the work team, by consideration of the following Agile concepts.

Readiness. The product owner learns the importance of doing due diligence on a work item before tossing it to the team. Each team creates its own *definition of ready*. Generally speaking, *ready* means that the team has enough information to do the work, there are no impediments or dependencies in place that would prevent them from doing the work, and they understand what it means to be "done." If the 'ready?' field in the backlog says "No," the team will not (and should not) commit to working on the story.

Sustainable pace. To work at a *sustainable pace* is to do work at a speed that can be maintained indefinitely. Expecting a team to work faster than a sustainable pace is a one-ingredient recipe for burnout, disgruntlement, and poor performance. Scrum includes built-in processes where the team decides how much work they are going to tackle. The product owner's best approach for maximizing value delivered to the customer over time is to choose well which stories will be the highest priority. She does this through analysis of the potential value of a story. This quantification of value is an aid when supplying customers with data about the choices they have to make.[4] Additionally, starting from the top-ranked work item, the team commits to work until they have reached their expected capacity for iteration.

Story-writing format. The three-part Agile story syntax, which articulates the user, the need, and the outcome, reinforces the habit of focusing on employee behavior and results.

Agile performance improvement provides built-in curbs on any inclination to disrupt flow. If you violate the rules or values of Agile and HPT you will overburden the team or waste precious capacity on work that does not accomplish anything.

A Tip of the Cap to Robert Mager

The three-part Agile story syntax is a wonderful device for articulating work items, ensuring that they are focused on value for the user. As Table 6-1 shows, the Agile story syntax was foreshadowed half a century ago by Robert Mager's definition of instructional objectives, also three parts:

- *Performance*: what the learner is able to do
- *Conditions*: important conditions under which the performance is expected to occur
- *Criterion*: the quality or level of performance that will be considered acceptable[5]

[4]I say "they" because in Agile the customer/client decides. In HPT, the consultant is considered a partner of the client, and they make decisions together. This is one of the more significant points of incompatibility between HPT and Agile. Overall I prefer the way Agile does it, because it seems more realistic to concede overall authority to the customer.

[5]Robert F. Mager, *Preparing Instructional Objectives* (Belmont, CA: Fearon Publishers, 1962).

Table 6-1. Mager Objectives Aligned with Agile Story Form

Commonality	Mager's Instructional Objectives	Agile Story Form
Performance	Performance. An objective always says what a learner is expected to be able to do; the objective sometimes describes the product or the result of the doing.	"so that I can ..." (Third in sequence of story form). This is the performance of the user.
Conditions	Conditions. An objective always describes the important conditions (if any) under which the performance is to occur.	"As a <user> ..." (First in sequence of story form). The condition is that the person is in the role of a user.
Criterion	Criterion (also called assessment). Wherever possible, an objective describes the criterion of acceptable performance by describing how well the learner must perform to be considered acceptable.	"I need <function> ..." (Second in sequence of story form). The criterion is the functionality that the story delivers, which has its own acceptance criteria.

Collaboration

> *If thousands are thrown out of employment, it suggests that they were not well employed. Why don't they take the hint? It is not enough to be industrious; so are the ants. What are you industrious about?*
>
> —Henry David Thoreau[6]

The *Agile Manifesto* tells us to favor "individuals and interactions over process and tools" and "customer collaboration over contract negotiation." Clearly collaboration is a foundational component of Agile. The Scrum ceremonies, the proliferation of Agile coaches, and the myriad of thought leadership on the topic of culture all attest to the challenges of collaboration, without regard for whether you practice Agile well or at all.

Three players, three one-to-one relationships: the customer and the product owner, the product owner and the development team, the development team and the customer. We look now at the exchange between each pair of players. Successful collaboration will manifest in three success measures: value perception, batting average, and customer satisfaction.

[6]Letter to Harrison Blake, November 16, 1857.

Why the product owner is special The product owner holds a unique place in the system. She collaborates not only with the players but with everyone in the extended ecosystem. She is the only person who sees the whole product and can truly view business problems systemically. We talk about creating working software, but that is merely the development team's focus. Somewhere out there others are handling tech support, training, sales, deployment, databases, and clouds, all on behalf of a catalog of products. It is the responsibility of the product owner to share a helpful amount of this information with each person. Then the team can consider how they might automate tasks or build bridges with related functions, or at a minimum have a better idea of what happens around their product. The full fruit of this idea is DevOps, wherein everything is automated and integrated, as discussed in Chapter 5.

The Customer and the Product Owner

The collaboration between the product owner and customer ensures that the efforts of the team are aligned with the needs of the customer. It sounds simple.

Customers can try to find products that meet their needs, and product owners can create products that hopefully catch on. Collaboration improves the chances of each succeeding.

There is a transactional nature to this collaboration, where each provides to the other things that they need (Figure 6-6). The customer provides business context, and the product owner uses that information to develop the backlog of possible work items or product features. The customer provides the "why" through his description of desired outcomes and business context. In response, the product owner provides the "what" through consultation and refinement of the backlog.

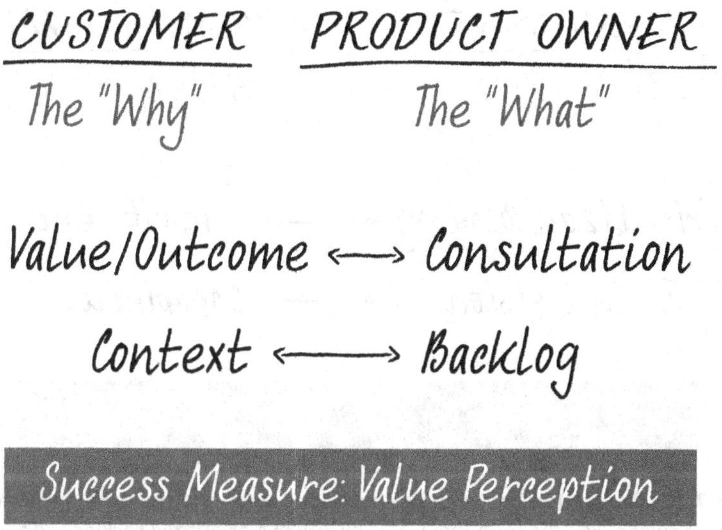

Figure 6-6. Collaboration between customer and product owner. The customer provides the "why" through his description of desired outcomes and business context. In response, the product owner provides the "what" through consultation and development of the backlog.

Scrum offers no ceremony defining the method of collaboration between the customer and product owner. The ongoing consultative conversation serves to work around this gap. The customer may express what they want in terms of output, but the product owner helps reframe the discussion (see Chapter 3), ensuring that potential backlog items are focused on the desired outcomes.

Success measure: *value perception*. Value perception is the customer's opinion of how effective the collaboration between the customer and the product owner is. Measure value perception by asking the customer directly how helpful the product owner's consulting is (on a 1-10 scale) in aligning the backlog with the customer's goals.

The Product Owner and the Development Team

The product owner brings the prioritized backlog to the development team (Figure 6-7). She provides a product vision, which is based on insights gleaned from the customer. In exchange, the development team provides a commitment to work on the items deemed to be of the highest value. Through hearing the backlog and the product vision, the team needs to adapt their capabilities to meet the demands of the work items. Ideally, the team will self-direct toward building skills, but the manager has a role here in composing a team that has the ability to do the work.

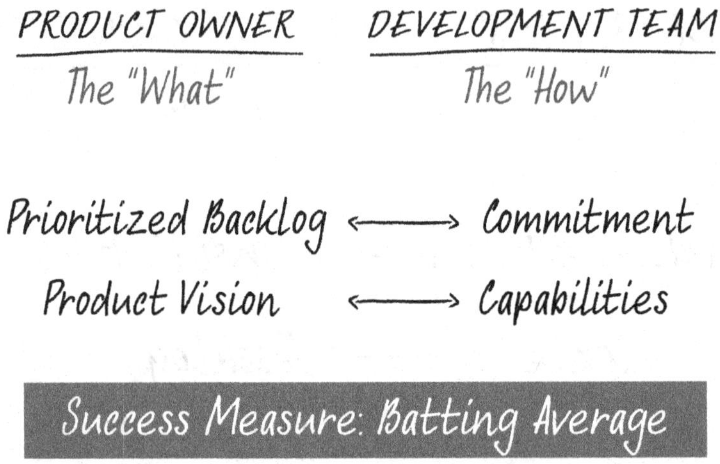

Figure 6-7. Collaboration between the product owner and the development team. The product owner gives the team the "what" by way of a prioritized backlog and a product vision. In exchange, the team provides a commitment to do the work and ensures that they have the capabilities to fulfill that commitment.

There are three Scrum events that formalize the collaboration between product owner and development team: sprint planning, daily stand-up, and sprint retrospective. With all of that built-in collaboration defined, this is the least problematic collaboration. If the product owner and the team just follow the guidelines established by Scrum, there should be continuous improvement. That is, the team understands what they are working on and reflects periodically on how they do the work. The most common gap in this relationship is if the product owner is not engaged with the team on a daily basis.

No. 1 Debate about Agile that shouldn't be a debate at all Is the product owner part of a scrum team? Answer: Yes. If you are working in a framework with an identified product owner, that person is part of the development team. Period.

Success measure: *batting average. Batting average* is a term I propose here to quantify the team's accuracy in predicting velocity.

Batting average = actual velocity / predicted velocity

For example, if a team commits to 40 story points at the beginning of a sprint and they complete 30 story points during the sprint, the batting average is .750, or 75 percent.

When the product owner is collaborating well with the development team, estimation practices improve. The team works at a sustainable pace and completes stories to which it is committed.

The Development Team and the Customer

The collaboration between the development team and the customer (Figure 6-8) closes the loop, finishes the deal, and sets the stage for future work.

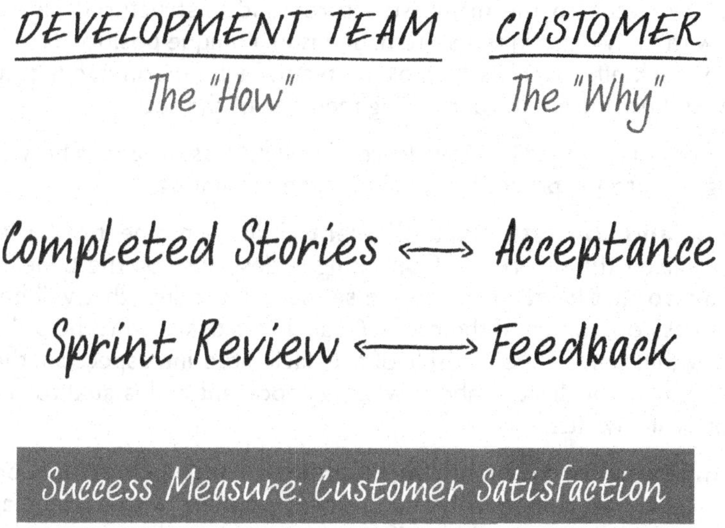

Figure 6-8. Collaboration between the development team and the customer. The team provides the customer with completed stories with the hope of acceptance. The team hosts the sprint review to facilitate feedback about the result of the work iteration.

The development team provides the customer with completed stories and the sprint review, a forum for the team to demonstrate its output. As the team completes stories, the customer accepts the work and provides feedback. The sprint review sets the stage for an ongoing collaborative working relationship. If the customer does not attend (or is not invited to) a sprint review, then this value exchange doesn't happen.

Too often, this is a broken piece of the puzzle. Teams deliver completed stories and never get to share them with the potential consumer. This is where teams risk delivering things that are of no use.

Success measure: *customer satisfaction.* When the development team is effectively collaborating with the customer, completed stories will be accepted, and the exchange of feedback will lead to continuous improvement. Customer satisfaction reflects this state, and it is measured using a single question (1-10 scale) asking the customer about the quality of collaboration with the team.

Improved Collaboration through Coaching

Many companies support the transition to Agile methods by providing agile coaches, who help teams and individuals navigate the challenges of changing to a new work method. A product owner often finds herself in the position of coach by virtue to the many (structured and unstructured) interactions she has with individuals in the system. She is in a unique position to help each player to work effectively as part of the team. Each person needs something different to become a fully functioning member of the team.

Through my study of Agile, I have learned several lessons about how to apply coaching skills to my practice of performance consulting.

Coaching and consulting are different skills. A moment of clarity came when I realized the difference. Consulting is designed for the benefit of the consultant, so that he can provide the service or product that will best align with business outcomes of the client. Coaching is designed to help the client explore within herself. As a result of this facilitated introspection, the client draws her own conclusions about what is important and is able to articulate what she really wants.

Coaching can inform consulting to make it more powerful. Consulting calls on you to rigorously analyze a business problem with a client, agreeing on the desired outcome and identifying the cause of a business problem. As I described earlier, clients typically approach the learning department with a solution in mind, but most of the time the requested solution is not aligned with the problem.

At certain points in the consulting conversation, it is beneficial to move into coach mode, applying higher levels of listening and questions that prompt the client to better articulate their vision or true desires for their business. Doing this takes more time, and takes the consulting on a less linear path. The coaching intervention can be more personally powerful, whereas the consulting conversation helps focus on a specific need for the client's constituency.

Sometimes you just coach. Although not prominent in the job description, the performance consultant finds herself in situations, formal and informal, where the consulting hammer is not appropriate for the screw that is presented. People simply need help finding ways to be more effective.

In recognizing the overlap between the coaching and consulting skill sets, the lessons for my own practice are powerful but nuanced. Anyone in a position of leadership, whether as a coach, performance consultant, or manager, has strong technical expertise. Coaching skills help complete the skill sets. The lessons learned about the human side of Agile and the power of coaching have the potential to propel your influence to new heights.

Responsiveness

Never play anything the same way twice.

—Louis Armstrong

So far, the description of agile performance improvement focuses on the closed system. The larger ecosystem includes management, project managers, bean counters, lawyers, strategy people, architects, anyone who makes red tape, and the outside world itself.

Glass half-empty: If there were no external forces, the collaborations would go better. If it weren't for management, there would be less distraction from the work, less inhibition and discouragement of creativity.

Glass half-full: All of these players have a job to do, and all of them hope and expect that they can do their part in helping the development team succeed.

How a worker bee gets annoyed with management Management oversight sometimes comes in for the wrong reason. If there are 15 bugs in a new software feature right now, it is likely that management will admonish the product owner or the team. But what is their motivation? What is the cause of that reaction? One would hope that the (product, people) manager had the best interest of the customer in mind. More likely, it is motivated by some line in a spreadsheet somewhere that shows how many bugs are in a current release. Once some project manager sees the 15 bugs, he will reflexively want to talk about the product manager or people manager about it, without reference to the context or its impact on the user. Guess what? If it made it into a spreadsheet somewhere, the team knows about it. If you trust the team, then trust them to focus on quality in an appropriate way.

The players in the agile performance improvement system need to effectively respond to all of the distractions, disruptions, and rigidity they encounter. The scrum master and the manager are there to help the teams manage these outside forces. Nonetheless, creating and maintaining flow and collaboration is really, really difficult to do, because . . .

Agile Is Antithetical to Large Corporations

Let us count the ways Agile is antithetical to inherent characteristics of large corporations. Here are some broad, sweeping generalizations for your consideration.

Compensation systems favor the individual heroics over team performance. Monetary incentives focus primarily on the performance of individuals, creating individual winners and losers to the discouragement of team work. Performance ratings are done on a bell curve that places 60–80 percent of employees in the "meets expectations" (read: average) category. All in all, these structures discourage team work and demotivate a goodly number of individuals.[7]

Structures are intrinsically command-and-control focused. For management to set expectations for owners, shareholders, and the marketplace, it is necessary to fix time and scope of product development. Fixed time and scope is the hallmark of waterfall methods, where extensive planning is all done up front. As we saw in Chapter 4, steadfastly marching toward a fixed time and scope project leads to a lack of responsiveness at the management level and disempowered teams who are afraid to make decisions. Overall, it's not conducive to innovation at any level.

Frequent top-down changes, big and small, cause disruption. Change does not equal progress. People think that any change (anything from a big reorganization down to nitpicky non–value-adding edits to a document) means that they are adding value. With agile teams trying to be self-directed in taking responsibility for the "how," people outside of the teams have trouble leaving them alone.

Just about everyone outside of the agile teams struggle to embrace uncertainty. There is a fundamental disconnect between Agile principles, which encourage adaptability to change, and corporate planning activities, which fix time and scope. Fortunately, we have emerging thought leadership in this area, with methods such as SAFe from the Scaled Agile Academy and Scrum at Scale from Scrum, Inc. The debate continues, but the agile community is attempting to address the challenges of scaling Agile to the enterprise.

Managers are conditioned to be directly involved. Having agile work teams means that managers are not part of the work team. Being removed from the work is a difficult adjustment for most managers, because they often are among the most proficient craftspeople. I have heard managers discuss the sense of loss and being lost in a new structure where they no longer do what they've always done. Frontline managers are a critical component of making Agile work in the enterprise, and they need environmental support as well. Executives need to articulate the expectations for managers in their redefined roles, and incentives need to reflect what their new focus should be.

---

[7]This basic critique of the traditional performance appraisal goes back decades. Thomas F. Gilbert touches on the topic in his autobiography *Human Incompetence*, and it is a legitimate school of thought among current-day HR consultants.

Upper management abdicates responsibility for addressing change management. Some executives think that their employees can be Agile without being Agile themselves. They think that becoming agile only means sending people to training classes and setting up teams. The change management skill set is absent in many executives, and internal or external consultants can help.

Many companies burn millions on Agile training and coaches without making progress. Sadly, they fail because they do not address whatever combination of or variation on these problems they have. It's a huge, largely unrecognized issue.

Many books about Agile come from a philosophical place that tries to overcome these problems with a prescribed system. But telling companies to plug and play a prescribed system is just a reinforcement of those innovation-crushing structures. If the culture and mind-set evolves, then the structures will follow. Every agilist's job, regardless of role, is to influence mind-set and culture, after which it should be evident to management which structures they should implement to support it.

I give you agile performance improvement, but there's no expectation that any aspect of it is universally applicable. Every situation is different. Every engagement is a new experiment in finding ways to successfully navigate new business context and collaborate with new people. You learn from experience, and you may get an opportunity to apply the same techniques more than once if you're lucky.

Model as consulting tool Years ago, my department created a model for project prioritization, a mashup of some Six Sigma and TQM techniques.[8] It was a spreadsheet formula for evaluating potential training requests on various components that might affect its relative prioritization—things like how many employees were affected, whether a comparable solution already existed, and how much time/money it would take to create it. We also developed a bank of questions to ask to define values requested by the model. After populating the component fields, the algorithm spat out a number. The higher the number, the higher the priority of the training project. We spent about three months creating the algorithm as a task team. Within about three weeks it was never heard from again. One of my colleagues was eager to try it, so she brought the model and a list of questions with her to a client discovery meeting. The client had no idea what she was talking about. The tool was full of training-speak and the model took no account of the nuances of the engagement. Disaster. I know there are plenty of successful consultants who hawk a model as part of their services. Too many times, I see external consultants come in and try to ram their proprietary model down the throats of an eager client. Again, every situation is unique. There is no magic bullet.

---

[8]Six Sigma and Total Quality Management (TQM) were popular quality approaches in the 1980s and 1990s. They were supplanted by concepts such as Lean and Agile.

Pressures on the System

Anyone in the larger ecosystem will apply disruptive pressure to the agile performance improvement system. Figure 6-9 shows the pressures on the system.

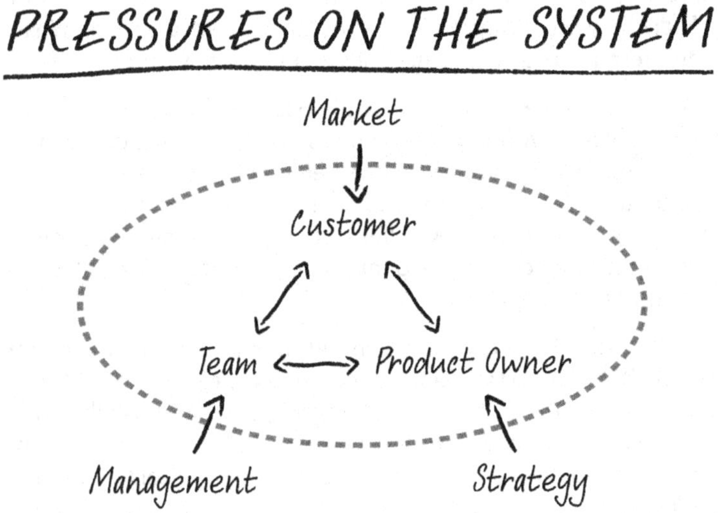

Figure 6-9. Pressures on the system. In practice, doing Agile gets difficult when the complexities of the outside forces place pressure on the closed system.

The *product owner* is the interface between the development team and the strategy people, which includes product management and all sorts of management. The product owner draws from them a variety of useful information—product and business strategies, architecture, access to data and customers—that will help refine the backlog.

The *development team* needs to interact with their discipline/vertical management and the demands of their discipline. They do also draw from them—standards, best practices, resources.

The *customer* has their own environment to manage. They work in a company as well, with its management structure, strategy, and the outside world of their outside world, the marketplace for their product.

We need to be wary of seeing agile performance improvement as a closed system. A closed system does not exchange anything with its surroundings, so the very idea of looking at any work approach as a closed system is idealistic and unrealistic. In fact, there is always ample exchange from the team to the larger system, and we need to account for it.

Improving Responsiveness

Everyone has a role in improving responsiveness to disruption and distraction. The *Agile Manifesto* value of favoring "responding to change over following a plan" tells us as much.

The scrum master holds a dual role, needing to guard against destabilizing outside forces and help the team practice Agile better. He needs to have two personas, one where he is facilitative, and one where he is able to successfully manage interaction between the team and, well, everyone.

The scrum master, while part of the development team, sits at the center of the agile performance improvement system. He is deemed a servant-leader who helps the team continuously improve by facilitating better flow, collaboration, and responsiveness.

Managers (and really anyone outside of the team) can do their part to help as well. The manager in an agile environment never directly touches the work. His job is to manage the environment so that people can focus on the job in front of them. For them, the performance consultant's toolkit (Chapter 3) is of use. Every day they should be asking, what is going on in the environment? Are people in a position to be successful? How can I use my influence to remove obstacles to teams?

Product owners have the best systemic view of anyone, as they nurture relationships and negotiate with the widest variety of people. Their anticipation and pattern recognition can head off a variety of problems as very few others could.

The development team discusses impediments every day at stand-up meetings. Work flow depends on those issues being raised expeditiously so the scrum master or manager can resolve them. Additionally, the team needs to tout its own credibility and innovation, so that everyone knows that they own the "how" and they know what they're doing.

What Can We Do?

The question is not whether disruption will occur. The question is how each of the players will respond to the pressures without allowing them to break the spirit of the team. Here is what we can all do to help the culture evolve.

Let executives know what is happening in the trenches. Executives are conditioned to focus on big-picture items, like financials, strategy, and major initiatives. They can easily be out of touch with the teams. Executives rely on advisers to provide data that tells the story of what is going on. It is usual for executives to have erroneous impressions of what is going on in the workforce, provided by people who are also not in touch with the workforce.

Did you say "out of touch?" Being out of touch is the punchline of the reality TV show *Undercover Boss*, where senior executives spend a week or two working alongside unwitting entry-level employees in their own company. It's formulaic but touching. The executive is flabbergasted by what is really going on in the work environment. Then at the end of just about every episode, the executive solemnly promises to improve the work environment and generally be more sensitive to the needs of the rank-and-file workers. Big bosses at all companies should watch that show.

Protect the work flow and collaboration. If your team is doing something that is working, let everyone know. Don't let the process and tools people force you to change your "how" in the name of best practices.

Educate everyone in the ecosystem. For years I worked within an agile practice as a provider of Agile training. I see a great thirst for knowledge about Agile outside of the development teams. People want to know more about how they fit in and their role in supporting agile teams.

Remember that everyone has a job to do. Managers need to manage; bean counters need to count beans; lawyers need to make sure we follow the law; project managers need to manage projects. For these people, getting the job done supersedes any disruption that they may cause to the agile performance improvement system.

Favor responding to change over following a plan! Things change, sometimes for good reasons, sometimes for not-so-good reasons. Evangelize Agile through your actions; always try to do what is best under the circumstances.

Defining Success

The remainder of this book explores how to define success with agile performance improvement. We can align the six success measures introduced in this chapter with the players, individually and collaboratively.

Player-specific measures

- Customer → Monetized value of output
- Product owner → Backlog quality
- Team → Velocity

Collaborative measures

- Team and customer → Customer satisfaction
- Customer and product owner → Value perception
- Product owner and team → Batting average

Those measures cover just about any meaningful outcome, from a team standpoint or from the perspective of the customer. Figure 6-10 shows those same six measures overlaid upon the agile performance improvement system.

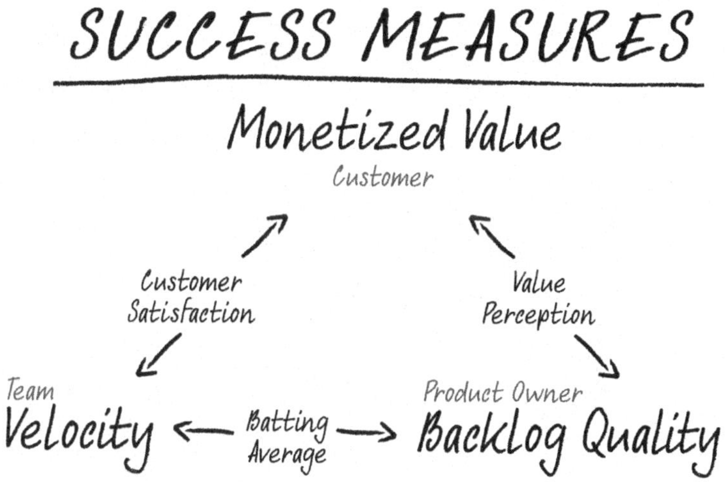

Figure 6-10. Success measures. Just about any meaningful measure of work success among the players is covered by these six measures.

What if there is a problem with an individual's performance on an agile team? Agile performance improvement favors team performance over individual performance. The player-specific measures don't consider the people on the team as individuals. Nonetheless, at any given time, some portion of an employee population will have individual performance issues. They can be in the wrong job; they could be incompatible with the team; they could have outside circumstances that distract them from focusing on the job. If a problem arises with an individual, it can be addressed by the team or by management, informally or through the established performance management process.

If by creating a baseline of these types of measures you see one or more of the measures becoming problematic, then it's time to apply the consulting and analytical techniques associated with the performance consultant's toolkit. If there is a problem, ask: What are you trying to accomplish? What is the cause of the problem? What solution can be devised to improve an outcome?

Thus endeth the introduction to the concept of agile performance improvement. The next chapter looks at some real-life examples of proving value through these success measures.

CHAPTER

7

Proving Value

Any kind of performance can be measured—reliably and with considerable precision. We can measure the performance of poets, managers, teachers, and politicians—not just that of production workers and athletes. The belief that the more complex forms of performance are not subject to measurement and quantification arises simply from ignorance about how to do it. Once you get the knack, performance that you once thought unmeasurable will usually be not nearly so difficult to measure as, say the radiation of Martian soil or the fertility of farm land.

—Thomas F. Gilbert[1]

It is difficult to correlate output, particularly the output of human performance, with value. But it can be done. It starts with knowing the desired outcome, identifying the causes of a gap, and remediating that gap through a solution. We learn this from human performance technology (HPT). We establish a baseline through existing (or if we must, fabricated) metrics. We try things and then make incremental adjustments as we go along, always focused on continuous improvement. This we learn from Agile. To prove value, these Agile and HPT techniques are blended. The agile performance improvement metrics provide six categories of success measures, which are divided roughly in two: those that measure value for the customer, and those that demonstrate improved team efficacy.

The latter will be explored in the next chapter. For now, I provide real-life examples of how to quantify the value of outcomes.

[1]Gilbert, Thomas F. *Human Competence: Engineering Worthy Performance, Tribute Edition.* New York: Pfeiffer, 1995.

The Rule My scrum team created what we now call The Rule: Undertake no story that has no defined customer value. The Rule helps a team to be rigorous, constantly focusing on why we are doing things.[2] After all, if it's not important to the customer, why should it be important to us? It is part of our team-defined definition of *ready*.[3]

Retrospectively, it's nauseating to reflect back on the disheartening consequences of embarking on a training project without alignment with business value. I count these deflating experiences from my experience developing training courses. You might have similar ones from your line of work.

- **Never Mind.** You work on an idea for a course for a long time before the business abandons the idea.
- **Dead on Arrival.** You produce a wonderful learning asset, and nobody takes the course.
- **Dead before Arrival.** You work on a course for a long time, but it never sees the light of day because the SMEs are more interested in perfection and risk-aversion than finishing.
- **The Big Bang.** Lots of people take the course during the initial rollout, and then nobody takes it afterwards.
- **Much Ado about Nothing.** Lots of people take the course, but no meaningful change occurs.
- **It Ain't Training.** Lots of people take a course as part of a holistic solution, but the business abandons their covenant to provide management or coaching reinforcement afterwards. The initiative fails, and training is to blame.
- **Secret Society.** You identify a viable existing business measure to monitor, hoping to align your efforts with improvement of the key metric, and the business won't give you access to their data.

---

[2]The product owner (or performance consultant) needs focus on defining and measuring value as a core capability, but the whole team needs to share the mindset, with or without Agile.

[3]As I write this, The Rule is only about one sprint old. We are the training department, and sometimes a training request is just a training request (hello, compliance training). Making a connection between a learning activity and business results is difficult and rare, despite the myriad tidy examples in the chapter.

Why So Stingy with Sharing Your Results? A month after 1,000 people take a training course, I send a follow-up email to the program manager. My question is: "Can you share any updates on the progress with the problem of system stability? For my work, I want to report back on how this problem is improving through the identified metrics, since the training is a part of the solution." A month and three additional follow-up emails later, I get a response that includes this zinger, "The training is a contributing factor to the stability, but not the only factor." What the response did not include was an update on the metrics.

Any time you are doing work that has no value to the customer, you risk encountering these disheartening customer behaviors. Of course, the customer does not always know what she wants, or she thinks she knows what she wants, but she's mistaken. If the front-end analysis is done in a way that sows confidence, then the team can concentrate on improving collaboration and work flow, while remaining responsive to change.[4] That is the agile performance improvement system in a nutshell.

Categories of Value

In the pursuit of proving value, my taxonomy puts the measures into three broad categories.

Monetized value measures are directly quantifiable in terms of money.

- Making money
- Saving money
- Repurposed labor

Convertible value measures are not directly monetizable, but the value is directly convertible into money. The success metric is monetized after applying a conversion multiplier. I propose to use these terms to concisely explain the idea of applying a multiplier to monetize a success metric.

- Retention
- Employee engagement
- Safety and security
- Customer loyalty

[4]By *front-end*, I refer to everything that is done before the product owner presents a story to the team during sprint planning.

Workforce efficacy measures track the performance or capabilities of teams or individuals. If the expectations for the work are aligned with outcomes, then improved efficacy metrics *should* lead to improved business results. Efficacy is quantifiable, but not easily valued.

- Employee capabilities
- Productivity
- Time to productivity

These categories have one thing in common: customers potentially care about them. Depending on the situation, different businesses focus on different metrics at different times. The measures can be applied to any work output, whether it's a new product or employee performance.

This chapter provides examples of specific metrics within each category along with real-life examples. As with the rest of this book, you will not get a playbook, worksheets, or step-by-step instructions. Ways of thinking trump any best practices.

Babies and Best Practices My attitude toward best practices (and parenting) is neatly summed up in a quote from the seventeenth-century English poet John Wilmot, the second Earl of Rochester: "Before I got married I had six theories about raising children; now, I have six children and no theories."

Monetized Value

The metrics in this category are expressed in money. Monetizing is the holy grail of measurement. Making money (top line contribution, including sales and other sources of revenue or a calculated dollar equivalent) is the easiest way to get an executive's attention. There are other measures that are directly monetizable, including saving money and repurposed labor. Let's start with making money.

Making Money

Most people, particularly in large companies, are in roles disconnected from the revenue part of the business. Even for those who are directly involved in revenue, like salespeople, it is difficult to make the connection.

Let's say a sales team sells more than they did before they went to a three-day training seminar. The sales training directly leads to more revenue, right?

Not quite. Think about all of the other factors that could lead to a change in sales performance. What if the business climate changes? What if the product development people just released new, appealing product features? What if support services have a new focus on customer loyalty? Have you ever wondered why you do an equivalently good job of providing your service twice in a row, and it works out one time and doesn't work out the other time?

That's the problem. It's difficult to isolate the impact of any single contribution to revenue. (Bob, are you saying we need to collaborate? Recommend holistic solutions based on cause analysis? Be agile? Be responsive to change? Stuff like that?)

Here is an example of when my team was able to nicely correlate associate the business's success with our efforts. That's about the best you can hope for.

Correlation vs. Causation A common analytical and rhetorical error is to equate correlation with causation. Just because two variables overlay one another on a graph does not mean that one caused the other. Correlation without causation: 99 percent of Americans with cancer have consumed milk. In HPT we talk about cause analysis, and you will find that valid observational data as proof of cause is difficult to achieve.

Real-Life Example 1: Suggestive Selling

Average check is an important metric in the restaurant business. It is calculated simply:

$$\text{Average Check} = \text{Sales} \div \text{Number of Customers}$$

Years ago, I was a hotel restaurant manager. In managing sales, there are two ways to improve restaurant revenue: get more customers and increase average check. For the latter, I regularly provided preshift training focused on suggestive selling skills. Depending on the day or week, we focused on selling more appetizers, more wine, or more desserts. The training helped some, but we started to see real results when I set up monthly contests to see who could sell the most of something. The incentive of winning a one-night hotel stay or other prize did the heavy lifting. Once the incentive was in place, the serving staff was engaged in thinking about more refined service or sales.[5] Once a prize was on the line, they suddenly became more self-organized, sharing tips for what worked and what didn't work. "Yeah, I described the German chocolate cake as 'delectable!' Aha!" *Prima facie* they were more highly engaged. The average check was up, along with comment card scores and team camaraderie.

---

[5]You never know what's going to work. Before we did the contests, I thought the mere idea of raising the average check would be incentive enough, since a waiter's income from gratuities is directly proportional to the dollar value of the food and drink they sell.

Our postshift discussions verified that most of the employees did change their behavior once the contest was announced. Interestingly, a few were put off by the idea, since they didn't like being competitive in this way. Nonetheless, we sold a lot more desserts and had a higher average check when a contest was under way. In between contests, the check average returned to previous levels. This leads to the question of why the effective suggestive selling behaviors would not continue when there wasn't a contest going on.

Extrinsic rewards can have a varied effect on intrinsic motivation and creativity. They should be deployed carefully according to the type of tasks at hand. Some jobs, like strawberry picking or data entry, offer little in the way of intrinsic motivation, because of the boring, repetitive, or routine tasks involved. In such cases, this type of reward system can work well.[6]

This episode was a lesson in the limited power of applying just one or two techniques to improve performance. Training alone or incentive alone can have a temporary effect on performance, but rarely sustainable. In Gilbert's performance engineering model, the work environment includes a variety of factors that work in concert to enable high performance (Chapter 2).

Saving Money

Incentive can also be used to save money. I worked in a luxury hotel that employed around 100 room attendants. They had a problem with their vacuum cleaner expenses. In short, room attendants were mistreating the vacuum cleaners, and most new ones didn't last a year. Progressive discipline and training on "how to properly handle your vacuum" had failed.

The answer? The head housekeeper installed a program where each room attendant would be given a brand-new vacuum cleaner every two years. They would own it. After two years of using it at work, they could take it home, and they would get another new vacuum cleaner to use at work. Once this incentive was in place, the cost of buying new vacuums and the hours spent maintaining the existing ones dropped dramatically. Ownership worked.

[6]Gerald E. Ledford Jr., Barry Gerhart, and Maiyu Fang, "Negative Effects of Extrinsic Rewards on Intrinsic *Motivation: More Smoke Than Fire," World At Work*, Second Quarter, 2013. Retrieved March 11, 2015, from `http://ceo.usc.edu/pdf/Ledford_Fang_Gerhart_2013_Intrinsic_Rew_WaWJ.pdf`.

Cost avoidance is a ripe source of performance improvement. Inefficiencies are everywhere. Labor is often a company's largest expense. Many large companies routinely save money through layoffs or *reductions in force* (RIFs).[7]

The Mathematics of RIFs

Sometimes a company has too many employees. The economy changes, the demand for the company's product or service goes down, the business slows seasonally, a changing business model evolves, or other reasons. If the company doesn't want to wait for the workforce to attrite (get smaller through people leaving naturally), RIFs are an expedient way of lowering payroll expenses.

The true cost of RIFs involve items on both sides of the ledger. Sure, you save money by way of salaries and benefits of the laid-off employees, but consider the other expenses it introduces:

- Severance and other payouts associated with termination
- Hiring and training new employees to replace laid-off ones[8]
- Unemployment insurance payouts
- Loss of knowledgeable, skilled, and high-performing employees
- Lower loyalty among embittered remaining employees, which leads to an increased risk of other employees quitting
- Defending the company (or proactively preparing to defend) against legal challenges associated with the layoffs
- Erosion of the company's brand as an employer

[7]In the corporate world today, *RIFs* and *layoffs* are two of many euphemisms used to describe getting fired. The original use of the term *layoff* was a temporary suspension of employment, with a hope of returning to work after a seasonal slowdown. If you get laid off from a cubicle job, you aren't getting recalled after the snow melts. You are looking for a new job.

[8]This happens often. In my observations, most large companies, unless the company is dying or going through a true business model change, eventually return to the previous number of employees after a major layoff.

In addition to the costs and systemic impact, layoffs or the prospect of them can encourage undesirable management behaviors. Managers may use the prospect as a proxy for sound performance management, hoping that the RIF cycle will do their dirty work for them. Others may hold on to a poor performer, with the expectation that they can offer them as a RIF later.

Ultimately, layoffs are just one way to save money. By monetizing performance, managers can establish the worth of their workforce, which improves everyone's employment prospects.

Real-Life Example 2: Empowerment Gone Wild

Once upon a time, in the call center function of a large regional bank, a senior vice president contacted me for help with a dire business problem. Over a four-month period, fee rebates granted through the call centers had increased by 59 percent, from $1.46 million to $2.32 million a month. Yikes!

The increase coincided with the kickoff of an "empowerment" initiative, where the call center agents were granted authority to make decisions on fee rebates. Previously, all rebate requests were escalated to supervisors, and these escalations were taking up an inordinate amount of supervisor time. In addition to freeing up supervisor time, the empowerment initiative was designed to support a new focus on customer satisfaction scores, which were below the industry benchmarks.

Call center agents had complained that they couldn't generate good customer satisfaction scores because they were not allowed to make decisions that would make the customer happy. If an agent thought that they could make a customer happy by providing a $30 rebate on a bounced check fee, it would require escalation to a supervisor. The escalation caused further delay in problem resolution, thus eroding customer satisfaction. The customer satisfaction scores were on the rise, improving from 61 percent to 69 percent (9s and 10s on a 10-point scale), but the dramatic increase in fee rebates overshadowed those gains.

The simplest way to fix the fee rebate problem would have been to take away the authority of agents to authorize rebates. Another idea was to issue detailed guidelines for fee rebates, but the procedures would have been unwieldy and would not account for all possible situations.

Although these actions would have curtailed rebates back to previous levels, there would have been negative consequences. The empowerment initiative would have been undermined, customer satisfaction would have eroded again, and supervisors would have again spent excessive time dealing with escalated calls.

After a lively debate, the leadership team came to agree that the agents should maintain their authority to provide fee rebates. The challenge was to find a way to maintain the momentum of the rising customer satisfaction scores without providing a rebate to every customer who asked for one, without engendering cynicism or undermining the empowerment and customer satisfaction initiatives already in place.

The business objectives were clear, but the causes of the situation were not. Before recommending a solution, I examined the situation closely, interviewing supervisors and conducting focus groups with agents.

Based on these activities, we determined the underlying causes. Clearly, providing rebates is the easiest way to deal with a difficult or hostile customer. Management did not establish criteria for providing rebates, and the agents did not have decision-making and customer service skills to resolve rebate requests properly.

A training class was the centerpiece of a holistic solution that also involved tweaks to policies, procedures, and supervisory practices. Table 7-1 displays the astonishing results. The training was effective, but the results would not have ensued if we hadn't viewed the problem systemically and addressed the causes.

Table 7-1. Calculation of Money Saved. After an initial surge in fee rebates authorized by call center agents, training and support provided employees with decision-making and customer service skills. As a result, fee rebates dropped without any erosion to customer satisfaction scores.

Date	January 2003	April 2003	August 2003
Stage	Empowerment initiative begins*	Time of training request	First full month after training
Customer satisfaction (9 or 10 on 10-point scale)	61%	68%	69%
Monthly fee rebate expense	$1,462,941 (Baseline 100%)	$2,321,556 (159%) +$858,615 from January	$1,552,555 (106%) -$769,001 from April

**Call center agents granted authority to make decisions about fee rebates.*

As we solved the empowerment-gone-wild situation, the monetary piece was so straightforward here that a *return on investment* (ROI) calculation was possible. Jack Phillips is notable in HPT for introducing ROI as a Level 5 to add to the four Kirkpatrick Levels (Chapter 2). Phillips wrote notable books on the topic, and his consultancy developed a robust ROI methodology that can be applied to solutions of any kind. The simple calculation of ROI is

$$\text{ROI} = \text{Benefit of solution} \div \text{Cost of solution}$$

In this case, the monetary benefit was a reduction in monthly fee rebates of $769,001 in the first month after the training was delivered.

The cost of the training initiative itself was around $200,000. This included print production of training materials, travel, and labor expense. Labor included time spent by call center agents (time spent attending the training) as well as staff employees who assembled and delivered the program. Thus, the benefit of the solution far outstripped the cost within the first full month after the training was completed.

$$\text{ROI} = \text{Benefit (\$769,001)} \div \text{Cost (\$200,000)} = 384\%$$

Rarely is a situation so straightforward, but that's an example of how a consultant can collaborate with business executives to save money.

Repurposed Labor

A variation on "save money" is *repurposed labor* (or labor not wasted).[9] Repurposed labor is the cost of time made available to be spent on more valuable things. With repurposed labor, you are spending the same amount of money, but the people you pay are focused on activities of worth.

Some examples:

- **The decision *not* to have people spend time doing worthless things.** An example is having employees spending their time working at their jobs instead of attending training that does not measurably contribute to solving a business problem or improving performance.

[9]A related term is *wastage*: effort that adds no value. In Lean and Six Sigma, the elimination of wasted anything is the core pursuit.

- **Deploying a solution more efficiently.** In the training business, this sometimes manifests in decisions about delivery methodology. For example, webinars and e-learnings are more expensive to develop than classroom experiences, but less costly to deliver. Consider the size and geographic distribution of the audience as well. If client comes to me with a solution in mind, and the solution that is actually delivered is less expensive, I call that saved money.
- **Helping employees to do less of a worthless activity.** Process improvements, knowledge sharing, and performance support focused on tips and tricks can all help work flow become less wasteful (lean, if you will).

Real-Life Example 3: Learning to Keep Time

Repurposed labor was a key focus when I supported the implementation of a new time tracking system for a large IT function. The new system provided a more efficient system for managing project labor. Before designing a training solution, we studied how much time people needed to learn the system. A control group of engineers learned to become proficient on the system without formal training, and it took them an average of 16 hours of self-study and practice. This became our baseline measure. Another group took a two-hour training class and an average of three additional hours of self-study to become proficient. The second group spent 11 fewer hours learning this system. Those 11 hours are now available to do other things besides training on the system. Table 7-2 shows how we use that information to calculate repurposed labor.

Table 7-2. Calculation of Repurposed Labor. A more efficient learning solution frees employees to spend time on worthy activities, like doing their jobs.

	Self-Study Only	Training plus Self Study
Time to proficiency	16 hours	5 hours
Cost of labor for all to become proficient	16 hours x $100/hour x 1,000 employees = $1.6 million	5 hours x $100/hour x 1,000 employees = $0.5 million
Repurposed labor	$0	$1.1 million

Some executives might be inclined to state this as $0.5 million in employee time spent on training. But the employees needed to learn how to use the system anyway. By viewing the more efficient solution as a benefit, there is $1.1 million of repurposed labor. Employees spent less time learning the system, freeing up that time to do other things, like their jobs.

Convertible Value

Convertible measures have a dollar value associated with them, but they are one or two degrees removed from being directly monetizable. Four metrics in this category are retention, employee engagement, safety and security, and customer loyalty. Let's look at them.

Retention

Retention is the percentage of employees who stay working somewhere. If you have 100 employees in year one, and 90 of them are still working there a year later, your annual retention rate is 90 percent.

Turnover is the inverse of retention, referring to the number of employees who left, either voluntarily or involuntarily. Turnover rate is the number of employees who leave divided by the average number of employees. If you have had an average of 100 employees over the course of a year, and 20 employees have quit or been let go, turnover is 20 percent.

Is All Turnover Bad? Not all turnover is bad—involuntary turnover is good and people who don't fit and leave on their own may also be beneficial. Companies can have low turnover, almost too low, which equates to more deadweight.

You can monetize turnover through a calculation of the replacement cost of an employee. Estimates vary greatly, but replacement cost is equivalent to at least 50 percent of a salaried employee's annual wage.[10] This calculation encompasses payouts to the exiting employee, recruitment of the replacement employee, and time on the job before the new employee becomes productive.

Retention data is of great use to the consultant. But to be useful, cause analysis must be performed. Seek answers to such questions as the following:

- Why are people leaving? What patterns are in the exit interview data?
- What factors in the work environment are dissatisfiers?
- Which job families, managers, or functions are losing people?

[10]The replacement cost of an employee, expressed as a percentage of annual wage, is lower for hourly employees and higher for executives. Estimates of replacement cost can be as high as 150 to 250 percent, depending on an employee's level and technical skills.

- Are you losing top, average, or poor performers?
- Were the quitters high-, medium-, or low-potential employees?
- Are highest-paid or lowest-paid workers leaving?

When examining trends around retention and turnover, external factors come into play. When the economy is good, the job market is good, and employees change jobs more often. Industries become more or less desirable, as we see in recent years[11] where technology companies have become more desirable employers than financial services companies.

Real-Life Example 4: I Need More Bus Boys

As a restaurant manager I supervised a staff of 30 employees. One year, the turnover rate for my crew was 100 percent, meaning 30 employees left. Some quit, some were fired. Based on that (frankly terrifying) number, you would think that it was a bad staff with a bad manager. Closer examination revealed something different. Twenty of the 30 employees were there all year, and the other 10 positions turned over about three times apiece. Fifteen of the employees were five-year employees (or longer), and none of the old-timers left during my three-year tenure.

Breaking the situation down by role, the problem was that I struggled to retain busboys. As the least skilled of the service staff, busboys were relatively easy to replace. But interviewing, hiring, and training a new employee every other week was burdensome to everyone.

I did some rudimentary analysis. The most common reason people left was for a better job that was outside of the hotel business. It seems that I was quick to hire people whose personality and character I liked, even if they were overqualified or had no experience in hotel or restaurant work. (I was smitten over and over by articulate and charming graduate students from the local university.) I changed my approach by passing over candidates who were not a good fit for the job on paper. Eliminating those people, I could look for those personal qualities I preferred in the person of someone who might want to work there for a while. As a consequence of this improved screening approach, the annual turnover rate improved from 100% to 40% the following year. In retrospect, those highly educated busboys weren't really great employees, and in that sense it proves the point that not all turnover is bad.

---

[11]The shift coincides with the financial crisis that triggered the Great Recession of 2007–9, when ambitious students started becoming more intrigued with tech start-ups and less intrigued with hedge funds.

Employee Engagement

Employee engagement refers to a person's psychological attachment to an organization or a transformational change within an organization. As with retention, meaningful use of the data comes only after identifying the underlying causes. However, the business case for monitoring and improving level of engagement among the workforce is compelling.

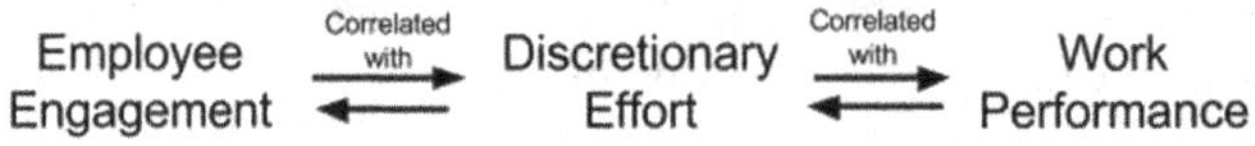

Not only is it logical, there is research to support such correlations. Employees who have a higher level of engagement try harder (they put out more discretionary effort). Higher discretionary effort is correlated with higher performance. They are also half as likely to quit as the average employee and nine times less likely to leave as those on the low end of the engagement scale.[12] Causation may not be so clear cut, but in my experience this correlation is quite persuasive with executives in terms of a larger performance improvement story.

A perusal of research on the subject shows performance correlations with other employee attitudes. In addition to level of engagement, researchers are exploring similar concepts under different names, such as employee satisfaction, engagement, and happiness.[13]

Engagement is an employee-reported metric that is collected through a survey. I use a multiple choice (Likert scale) question that provides the respondent with a range of statements. The employee chooses the one that best describes him or her. Rather than showing a mean, I show what percentage of employees are at 4 or 5 on the five-point scale. Now you have one number that shows what portion of the population is in *the engagement zone*.

Real-Life Example 5: Commitment Issues

The employee engagement metric is a powerful jumping-off point for examining the progress of any transformational effort. Level of engagement reflects the heart and the mind, and it evolves as the business evolves.

---

[12]Corporate Leadership Council, "Driving Performance and Retention through Employee Engagement. A Quantitative Analysis of Effective Engagement Strategies," retrieved from `http://www.usc.edu/programs/cwfl/assets/pdf/Employee engagement.pdf`.

[13]Yes, *happiness* is apparently now a term of art in the field of industrial and organizational psychology. The term also has some buzz in the Agile world, with some saying that "happiness leads to team velocity." Is happiness what lies at the intersection of Agile and human performance technology?

A 1,000-person business unit was transforming from waterfall to agile methods. They did the things that are normally done during a change initiative: people were trained, reorganized, and so on. I was able to convince the business unit executive to conduct a baseline assessment focused on employee engagement (presented in the survey questions as "my commitment") and repeat the process every six months.

By asking the same question at six-month intervals, the data paint a vivid picture. When I presented the information in Figure 7-1 to a small group of executives within this organization, they had plenty to talk about.

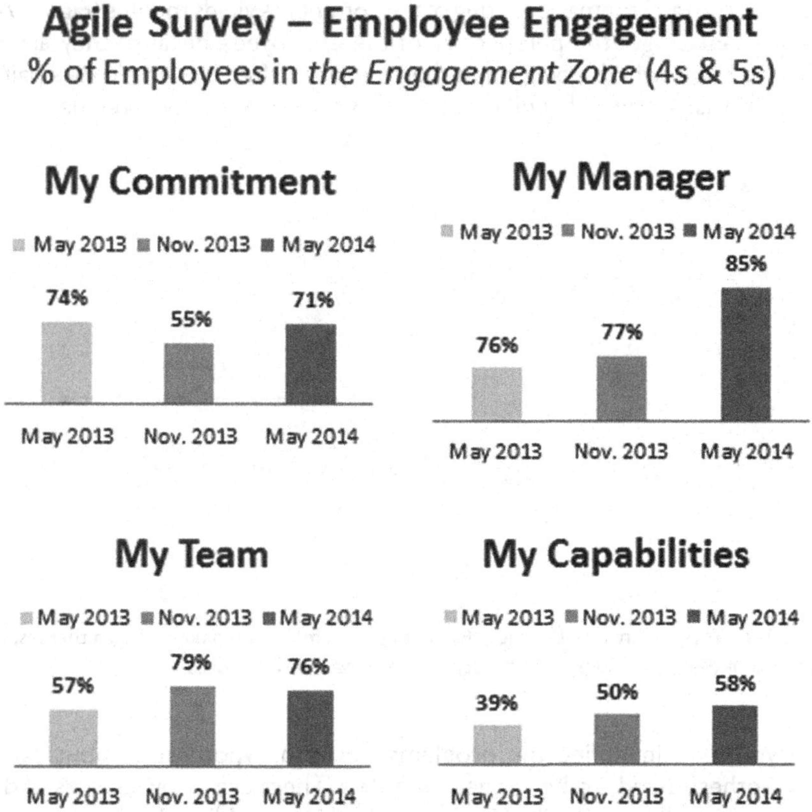

Figure 7-1. Presentation of responses to the employee engagement question, broken down by role. This result shows the movement in the metric at six-month intervals.

I like to explain the data and initially let them interpret it. After all, they understand the business context better than I do. They will have ideas immediately. Here, one of the first things the executives noticed was that the team members have the lowest level of engagement. They speculate on the reasons for a few minutes, but it's only speculation.

Though the quantitative responses are fodder for discussion, responses to an accompanying open-ended question add texture. We asked: What barriers exist that are preventing you, your team, or the organization from flourishing in Agile? That one question invites employees to speculate on causes, and we received about 800 comments.

An aggregation and thematic sorting of the comments yields themes (Figure 7-2). It's important to get the perspective of the employees, because they are the ones who know what's going on in the trenches. Often the employees paint a picture that is considerably different from what the executives tell us.

Agile Survey

Top Comment Themes

Theme	Comments	Summary
1. Team composition	174	Lack of proper skills sets; people on multiple teams; no product owner; colocation
2. Management	87	Executives, managers causing various problems; command and control; pressure on teams
3. Positive outlook	84	We are optimistic and making progress
4. Sprint planning	72	Teams struggle with planning; need help breaking stories into smaller pieces
5. Trust	61	Team lacks trust; need to be more collaborative

Figure 7-2. Top comment themes. By sorting the employee comments into themes, you get an idea of the most widespread perceptions among the work force.

Once you have identified the problems, you can hypothesize about causes. The hypothesis needs to be verified with data. There are many sources of data, as I've discussed throughout this chapter. In this case, I like the focus group.

One of the questions I get asked most often is: Why don't you do focus groups first, at the same time as the survey? Doing focus groups without any focus is, well, unfocused. Use the survey process to gather broad information, and then use the focus group to gather information about those topics about which you want to know more. If you are going to gather people for an hour to talk to them, the time needs to be used well. A deplorable amount of time is wasted on unfocused focus groups.

Teenage Drinking When I was in high school, I participated in a focus group asking what we thought about juice boxes, which had recently been invented but were not popular yet. They didn't ask us about every type of drinking container we encounter through our lives. They asked us what we thought about this particular dispenser, the juice box. Through the conversation, we touched on the soda can, the half-pint milk container, and others. But by honing in on the juice box primarily, the researchers were able to collect in-depth information about what potential users thought about the juice box. (For the record, in 1980 I thought the idea of the juice box was dumb. Shows what I know!)

Analyzing the deeper information gathered from the focus groups puts the consultant is in a good position to make recommendations that address the root causes. In this case, we said: Continue the push to capture the hearts and minds of the employees, through executive messaging, coaching support, and management reinforcement.

Without going into too much of the detail of what we found, there are three themes that now populate our transformation backlog:

- Executive messaging
- Coaching support
- Management reinforcement

We can tackle these themes using agile methods. We will create stories, with defined outcomes, which address the causes of low level of engagement. Once we develop the backlog, we scrum. The product owner prioritizes the stories in collaboration with the customer, and the team tackles the stories.

The focus on our backlog is substantially different than what it would have been had we only listened to the speculation of the executives or only listened to the voice of the employees. Everyone in the business unit is biased in some way. Only a third party can approach this analysis objectively, without any bias except for finding the truth. When asked by an outsider, with credible assurances of confidentiality, the employees tell the truth. The truth is the basis for action.

Management can monetize employee engagement as a convertible value by applying a conversion multiplier on an individual, team, or organizational basis. In this case the multiplier would be related to productivity. To isolate a causal relationship with productivity, a company would need to perform an extensive study of the performance differential between highly engaged employees and the others. Quantifying and monetizing that performance differential is theoretically useful but probably not cost-efficient.

As exemplified in Figure 7-1, addressing causes can produce a rise in engagement level over time. In most consulting situations, that is enough.

Safety and Security

The safety and security of employees and customers is monetizable in a few basic ways.

- Employee time out of work due to an accident or injury, which could involve loss of team productivity or disability
- Lawsuits involving physical or nonphysical violence between or among employees and customers
- Insurance premiums, which depend on variables such as provision of specified training or number of claims

Preventive measures can improve an assessment of risk, but it is not monetizable until after a mishap occurs. If there is a catastrophe, reputational risk comes into play, as it will cost the company in lost business or lawsuits.

Real-Life Example 6: You Threatening Me?

Once I was called in to support an awareness campaign for a workplace violence prevention policy at a large bank. Green at performance consulting, I asked the sponsoring security executive what his measure of success was. His response was, "Well, we've noticed an uptick in reported cases of violence or threats in the bank branches. We have had 300 in the past six months, which is more than one per day. We want that number to go down." The new policy, he continued, will make for a safer workplace. "We need people to know that it's not okay for customers to yell at you. It's not okay for a fellow employee to threaten you. If one of these things happens, there is help though corporate security." It was a poignant message, and I admired the effort of the security organization.

Fast-forward six months. We implemented a campaign around the policy, including training for thousands of employees, a video, posters, and communications. The objective of those activities was to raise awareness of the policy. People learned what to do in threatening or violent situations and how to report incidents.

Afterward I asked, "How are we doing with reducing workplace violence?" The answer: Reported incidents of workplace violence have doubled.

The executive understood what this meant: The initiative succeeded in heightening awareness of the policy, which resulted in more reported incidents. It also highlighted the idea that there must have been a lot of previously unreported threats and violence. In that sense, the initiative did exactly what it should have done. The objectives were misstated, and I learned a lesson in aligning success criteria with learning objectives.

As part of the sustainment activities that followed, workplace violence prevention training became a required onboarding activity for new-hires, and a regular cadence of refreshers became part of the annual compliance training routine. Stabilizing the variable of awareness enabled the security team to better assess the rate of these incidents occurring. The rate of reported incidents peaked in the wake of the awareness training but steadily decreased in the years following.

Customer Loyalty

Today, managers in every industry have access to *customer relationship management* (CRM) techniques and technologies that can readily quantify the value of customer loyalty. It can be complex, but it's doable. As with these other money metrics, the consultant's role is to perform cause analysis and identify success metrics before recommending a solution.

Real-Life Example 7: Who's Your Daddy?

While I was drafting this chapter, I received a phone call from GoDaddy, the domain registrar and hosting service. I had just registered two domains. The young man introduced himself, and said he wanted to make sure I knew that they had customer service available to support me as I set up my new website. Wow, I thought, I spend just $30 with them, and I get a phone call telling me that they are at my service. That is extraordinary.

Somewhere at GoDaddy is a customer loyalty metric. By giving me a two-minute phone call (which couldn't cost them more than a few dollars), they are still making money on me. Their cost to provide service will increase if I actually call for support, but that is unlikely for most customers.

More important, the call, identified as being from the "customer development" area, was clearly an effort to engender loyalty. A customer loyalty success metric would have to do with how much money I spend after receiving the phone call, and through it they can quantify the value of my relationship with them. In addition, they sent me a customer satisfaction survey, which they can correlate with any number of factors, including the specific agent who called me and how many times I call user support. They have set up monetizable metrics that will be useful in diagnosing human performance issues.

It worked. In the future I will be inclined to spend more money with them. The agent was conversant about the GoDaddy-sponsored racecar that runs in NASCAR events, even though he admitted he didn't know much about it before starting to work there. So the customer service is nicely integrated with their overall branding and sports sponsorship campaigns.

Conversion Multiplier

To monetize the convertible value metrics, you apply a conversion multiplier.

Value = Performance measure x Conversion multiplier

The value is the product of the performance measure (a number) and a conversion multiplier (a monetizable metric). Conversion multipliers must be supplied by the customer, as they reflect how they value performance. Of course, consultants can make suggestions! Table 7-3 presents examples.

Table 7-3. Conversion Multipliers. The product of the performance measure and the conversion multiplier is a monetary value.

Metric	Performance measure	Conversion multiplier
Turnover	No. of employees who left	Replacement cost of an employee
Employee engagement	No. of employees in the engagement zone	Difference between highly engaged and other employees (by way of monetized productivity)
Safety and security	No. of incidents (accident, violation, legal problem)	Liability cost per incident
Customer loyalty	No. of customers who stay as a customer	Value of a customer relationship over time; value of a renewal

The product owner can forge trust and credibility by applying the performance consultant's toolkit. "Let's look at what metrics you want to change, and let's assign a dollar figure to it."

Although convertible value metrics are powerful, there are potential potholes in the road to making good use of them.

Data are readily available, but they move in slow motion, usually only calculated over the course of many months or years. Executives who are thinking about an initiative that starts in the current quarter are seldom prepared to wait a year to see results.

About Heavy-Duty Data Analysis Conducting a proper analysis of convertible value data can require the services of a specialist, PhD type. They tend to be expensive, and they tend to work quite deliberately. I'm not a specialist PhD type, so I hack my way through using the techniques you find in this book. It tends to be less scientific and more expedient than what the PhD types do. But I find that many executives excuse the lack of rigor in favor of agility and a sensible interpretation. You're really advising them based on the evidence that you have compiled, the wisdom of your experience, and the deepness of thought that the analysis reflects. Whether it's all scientifically valid (or whatever) is of no concern to many executives.

It takes finesse to talk about the HR metrics coming out of a learning function. It should be obvious that you will have difficulty aligning a training class with an improvement in, say, turnover. Although some folks do quit because of limited career growth opportunities, I don't often hear about people leaving because they didn't get enough training.

Don't underestimate the power of the convertible value measures. As a consultant, you can use them as tangible outcomes to buttress your narrative about how remediating the causes of off-kilter metrics will make long-term sense.

Workforce Efficacy

Workforce efficacy refers to how effective the employees are at doing their jobs on an individual, team, or business unit basis. Clearly, there is goodness in having a more effective workforce—words like *efficiency*, *competence*, and *productivity* come to mind. While the lexicon is common, among the value measures outlined in this chapter, they are the most tenuous.

You cannot always draw a straight line between efficacy measures and results. Sometimes, the connection is clear. For example, billable employees such as lawyers or people in piecework jobs make money in direct proportion to the services they provide. But for most employees, there is a degree of separation between performance and outcomes.

What follows is a description of a few categories of workforce efficacy metrics, together with appropriate caveats.

Employee Capabilities

As we saw in Chapter 2, the genesis of a human performance gap usually lies in the work environment and not the capabilities of the employees. That is, training alone will not fix the problem.

Nonetheless, requests to remediate employee capabilities are common. This is what learning functions are good at: establishing learning objectives and creating learning experiences that teach people how to satisfy the objectives through behavior and skills. The challenge is aligning the skill set with performance outcomes.

Isolating the Impact of Learning I used to love the phrase "isolating the impact of learning." The expression is still part of my working vocabulary, but I don't love it as much as I used to. As we saw in Chapter 2 with the 85 percent rule, only rarely can we draw a straight line between a training intervention and a business result. Now I say only rarely can we associate a training intervention with a business result.

Job definitions, including competency models and job descriptions, provide a behavior-oriented description of what duties and skills incumbents need. Organizations will do different types of assessments to figure out what skills are needed to succeed and what skill gaps exist in the current workforce. These activities and the related cause analysis can help isolate development opportunities for individuals and organizations.

In addition to the analysis process I described in the context of employee engagement, there is one other concept to cover here. It is the performance exemplar.

A *performance exemplar* is the employee (or team) who performs the best. These are the stars. We wish all individuals and teams would perform more like the exemplars. Competency models and job descriptions are large, complex, and generally unwieldy. Studying the exemplars is a good way to isolate those critical few behaviors that distinguish great performance from ordinary performance. The logic says that if more people did more of what the exemplars did, performance overall would improve.

There is a big disclaimer here. Sometimes, the exemplars have a *je ne sais quoi* that cannot be developed in others.

Some workers are not capable of doing what some exemplars do or lack the inherent motivation. While there are things to learn from those who have achieved excellence, performance results from a convergence of capability and motivation.

The *je ne sais quoi* can be influenced by intrinsic motivation and/or derived from innate talent. Most of the great ones have certain characteristics in common. Think of the greatest authors, musicians, athletes, or burger flippers you have known or witnessed. They work hard, and they have a love for what they do. The transcendent ones also have genetics on their side. None of that can be managed into existence. It can only be ruined.

Real-Life Example 8: The Unexpected in Sports

The world of sports is rife with examples of how the *je ne sais quoi* can take results in expected directions. Sometimes individual stars and superstar teams disappoint; sometimes the ordinary do something extraordinary. Look at what can happen.

Tyler Seguin. This top hockey prospect was drafted second in the 2010 NHL draft by the Boston Bruins. There was never a question of his talent, until he scored only one goal in 22 games during the 2013 playoffs. The team, fans, and media soured on him, and he was traded to the Dallas Stars. Once he arrived at Dallas, he flourished, establishing himself among the elite scorers in the NHL.

Scottie Pippen. Known as one of the greatest all-around basketball players ever, Pippen was traded to the Houston Rockets in 1998 after winning six NBA championships with the Chicago Bulls. As Michael Jordan's "second banana," he developed a reputation as one of the most unselfish and team-oriented players. Nonetheless, his tenure with the Rockets, alongside fellow greats Hakeem Olajuwon and Charles Barkley, ended inauspiciously after one season. The Rockets made an ugly first-round playoff exit, and the team was broken up among bitter public sniping among all three stars.

Brazil's football (soccer) team. Playing on home turf, Brazil fielded a team of superstars for the 2014 World Cup tournament. Brazil was heavily favored with 3-1 odds. Eventual champion Germany shocked the world as they punished Brazil 7-1 in a semifinal match.

USA 1980 Olympic Hockey Team. The United States defeated the mighty Soviet Union team, perhaps the greatest hockey team ever assembled, by a score of 4-3, setting the stage for the team to win an unlikely gold medal. The "miracle on ice" was pulled off by a team of college players, none of whom ended up being professional stars.

The message here? You never know. These individuals and teams all had their fortunes changed by *je ne sais quoi*. This chapter is about engineering performance, but there's only so much you can do.

Productivity

Most business people are familiar with the concept of productivity in terms of manufacturing and its analogue to their profession. My discussion will not extend this conceit. If you are producing widgets, success metrics include things like number of widgets produced per hour, percentage of widgets with no defects, and length of time it takes the widget to travel through each stage of the process.

As long as your team is working on the right things, team productivity contributes to business outcomes. If they are working on the wrong things, then team productivity doesn't matter. As my fortune cookie intoned on New Year's Eve:

> *Before you wonder "Am I doing things right," ask "Am I doing the right things?*

Real-Life Example 9: Paper or Plastic?

If you are confident that you are working on the right things, team productivity measures are a worthy pursuit. Measures of productivity seem like they are simple. A straightforward example comes from the grocery business. In most large grocery stores, a key measure of cashier productivity is *items per minute* (IPM), referring to how many products are scanned into the cash register for each minute of work. A good IPM score is 30. However, even IPM, a seemingly reasonable and true measure of cashier performance, is subject to mitigating or offsetting factors. Any number of environmental conditions—malfunctioning cash registers, poor lighting, missing stickers on produce—can render the simple IPM metric unreliable as a direct reflection of cashier productivity. It's never simple.

The possibilities for productivity metrics are endless. Every profession has them. Ask your customer or client which one they use.

In any case, treatment of productivity metrics works similarly to the approach I described for employee engagement.

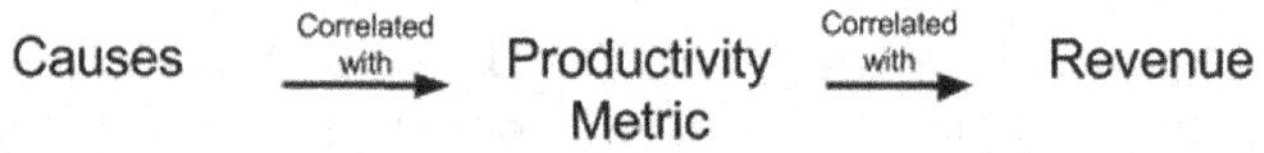

Presumably there is a correlation between the productivity metrics and revenue. If there is a problem with productivity metric, the consultant helps find out why and recommend solutions that remediate the underlying causes.

Time to Productivity

How long does it take for an employee to start contributing? *Time to productivity* is the length of time it takes an employee to become competent and productive in the job.

Think of the factors that go into a new person becoming competent and productive in their job. A few are:

- Skills and experience that the possess prior to arriving (recruiting)
- New-hire training (learning)

- A welcoming environment (management)
- A good match between the skills and attitude required to succeed as part of a specific team and the person hired (human resources)

It's a wonderful metric in theory. Unfortunately, I have never seen someone measure it in a usable way. It's too hard to pin down when a person reaches "productivity," even if you are talking about an environment where a large workforce all perform the same tasks repetitively, like tuning pianos or doing oil changes at an auto repair shop. If you are talking about rote or repetitive tasks, like picking strawberries, it doesn't take long for the worker to learn the skill. Eventually, time to productivity takes a backseat to sustained productivity, and using this metric is a tough sell.

But what if we are talking about a highly skilled job that requires three years to reach full productivity?

Real-Life Example 10: Go Away, Newbie!

I once supported an investment management function at a financial services company. Portfolio managers made decisions about what stocks to trade after examining a wide variety of information resources. One of the sources of information was a cadre of analysts who researched companies and created models to express why they thought a portfolio manager should buy, sell, or hold a stock.

Full productivity for an analyst means that their buy/sell/hold recommendations influence portfolio managers' decisions. If a portfolio manager buys a stock because the analyst recommends it, and the price of the stock rises, then it can reasonably be said that the analyst is productive.

It was a running joke that portfolio managers would not listen to new analysts (campus hires) until they had been on the job for three years. During new-hire training, analysts were instructed to print out and carry around their financial models everywhere in case they ran into a portfolio manager who might be interested in hearing about it. Any time a portfolio manager left his office, he ran the risk of being accosted by an eager analyst at the coffee machine or in the bathroom.

Any attempt to change that dysfunction would require a major shift in culture. Doable, but not expedient. What if they had worked with the three-year time to productivity as an assumption, and modified the approach accordingly?

- Instead of front-loading six weeks (!) of immersive classroom training, why not spread out the training over a year, or two, or three? This will improve learning by giving the analysts opportunities to practice what they learn as they learn it.

- Instead of encouraging analysts to chase portfolio managers into the bathroom to show them their models, how about modifying the system in way that gives the work an opportunity to be heard? The analysts are talented and ambitious people, but many of them quit because they felt they had no influence.
- If portfolio managers don't listen to analysts until they have three years of experience, why hire them? The straight-out-of-school prospects are less expensive to pay, but more expensive to recruit. Why not hire experienced analysts? Or if portfolio managers have enough information from other sources, why have so many analysts?

I floated these ideas, but never got traction with any of them. "We've always done it this way" summarizes the attitude I encountered there. Maybe in different circumstances I could have done better with it. Maybe a better presentation of data would have more influence. Or maybe it's tough for an individual contributor to propose a fundamental shift in the ways of doing business.

So What?

Working as a consultant out of a support function, such as learning or human resources, presents a significant credibility problem. Namely, it is difficult to establish business value being several degrees removed from the core business function.

For a learning consultant, the key is to reframe situations to focus on performance and not learning. Instead of asking, "What training do people need next?", we should ask, "What problem are you trying to solve, and what are the causes of it?" As the examples in this chapter have shown, barriers to success usually have very little to do with training.

This chapter revealed my bag of tricks for establishing meaningful data that influence how an executive runs a business. My strategic influence kicks in when the data tells a compelling story. Too many of my colleagues rely on training data, expressed in terms of the Kirkpatrick Levels. To influence human performance, you need to leverage data that means something to executives. Much of that data exists; you need to mine it and mold it toward compelling business outcomes.

This chapter looked at ways to define and influence customer value. The next chapter will examine the team dynamics within the agile performance improvement system.

CHAPTER

8

Continuous Improvement Lore

At regular intervals, the team reflects on how to become more effective, then tunes and adjusts its behavior accordingly.

—Principles Behind the Agile Manifesto

At the conclusion of each sprint, Scrum calls for the team to hold a *retrospective* meeting. It is the lynchpin of continuous improvement and responsiveness to change. By scheduling this event regularly, every one, two, or four weeks, depending on iteration length, the team finds focus on improving performance, much more often than in non-Agile practices, where reflection usually occurs only at the conclusion of a big project or at some other long interval.

The guidance and so-called rules for the retrospective are few.

- The meeting is for the team only—no managers or other chickens allowed.
- Team members reflect on what went well and what did not go so well.
- The team commits to one action for improvement

The team action around the retrospective applies the same skills that the agile consultant uses to develop a story. Once the team settles on a problem to address, it identifies causes, defines success criteria, and develops a story that is focused on an outcome. The improvement comes between retrospectives, when the team completes the story developed in the meeting. The retrospective formalizes the commitment and helps build trust within the team.

Continuous improvement lore includes stories from my experience, arranged around the agile performance improvement success measures presented in Chapter 6 and shown in Figure 8-1. All of the team actions pertain to modifying team processes, improving collaboration approaches with customers, or responding to pressures from the world outside of the team.

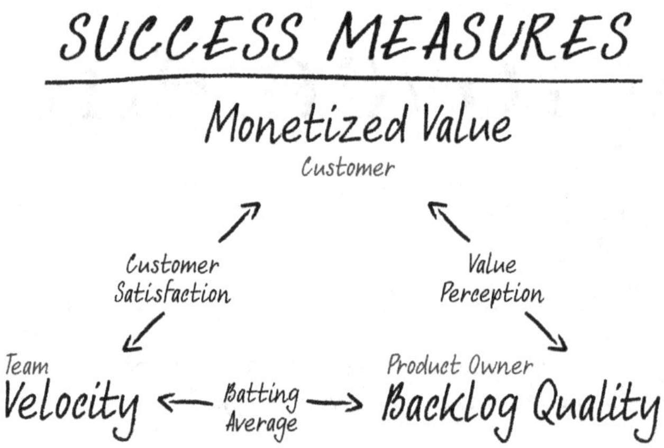

Figure 8-1. Success measures. Success with agile performance improvement is measured through six success measures that reflect the team's ability to improve its work efficacy, collaborate with customers, and respond to pressures.

My taxonomy of continuous improvement includes five success metrics within two categories, and it is the basis for the structure of this chapter.

Team efficacy metrics focus on the collaboration between the product owner and the rest of the team.

- Backlog quality
- Velocity
- Batting average

Customer collaboration metrics concern the relationship between the team and the customer.

- Value perception
- Customer satisfaction

The team can pluck success measures from the standard categories and metrics introduced here, or they can select ones of their own invention. There are six success measures for agile performance improvement. Monetized value was covered in Chapter 7. This chapter focuses on the other five measures.

All of these metrics will deteriorate as disruption occurs. Later in the chapter, I discuss the importance of being responsive to pressures on the agile performance improvement system. It is the key to being agile while maintaining overall productivity.

The most important things for the team are to hold retrospective meetings faithfully and keep continuous improvement as a mantra.

About the Team When I refer to anecdotes about *our team* or *my team*, it reflects my collective experiences being part of scrum teams over the past few years at different companies.

Team Efficacy

> *The nightmare scenario is to get to the end of the iteration with 90% of the tasks complete, but no stories complete.*
>
> —Uncle Bob Martin[1]

Team effectiveness comes with team maturity. It is rare for a newly formed team to perform to their full potential. "Team actualization" (Figure 8-2) describes the progression of a team to a state of high-performance. There are two dimensions to team actualization: the adaptation of the team's collective skill set to the work at hand (technical practices), and the improvement of the team's ability to collaborate and adapt (agility).

---

[1]Robert C. Martin, *Agile Software Development: Principles, Patterns, and Practices* (Upper Saddle River, NJ: Prentice Hall, 2003), p. 22.

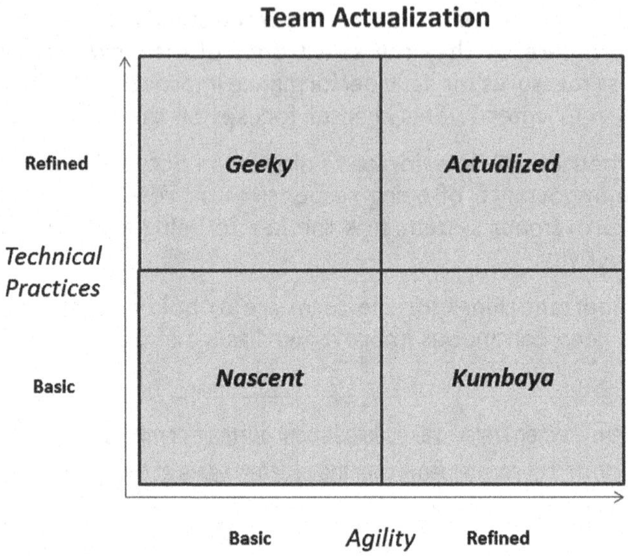

Figure 8-2. Team actualization. As a team matures, it refines both its technical practices and its agility to become actualized, a fully realized level of high performance.

I here propose new terminology to describe points on the journey to *team actualization*, the achievement of full potential for high performance. When teams form and learn to work together, they are "nascent": it's the honeymoon period when not much gets accomplished. Having strong technical practices with weak collaboration is "geeky": the team has refined technical processes but does not collaborate well. Strong collaboration with weak technical practices is "kumbaya": everyone works well together and faithfully performs Agile, but they have not figured out the technical aspects of the job. The geeky and kumbaya teams have one thing in common: they do not get much done. If they do get things done, they do not deliver much value to the customer. "Actualized" describes a team that is at or near its potential. They are a high-performing team, delivering worthy output frequently.

Three metrics directly reflect efficacy of teamwork. As these improve, collaboration and flow improve, and the team delivers.

Backlog quality refers to stories' readiness for a team to work on. Grooming the stories is the responsibility of the product owner, but deficiencies in grooming cause problems for the team and the customer.

Velocity refers to the amount of work that the team completes per sprint. It is the "official" Agile team productivity metric.

Batting average refers to the ratio of story points completed to story points committed (see Chapter 6). The expectation is that teams will finish all stories to which they commit.

Let's start with the metric over which the product owner has most influence: *backlog quality*.

Backlog Quality

It was the worst of times. We just ended an acrimonious three-hour sprint planning meeting. Everyone on the team thinks I don't know what I'm doing, and they might be right. As the product owner, it seemed that every time I introduced one of the stories that I had so lovingly groomed, there was pushback. There were questions about aspects of the story that I thought were obvious. There were doubts about whether they could finish the story within the prescribed four-week iteration. We left the meeting with planning unfinished, and the scrum master had to schedule two hours more for planning the next day.

The effectiveness of the product owner's work is measured, in one way, by backlog quality. A backlog populated with poorly groomed stories sets the team up for failure.

- The team feels compelled to commit to stories that are too big to finish within the iteration.
- The team does not have sufficient information to do the work.
- Dependencies and impediments stand in the way of the team working on stories.[2] They are not "ready."

Sprint planning shines a light on backlog quality. If your sprint planning meetings are going longer they should; if the team is less happy with itself at the end of sprint planning than it was at the beginning; if the team is rejecting stories; if the team is figuring out basic elements of the story during sprint planning, you probably have a problem with backlog quality.

The product owner owns backlog quality. If the team points to backlog quality, they point at the product owner. A good team will tell the product owner she can improve the backlog or how it is presented to the team.

> As a team member, I need stories in the backlog to be groomed well, so that I can commit to the stories confidently and without potential impediments.

[2]In Scrum, an *impediment* is an issue that is blocking a story from getting done. Typically, the scrum master fields the impediments from the team during the daily standup and then works to resolve them.

I've been that product owner whose backlog quality caused problems for the team. At first my response was to spend more time refining stories in the backlog and more time working with customers. Individual heroics are not enough. The team learns that although the backlog is the responsibility of the product owner, it takes a team to make the backlog.

Before the backlog quality became acceptable, I held individual meetings with each team member before every sprint. I shared the current state of the backlog, and we discussed stories that fall in the wheelhouse of each person. The best surprise is no surprise. By the time we got to sprint planning, everyone knew what was coming. By collaborating on refinement of stories, everyone contributed to grooming the stories to which they would commit. The improvement we experienced was not just because of the process. The process sets up opportunities to develop more effective working relationships within the team, which is what really led to the better backlog quality.

Within six months, sprint planning took half as long, and we liked each other twice as much.

Velocity

It's the end of the sprint. Our team committed to 16 stories representing 94 story points, and we completed 0 stories totaling 0 story points. For those of you without a calculator handy, that works out to a team velocity of zero. It was not a matter of the team not working hard. We tracked task hours, and people were doing plenty of work. Nonetheless, it was a disaster.

About Story Points Many agile teams use story points to estimate the relative effort and complexity of a story. The value of a story point is team-specific. A five-point story by Team A necessarily bears no comparison to a five-point story by Team B. Team-specific estimates become refined over time as the team learns to calibrate its own productivity. The power of the story point is that it asks the team (not management) to estimate what is needed to complete a piece of work. Before the team commits to work, it estimates the size in story points. Before it estimates in story points, it must understand the expectations for what has to be done. If the product owner cannot provide clear and meaningful acceptance criteria, then the team cannot commit to completing the story.

If no stories get done, things of value are not delivered to customers. If things of value don't get delivered to customers, they wonder what the heck we have been doing. If customers wonder what the heck you have been doing, they stop using (or funding) your function.

> As a team member, I need the team to have impediments and dependencies out of the way, so that I can finish stories.

In Agile, velocity is the measure of team productivity. The key to velocity is in finishing stories, not just working hard. To finish stories, the team needs to envision, during sprint planning, what needs to happen to get things done. They need to anticipate what things stand in the way of getting a story done. They need to *not* commit to stories that they cannot finish.

The practice of Scrum asks the team to plan the work at the beginning of the sprint. As the team commits to stories, they estimate the relative effort of each story using story points. Planning and estimating are two very straightforward ideas, but ones that have caused perhaps the most consternation among Scrum practitioners.

What makes planning and estimating so difficult? I have participated in retrospectives focused on this topic many times, and I observe that several factors are at play.

- People tend to overestimate the effort required to complete work items. Typically, one week into a sprint we see team members saying thing like, "this is going to be harder or more complicated than I thought."
- Developers (of software, e-learning, and other things) underestimate the impact of dependencies and impediments. The work itself may require little effort, but the time spent idle sitting in queues can significantly delay completion of a work item.
- People tend to spread themselves thin, working on many different things at once, losing focus and productivity as they mentally toggle from one complicated matter to another several times a day. Toggling from one priority to another is a natural avoidance technique for when dependencies and impediments appear.

Some combination of those factors led us to Uncle Bob's nightmare scenario of many tasks completed and no stories done.

Batting Average

The ensuing sprint saw our team complete more than zero story points. In Sprint 2 (Table 8-1), we committed to 90 points worth of stories and completed 17 points worth of stories. Going from 0 to 17 is a wonderful improvement in velocity, but our average was below the Mendoza line at .189 (18.9 percent completion rate).[3] We've started to get some things done, but we are failing to finish the majority of stories to which we committed.

Table 8-1. The Journey to a Higher Batting Average

Iteration	Stories Committed	Story Points Committed	Story Points Completed	Batting Average
Sprint 1	18	94	0	.000
Sprint 2	17	90	17	.189
Sprint 3	12	65	24	.369
Sprint 4	9	50	28	.560
Sprint 5	10	45	20	.444
Sprint 6	9	44	38	.863

> As a team member, I need to be discriminating in selecting stories, so that I can finish the stories to which I commit.

The team concluded that we need to commit to fewer stories. We applied a kanban practice called *limiting work in process* (WIP).[4] The team agreed to a limit of two stories per person at a time. Queuing theory suggests that two is the ideal number of work items to own at a time. If you have one story, you risk being idle when an impediment arises or you just have to wait for someone. More than two stories and you lose productivity due to having too many context shifts.

---

[3]Major League Baseball's Mario Mendoza was a weak-hitting infielder after whom the dividing line between competent and incompetent batter is named. To be "below the Mendoza line" is to have a batting average below .200. Mendoza himself batted .215 for his career, which spanned from 1974 to 1982.

[4]*Work in process* refers to the number of stories to which a person or team is committed at a time. A *WIP limit* puts a cap on the number of stories.

Kanban and ScrumBan *Kanban* is a method of production in which work is done in small pieces using a continuous pull system instead of the iterative sprint planning that we see in Scrum. Limiting WIP is one of the defining features of kanban. *ScrumBan* is a hybrid method that adds a WIP limit to the defined iteration length of Scrum.

As part of our new team rule, we specified that each person would work on two stories at a time, but once they finished a story, they could commit to another. Batting average can go above 1.000 as people pick up new stories after meeting all of the commitments from sprint planning.

Limiting WIP made the team more discriminating. Being serious about completing all of what was committed to, the team subjected the backlog to more scrutiny. In sprint 3, we committed to fewer story points than we had in sprint 2, and we completed more. Our batting average improved from .189 to .369, a significant jump, but we still had a long way to go.

Task-Level Estimation Many Agile teams break stories into tasks and then apply time estimates to each task. This practice allows for more than one person to work on a story, or for each task to be taken on by someone else in a pinch. Story-level estimation versus task-level estimation is a pervasive and dogmatic debate in the Agile world. I happen to subscribe to the school that says, "You don't need to break stories into tasks during sprint planning, unless of course the team decides that it needs to." If you feel an urge to break stories into tasks, then maybe your story is too big. In any case, the method for estimation belongs to the team.

The team continued to make refinements in technical and collaboration approaches, leading to improved backlog quality, velocity, and batting average. Some sprints were better than others, but there was an overall trend toward greater team efficacy. By sprint 6, the team's batting average rose to .863.

Even with that success, we still suffered from overestimating what we could accomplish. Part of the problem is the urge to push ourselves to do more work. This is a form of posttraumatic stress created by years of being conditioned to crank out as much work as possible without regard for the value the work brings to the customer. Look back at work you have done, or new things your team has created. What portion of those adds discernible value?

Years ago, I examined a report about the usage of new training courses delivered by way of our learning management system. We had a large learning operation that produced upward of 100 new learning assets per month. The report showed that 80 percent of new courses were virtually unused, consumed by less than 1 percent of the employee population. These courses were mostly e-learnings, which are incredibly expensive to produce—the standard multiplier is 100 hours of labor to produce 1 hour of content. At that rate, it would have been cheaper to have the subject matter expert train each person individually. Essentially this learning function was wasting 80 percent of its resources creating courses that nobody used. Believe me, there was plenty of management pressure to continue working at a frenetic pace to crank out the 100 courses a month. Success of this function was measured primarily by metrics that nobody cared about: production of training courses, total course completions, and participant reaction (smile sheets). Clients patronizingly praised the function. The function stayed viable by keeping its ratios of employees to population in line with industry standards.

Team efficacy is good, but focus first on adding value for the customer.

Customer Collaboration

> *The customer's perception is your reality.*
>
> —Kate Zabriskie[5]

Two metrics reflect how well the development team collaborates with the customer: customer satisfaction and value perception. *Customer satisfaction* asks the customer to evaluate the output of and collaboration with the team. *Value perception* is a label I propose to describe the customer's opinion of the product owner's contribution. Let's explore each one.

Value Perception

I had just started a new position as a program manager. Andrea, a dedicated and fastidious instructional designer, warned me. She carried with her just one sheet of paper, a diagram of sliced concentric circles populated with the names of 80 training topics. It looked like a dart board. Overwhelmed, she shakes the already crumpled sheet, "We need to create training for *all* of these things!"

As a performance consultant in a new role, I was reminded that charity starts at home. Before I can do my thing with customers, I need to do my thing with my colleagues.

---

[5]See http://www.businesstrainingworks.com/training-resources/free-customer-service-quotes.

I'm always wary of a training request that sounds like an attempt to create (the anti-Agile) comprehensive documentation.[6] Surely we don't need to create courses for all of these topics. The consulting questions come fast and furious.

- Who's asking for all of this training?
- What methodology does this training need to be? Are they e-learning, or are we doing classroom?
- Who is going to take all of this training?
- What are the learning objectives?
- What performance problem are we solving by providing the training?
- What will happen if we don't create this training?

Surely we don't need to do all 80 projects at once. As an agilist, the questions come just as fast.

- Okay, we have 80 training topics, which one should we start with?
- For each of the 80 topics, can we break them down so that we can create a potentially shippable increment within one iteration?
- For each of these topics, have we written them in the story form, so that the persona, outcome, and reason are defined?

If we had done as Andrea wanted, we would have spent the ensuing couple of years creating 80 (very likely) useless training courses and not doing anything else.

Guess how many of those topics got developed into training. Guess how much trouble we all got into. The answer to both questions is zero.

> As a product owner, I need to develop and prioritize the backlog with a rigorous focus on delivering value, so that the customer perceives value in the engagement with our team

Instead, the consultant returns to the customer, applying the skills of performance consultant's toolkit (see Chapter 3). It's fair to say that the customer would be happy if we produced the 80 courses in a timely manner. But it is unlikely that he would perceive us as meaningfully contributing to his success. Effective collaboration enables the performance consultant to develop a product backlog that is aligned with what the customer is trying to accomplish.

---

[6]Recall the Agile Manifesto has come to value working software over comprehensive documentation.

There is no value in squandering precious resources creating crap that nobody cares about. Value is not in producing more things. Value is in producing worthy things. This is where generations of people in fields such as training, communication, and software development have gotten themselves into trouble. How many times do our customers encourage us to produce more and faster with no apparent value contribution?

The monetary value of consulting can be established through repurposed labor or other cost avoidance (see Chapter 7). The *perception* of value can be measured simply through one question. I use this one: on a 1–10 scale, how likely would you be to recommend the product owner to others? The response to this question reflects the value that the customer associates with the product owner's contribution.

Customer Satisfaction

How is your relationship with your customer? How do you know you're successful with them? How do you plan to improve the collaboration with and value delivery to the customer?

When my boss starting asking me these questions, I did not have good answers. Sometimes we get so wrapped up in doing work and focusing on the cohesion of the team, we almost forget that we have customers. For months, we had been skipping the sprint review event. It was easy to find excuses. Our velocity was zero, so we were embarrassed. It seems like we didn't produce very much this sprint, so our demonstrations would not be very exciting. We are going to have some great accomplishments in the next sprint, so we might as well wait until then to hold a really hearty sprint review. All of these rationales are natural, but they shirk the truth.

If the team fears the customer perception of what we are producing, it is a great time to start monitoring it, creating a baseline. If our performance is bad, at least bring that into the open.

So we had a sprint review, which is effectively a retrospective on the work with the customer. We invited every executive we serve, every project sponsor and subject matter expert with whom we regularly work. Out of 15 invitees, only 2 showed up. What a wonderful and encouraging affair it ended up being! We were reminded that the customers are vested in our success. By having an explicit discussion on how our collaboration with them was working, we got feedback and ideas, along with a renewed commitment to make things work better. From that day forward we faithfully hosted a sprint review, no matter how unappetizing the thought. We realized that no good could come of skipping it.

So, how do you measure if your customers are satisfied? It's simple. As with value perception, you ask them.

At the end of the sprint review ask one question. On a scale of 1–10, how likely would you be to recommend our team's services to others?

One Question? I use one question each to gauge the customer's value perception (of the product owner) and satisfaction (regarding the team). This idea is based on the net promoter approach that measures loyalty in relationships. Asking one question focused on your key result adds a welcome simplicity to normal customer satisfaction assessments.[7] There is no implicit causality between loyalty and business results, but it will be difficult to get business results without strong customer loyalty.

The data you get from the one question and the feedback during the review is fodder for the team to create a story about improvement. Again the team takes on a consultative mind-set. They need to figure out what the customer wants and how they want to work with us. They need to explore root causes of problems that exist. They need to develop solutions that address the causes. The team needs to refine the covenants it has with itself and the customer.

> As a development team, we need to encourage open dialogue between the team and the customer, so that we can build trust and provide the customer with worthy output.

In consideration of this story over months, we adopted a few practices that helped us strengthen the team's relationship with customers.

Have sprint reviews. With short sprints it can seem like there is nothing to show, but you show anyway. It's an opportunity for the team to talk to the customer about the work.

Measure customer satisfaction. It doesn't need to be complicated or scientific. Ask the same question once per iteration.

Create a covenant with the customers. Even if it's just a few sentences to start with, a charter delineates clear expectations about the work output. A product roadmap is an agreement on a longer range plan, and discussing it can strengthen trust with the customer. It also provides transparency and peace of mind.

---

[7]See, for example, Frederick F. Reichheld, *The One Number You Need to Grow,* Harvard Business Review, December 2003; available at `https://hbr.org/2003/12/the-one-number-you-need-to-grow` (retrieved March 20, 2015).

The customer satisfaction metric belongs to the team. The sprint review event is the one time that the team has the full attention of the customer. While some business people will be in touch with team members, primarily the product owner has the relationship with the customer.

Pressures on the System

> *I feel my heart glow with an enthusiasm which elevates me to heaven; for nothing contributes so much to traquillise the mind as a steady purpose—a point on which the soul may fix its intellectual eye.*
>
> —Mary Shelley, *Frankenstein*

The players within the agile performance improvement system (see Chapter 6) reside within a closed loop containing the customer, the product owner, and the team. As a team within a larger entity, it is impossible ignore or shut yourself off from pressures of the larger ecosystem (Figure 8-3).

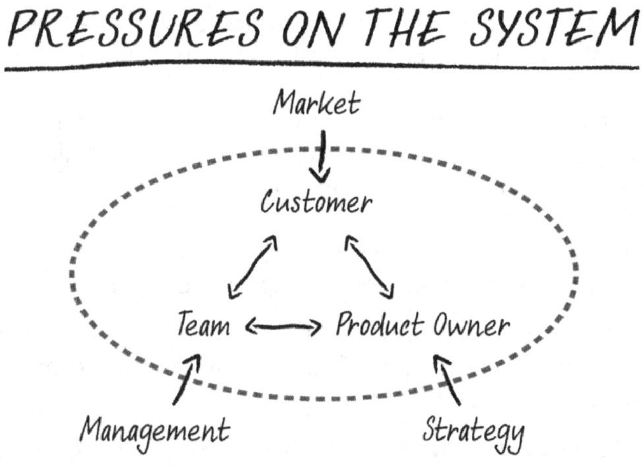

Figure 8-3. Pressures on the system. To look at agile performance improvement as a closed system is idealistic and unrealistic. A closed system doesn't exchange anything with its surroundings

Each player has other circles within which they work. The *work teams* roll up to traditional layers of management and maintain associations with their professional disciples. The *product owner* supports a larger product strategy. *Customers* contend with the market for their products. Everyone deals with the demands of corporate governance and oversight, which includes the finance people, compliance, the lawyers, the project/portfolio managers, and who knows what else.

All of these pressures present convenient excuses for a team to *not* fulfill their commitments. But really, maintaining focus on commitments while remaining responsive to change is the game. Success amounts to this: don't let disruptions, impediments, and pressures prevent you from meeting your commitments.

The metrics of responding effectively can be applied to any disruption related to management, strategy, or market. They include:

- Accurate estimations of team velocity
- Consistent batting average
- Low number of impediments
- Quick resolution of impediments

This section is not called "dealing with, contending with, or putting up with the pressures on the system." It is about that Agile value of responding to change.

Management

At our daily standup, one of our team members, Julie, reports: "I haven't been working on my stories the past couple of days. I got an urgent request on Tuesday morning from Paul, the head of HR. He needed me to put together a quick job aid to support the new features of the compensation management system. He said managers are confused about how to log in and navigate, and he wants to send this information out to everyone by Friday."

The Ad Hoc Requester. Beware the ad hoc *requester* persuading you with a promise that the work will be "quick." When fielding a request, clarify what they want. The team is better equipped to figure out the how, including how long and how much effort it will take.

Urgent things come up sometimes. But our team was finding that these so-called emergencies were coming up during every sprint. Typically the ad hoc requester outranks the team member fielding the new request, someone in our reporting hierarchy, or one of our client executives.

On one hand, we claim to be agile. Everyone should expect that we are responsive to change. Our team had that can-do mind-set, as Julie showed here. She valiantly produced the job aid in time for Paul to send it out by Friday. This gesture sowed good will with Paul.

On the other hand, if we are responsive to every urgent request, we will never be able to consistently deliver on the stories to which we committed through sprint planning. In this case, Julie spent the better part of a week on this request. Within a two-week sprint, that is a lot of time.

For months, the team debated this issue. Finally, we came up with this story:

> As a team member, I need a procedure to field ad hoc requests during the sprint, so that we can stay focused on our commitments but still remain responsive to the urgent needs of management and customers.

The problem is that the new request, however appealing, urgent, and important it seems, necessarily displaces work that the product owner identified as a high priority, and the team made a commitment to the customer to deliver it.

When agile performance improvement works correctly, team members focus on fewer projects that get done well and deliver value. That is, until disruption occurs.

The Scrum rules tell you to inform the requester of new work, as tactfully as possible, that this new work should be added to the backlog and prioritized for the next sprint. Operationally, the scrum team member should refer the requester to the product owner to vet the request and determine what its true priority is.

Rarely does it work that way. The instinct is for the team member to take on the request without pushing back, given that the request is from a person who is higher up in the food chain.

In reality, most of these requests can wait. Is it better to drop everything and dive into the new request, or is it better to have the person go through the planning process? If the latter, the request will receive proper vetting by the product owner, whose job it is to look at each request in the context of everything else that is a possible priority. Additionally, the product owner has the skills to determine what the best solution is in terms of solving a problem or contributing to improved performance of the team.

As a result of our retrospective conversation, the team agreed to direct potentially disruptive requests for new work to the product owner. At times this can put the team member in an uncomfortable position. But the result was that the team can keep focus on their commitments. With short iterations, the next prioritization and planning cycle is right around the corner. Asking a requester to wait a couple of weeks for proper vetting and focus is a small price to pay for a product or feature that will add value.

The Scrum process failed by allowing the disruption to occur, but the very fact that we practice Scrum exposed this truth. Without working off of a prioritized backlog that the product owner continually refines, you risk loss of time and diverted focus that can cripple your team's ability to deliver value. After the retrospective process helped us learn to handle wayward requests, our team is keen to navigate disruption.

Strategy

Our team designed a one-day classroom course to develop the soft skills of managers. I looked forward to piloting and fine-tuning the course in preparation for a large rollout. I assumed that Natalie, our lead instructional designer on the project, would facilitate the pilot and train-the-trainer sessions of the class. Then I learned that she had absolutely no experience with classroom facilitation or trainer preparation. Natalie had a background in e-learning design and development, and she had wonderful skills in that area. Relatively new to the team, I realized that our group was set up to be an e-learning factory.

Sometime between when the team was formed and now, the demands of our job changed, and our learning strategy evolved more toward soft skills and live training, as opposed to automated training. This was a strategic disruption to our team, albeit one that unfolded gradually.

> As a development team, we need to adapt our skill set to accommodate the backlog, so that we can deliver a continuous stream of value to the customer.

A series of retrospectives caused us to examine the skill set we needed on our team to execute the strategy. This was a self-organizing effort on a small team, not a heavyweight corporate initiative. We looked at the overall direction of the backlog, and identified our collective skill gaps. We remediated the issue with professional development, which enabled the team to stay together.

Other strategic disruption comes to the team by way of the product owner, who usually enjoys a dotted-line or solid-line relationship with product strategists.

> As a product owner, I need to align my work with the larger corporate or product strategy, so that our team contributes to the long-term vision of the organization.

Our team struggled in part from focusing too much on sprint planning, taking very literally the notion of maximizing value on a sprint-to-sprint basis. We find that our planning is too myopic, too in the moment, and we lose track of the big picture. Integrating long-term thinking into product development while using Scrum is a tall task.

Long-term thinking should concern the team but it should concern the product owner more. Teams are disinclined to trouble themselves too much with work beyond the current planned sprint. But high-performing teams must know about and contribute to the strategy. I've learned that there can never be too much transparency. There can never be too much planning between sprint planning events. As a product owner, I might understand and be in favor the product strategy, but the team needs to be brought into the fold.

Market

Market pressures originate with the customer, and they tend to have a dramatic effect on the work team. The customer could suddenly become more demanding. They could disappear for a while due to reorganization or other distraction. They could be developing a new strategy. There could be sudden changes in the market for the product, such as new competitors or shifts in the economy. Any of these conditions could reflect market pressures that the customer experiences.

Responsiveness to market pressures can only be measured in one way: by the success of your customer.

> As a team, we need to be responsive to rapid changes in the customer's business climate, so that the customer can succeed in the marketplace.

What follows is the story of team that needed to respond to rapidly changing conditions in the market.

September 12, 2013, San Francisco Bay (Figure 8-4). The eleven-man crew of Oracle Team USA steps off their boat and heads to a nearby café, joining their design team for a circle-the-wagons meeting. They had just lost two races in convincing fashion to Emirates Team New Zealand. The Kiwis led 6-0, with nine race victories required to win the America's Cup. Las Vegas offered 700-1 odds of Team Oracle coming back to win.[8] What happened in the next eleven days of racing was made possible by the US team's agility in finding ways to improve the performance of their boat.

---

[8]Stephen Orsini, "Bieker's Cavitation Fix," Sailing World, October 21, 2013; available at `http://www.sailingworld.com/racing/biekers-cavitation-fix` (accessed January 12, 2015).

Figure 8-4. Emirates Team New Zealand leads Oracle Team USA across San Francisco Bay at 40+ mph during the 2013 America's Cup Finals. The Kiwis built an early 7-1 lead in the match racing regatta. The Americans came back to win the cup, but only after the team showed extraordinary agility in making small adjustments that made the boat faster.

Oracle Team USA spent years developing a fast boat. They dominated competition in the months leading up to the finals. However, Team New Zealand's improved boat set-up and boat-handling techniques catapulted them into a dominant position in the finals. For Team USA, facing a faster and better-sailed boat represented a sudden change. To succeed (win), the sailors and designers needed to adapt quickly. Team USA demonstrated many of the characteristics that agile performance improvement emphasizes.

They focused on the outcome. Team USA needed to regain superiority on the water and win races, and they had no time to waste.

They were responsive to changes imposed by the market. The emergence of New Zealand's suddenly faster, better-handling boat forced Team USA to be responsive.

They collaborated on prioritizing the backlog. The response was agile. The changes were not dictated by a titular leader, the skipper, or the general manager. They considered input from all members of the crew and the design team.

They addressed root causes. The focus of their cause analysis was to analyze differences in how the two boats sailed. The symptom of the boat's sluggishness manifested itself in "lee helm," which is a condition where the boat wants to steer off course away from the wind. Lee helm is a reflection of an unbalanced boat, making the boat slower and more difficult to maneuver. The problem was not in the rudder (the foil with which you steer the boat), but in the rest of the rigging. Find and address the causes of the lee helm, and the boat should become more stable and sail better.

They experimented with small changes. By examining the performance of the Team New Zealand boat, Team USA decided on changes that would move the boat's center of effort lower and aft (to the rear of the boat).

At the end of each racing day, the design team examined photogrammetric data and talked to the crew, making further adjustments. Ultimately, these adaptations made the boat more balanced and faster. Two weeks later the Oracle team finished the rally, winning the final race by a convincing 44 seconds and clinching the series 9-8.

Team USA may not have studied the Agile Manifesto, learned to apply Gilbert's behavior engineering model, or practiced Scrum. But their success shows what can happen when the skills introduced as agile performance improvement come to life.

Retrospective Lessons

> *Do the difficult things while they are easy and do the great things while they are small. A journey of a thousand miles must begin with a single step.*
>
> —Lao Tzu

The outline of this chapter is as overwhelming as Andrea's concentric circle of 80 training topics. Over time, a team will want to have it all: an effective team, productive relationship with customers, and adaptability to changing conditions. But you can't fix all of that at once. All you can do is pick one thing to work on at a time, like Agile. Analyze causes and define quantifiable outcomes. That's human performance technology. Then you do the best you can on that story, and measure the result. Over time you get better. The team learns to deliver value through collaboration, flow, and responsiveness to change. That's agile performance improvement.

The lessons for any team in any discipline are the same. We need to commit to less work and have more focus on getting things done. This simple idea is a large hurdle for most employees and most teams, who are conditioned to crank out as much stuff as possible. How about we only work on the products that will add the most value? How about we crank out less stuff but make that stuff better?

As an education product owner, I grapple with these questions from our clients as well. The beginning of the conversation, paraphrased:

> *Client:* I need these 18 things by the end of the month.
>
> *Me:* That's not possible. We don't have the capacity to do that much work within that amount of time.
>
> *Client:* Can you get more resources?
>
> *Me:* I might be able to, but maybe we should talk about what is most important to do first.

This becomes the start of a reframing conversation about what they hope to accomplish overall, and what employee capabilities need to be developed. Almost invariably, we can add more value by tackling 18 things one or two at a time, prioritizing them well and aligning them with the desired outcomes of the business.

In a traditional world of work, where training people are order-takers and teams try to crank out as much work as possible through sheer willpower and overtime, we would have undertaken the 18 things at once. The output would have been shoddy and incomplete, and the value to the customer would have been difficult to recognize. By limiting WIP and using solid performance consulting skills, we raise productivity of the team and add more value to the business.

People ask me variations of this question: is agile performance improvement a method with a prescribed implementation approach and a litany of rules? Well, it may be in another book if my readers ask for it.

For now, it's just a way of thinking and doing that bridges the best of Agile and HPT. I invite colleagues to help me to develop this nascent concept further.

Technologists have seen how to apply the analytical and interpersonal techniques of HPT to the solution of any business problem. Doing so ensures that the team is working on stories that deliver value to the customer. Nonsoftware people have seen how to apply the principles and practices of Agile software engineering to the design and development of any creative output. Doing so helps teams deliver output more frequently.

The lessons we learn from the elders of both fields make agile performance improvement possible. Whatever methods or models you use, the goal is to produce worthy performance by maximizing the value of interactions among product owners, work teams, and customers.

Glossary

Terms coined or specially adapted for the present work are marked with an asterisk.

85 percent rule. A possibly apocryphal notion that 85 percent of performance deficiencies are due to environmental factors. Only 15 percent are related to the individual factors, including knowledge and skills.

acceptance criteria. A description of what the *customer* (q.v.) expects the output to do when a work item is complete.

actualized.* A state of a team that has realized its potential for high performance through the frequent delivery of worthy output.

ADDIE. An acronym for analyze, design, develop, implement, evaluate. This is a development process, popular among learning and development professionals, that defines steps necessary to create solutions that are focused on defined learning objectives, instructionally sound, and thoroughly tested and evaluated.

Agile. A group of software development methods based on *iterative* (q.v.) and *incremental* (q.v.) development, where requirements and solutions evolve through collaboration between self-organizing, cross-functional teams striving to deliver value to customers faster. The present work adopts the convention that adjectival form of *Agile* is *agile*, with a lowercase *a*.

agile engineering practices. Work methods that support the *agile* (q.v.) mindset, leading to greater *velocity* (q.v.) and quality. There are dozens of them, but the most commonly discussed are *automated testing* (q.v.), *test-driven development* (q.v.), *refactoring* (q.v.), and *continuous integration* (q.v.).

Agile Manifesto. The 68 words that introduced the term *Agile* (q.v.) as a software development concept and defined its values. Its creation during a 2001 get-together at Snowbird ski resort in Utah was the seminal event in the history of the Agile movement. Any like-minded person can sign it.

agile performance improvement.* A work approach and a way of thinking that blend the best of *human performance technology* (q.v.) and *Agile* (q.v.) software development methods.

agile performance improvement system.*The working relationships among the three *players* (q.v.)—*customer* (q.v.), *product owner* (q.v.), and *development team* (q.v.)—practicing *agile performance improvement* (q.v.).

agilist. One who practices the techniques of *Agile* (q.v.).

articulation flow.* The movement of ideas and expertise from one *player* (q.v.) to another through the *agile performance improvement system* (q.v.).

automated testing. A process wherein code is inspected for *defects* (q.v.) using software instead of, or under the supervision of, quality engineers.

backlog. A list of possible *stories* (q.v.) that will lead to the development of new product features.

backlog quality. A measure of *product owner* (q.v.) effectiveness in developing a *sprint backlog* (q.v.) or *product backlog* (q.v.) that helps improve a variety of metrics, including cumulative flow, length of *sprint planning* (q.v.) meetings, and propensity for the team to get annoyed with the product owner.

batting average.* The ratio of predicted to actual *team velocity* (q.v.), which reflects the accuracy of team predictions for its own productivity.

behavior. Execution of a task that can be verified by observation.

behavior engineering model (BEM). Thomas F. Gilbert's categorization of individual and environmental factors that influence behavior. As a framework for analysis, the BEM helps the analyst pinpoint causes of *behavior* (q.v.) or *performance* (q.v.) deficiencies, so that impactful solutions can be designed to remediate them.

bidirectional prefill authority.* Verification of a truth by searching for an association in two different ways. For example, type "Martin Fowler" in your browser and *refactoring* (q.v.) prefills the results. Search for "refactoring" and Martin Fowler prefills the results. Therefore, Fowler has a strong association with refactoring.

bug. See *defect*.

capability. The total skill set that the workers possess, comprising all the performance they are able to deliver.

cause analysis. A methodical determination of why something is the way it is, so that solutions can treat the reason for a state of being, not the symptom.

CI. See *continuous integration*.

clean code. The product of practicing professionalism as a software craftsperson, where the code is sound, elegant, and not crappy. Uncle Bob Martin is its main advocate, writing two books on the topic and spearheading the *Manifesto for Software Craftsmanship* (q.v.).

client. See *customer.*

code. Specifications for the design of a product feature, including nonsoftware output.

code inspection. See *manual debugging.*

code repository. A common location for storing the current version of *source code* (q.v.).

code smell. Something in *source code* (q.v.) or a design that stinks, indicating that something beneath the surface is wrong.

continuous improvement. A guiding light for *Agile* (q.v.) teams as they enhance their agility with each *sprint* (q.v.).

continuous integration (CI). The full realization of automation in software development, where every time *source code* (q.v.) is checked back into the repository, it is automatically tested and integrated into the production version of the software.

conversion multiplier.* A factor, defined by the customer, by which a *convertible value* (q.v.) metric can be translated into monetary value.

convertible value.* A set of success metrics that are not directly monetizable but can be translated into *monetized value* (q.v.) by application of a *conversion multiplier* (q.v.).

craftsmanship. Professionalism in the spirit of an artisan.

customer. A *player* (q.v.) in the *agile performance improvement system* (q.v.) who requests or will consume the product output.

customer satisfaction. The state of a *development team* (q.v.) that effectively collaborates with the *customer* (q.v.), completes *stories* (q.v.) that will be accepted, and exchanges feedback, leading to *continuous improvement* (q.v.).

daily scrum. See *daily standup.*

daily standup. A *Scrum* (q.v.) *event* where team members report on what they worked on yesterday, what they will work on today, and what *impediments* (q.v.) to progress exist.

death march. The road to seemingly certain project failure, where a team shares and is consumed by feelings of hopelessness and despair.

defect. An error in coding that causes a product feature to behave in unexpected or unintended ways.

definition of done (DoD). A general set of team-specific standards that are applied to every *story* (q.v.).

definition of ready. A team's articulation of how they determine if they can commit to a *story* (q.v.).

design improvement. See *refactoring.*

developer-in-test. See *quality assurance engineer.*

development team. A cross-functional group of people who design and create product features; collectively, one of the *players* (q.v.) in the *agile performance improvement system* (q.v.).

DoD. See *definition of done.*

done. The state of a *story* (q.v.) having achieved the generic, team-defined characteristics of completion, along with satisfaction of the *acceptance criteria* (q.v.) that are specific to the story.

efficacy. The product of flow and collaboration in the *agile performance improvement system* (q.v.).

****emergent analysis.*** The impetus for a recommendation that manifests after proactively identifying patterns and *performance* (q.v.) opportunities through *front-end analysis* (q.v.).

employee capabilities. The skills and abilities of an individual worker; what they are able to do.

end of sprint review. See *sprint review.*

epic. A *product backlog item* (q.v.) that is too big to be completed within one *sprint* (q.v.) and thus needs to be broken down into multiple *stories* (q.v.).

estimation. A team's prediction of how much effort it will require to complete a *story* (q.v.).

executive request. A demand from business leader, who is typically an initiative sponsor or executive stakeholder.

exemplar. An employee (or team) who performs the best and whose habits and behaviors distinguish ordinary from extraordinary *performance* (q.v.).

extreme programming (XP). An *agile* (q.v.) software development method that takes engineering practices to an extreme level.

formative evaluation. Activities done before implementation to test solution efficacy; a pilot.

front-end analysis. The work that is done before the *product owner* (q.v.) presents a *story* (q.v.) to the team during *sprint planning* (q.v.), which improves the odds of providing a solution that enables improved *performance* (q.v.). The skill set includes consultation, analysis, and prioritization.

gap analysis. Examination that defines the difference between current and desired *performance* (q.v.).

geeky.* A team state of having refined technical practices with weak collaboration.

grassroots request.*A demand intended to accommodate a team- or domain-level need. This is the most common type of request, often focusing on the support of an initiative.

high-performing. A level of team maturity where it is frequently delivering worthy (q.v.) output.

historic velocity. Productivity in previous *sprints* (q.v.).

holy grail.*The ability to monetize the contribution of a *development team's* (q.v.) efforts.

human performance improvement. See *human performance technology*.

human performance technology (HPT). A systematic approach to improving the productivity and competence of a workforce, the standards of which are defined by the *International Society for Performance Improvement* (q.v.).

I ♥ Training.* A school of thought that sees training as a standalone solution to business problems and reinforces mantras like "Training Is Fun!" and "All Curious and Inquisitive People ♥ Training!"

impediment. A barrier or issue that threatens the team's ability to complete a *story* (q.v.).

incremental. Referring to the delivery of small bits of work within a short *iteration* (q.v.).

information flow.* The movement of shared data and expertise required to complete valuable work through the *agile performance improvement system* (q.v.).

instructional design. Methods used in the design, development and evaluation of learning solutions. In recent decades, the term replaced the now archaic term instructional systems design (ISD).

instructional systems design (ISD). See *instructional design*.

International Society for Performance Improvement (ISPI). A professional affiliation for practitioners of *human performance technology* (q.v.), which maintains the Certified Performance Technology (CPT) standards for the field.

ISD. See *instructional design.*

item. See *story.*

iteration. A recurring period of time during which a team completes a specific set of work priorities; in *Scrum* (q.v.), synonymous with a *sprint* (q.v.).

iterative. The characteristic of specifically defined work periods within which a team designs and develops product features.

kanban. A method of production in the same family as *Scrum* (q.v.), where work is done in small pieces using a pull system instead of *sprint planning* (q.v.) and without the fixed *iteration* (q.v.) length of Scrum.

Kirkpatrick Model. The classic training evaluation framework, introduced by Donald Kirkpatrick in the 1950s. Four levels measure reaction, learning, skill application and business results in relation to a learning intervention or other solution.

kumbaya.* A state of strong collaboration with weak technical practices, where everyone on a team works well together and faithfully performs *Agile* (q.v.), but they have not figured out the technical aspects of the job.

lean. A manufacturing process focusing on the elimination of waste of time and resources.

legitimation request.* A demand to convert content (training developed in the field or purchased from a vendor) into an official course.

level of engagement. An employee's psychological attachment to an organizational or a transformational change.

learning management system (LMS). An application that houses and delivers training content and maintains records of all of the courses that employees have taken.

LMS. See *learning management system.*

long-term plan. See *release plan.*

Manifesto for Agile Software Development. See *Agile Manifesto.*

Manifesto for Software Craftsmanship. A statement of values, spearheaded by Uncle Bob Martin, dedicated to demonstrating the rigor, professionalism, and discipline that goes into creating good—that is, useful and free of *defects* (q.v.)—software code. Any like-minded person can sign it.

manual debugging. The slow and error-prone process in which quality engineers pore over code to find known bugs.

model of performance. Documentation that describes the behaviors that a person needs to exhibit to do a job.

monetized value. Success measures that are directly quantifiable in terms of money.

nascent.* A team state of forming and learning to work together, during the honeymoon period when not much gets accomplished.

order taking. A situation where the *performance consultant* (q.v.) is recast by the *customer* (q.v.) as a diner waitress, expected to carry out requests efficiently and without question.

pair programming. A technique from *extreme programming* (q.v.) where two programmers work together, sharing one computer. One person "drives" by handling the keyboard, and periodically the second person takes control of the keyboard.

PBI. See *product backlog item.*

peer programming. A variation on *pair programming* (q.v.) where two people commit to each story.

performance. Quantifiable work output; what a learner is able to do.

performance consultant. An adviser to executives who performs analysis for the purpose of recommending solutions that address causes and support specific business outcomes.

performance engineering. See *human performance technology.*

performance exemplar. See *exemplar.*

performance gap. The difference between desired and current work output, the determination of which is done through *gap analysis* (q.v.).

performance improvement. See *human performance technology.*

pilot. See *formative evaluation.*

player.* Any of the entities that comprise the *agile performance improvement system* (q.v.), which includes the *customer* (q.v.), the *product owner* (q.v.), and the *development team* (q.v.).

PO. See *product owner.*

product backlog. See *backlog.*

product backlog item. See *story.*

product owner (PO). The member of an *Agile* (q.v.) team who translates the desired *customer* (q.v.) outcomes into *product backlog items* (q.v.) that will add the most immediate value for the *customer* (q.v.).

product vision. A statement of what a creation will be once all features are in place.

programmed learning. A now-archaic term suggested in the 1950s by behaviorist B. F. Skinner to describe a way to apply his principles of operant conditioning to the pursuit of human learning.

promiscuous pairing. A variation on *pair programming* (q.v.) where programming partners are rotated often.

QA. See *quality assurance engineer.*

quality assurance engineer. A tester of software code.

ready. As applied to teams, being in a state of having enough information to commit to a *story* (q.v.), where there are no *impediments* (q.v.) or dependencies in place that would prevent them from doing the work, and they understand what it means to be *done* (q.v.).

refactoring. A technique for changing the internal structure without changing the external functionality; a fancy term for "tidying things up."

reframing. A consulting technique that encourages the requester to look at the business problem from a *performance* (q.v.) point of view, rather than assuming that a training course will solve the problem.

release. The availability of a new version of software or other product feature, typically occurring after several *sprints* (q.v.), but sometimes happening as fast as several times a day.

release plan. The set of *product backlog items* (q.v.) that is to be completed over the course of a *release* (q.v.).

repurposed labor. The value of time made available to be spent on more *worthy* (q.v.) things.

retention. The percentage of employees who stay with the company, the inverse of *turnover* (q.v.).

retrospective. A *Scrum* (q.v.) event where the team reflects on how they worked together during the recently concluded *iteration* (q.v.). At the conclusion of the event, the team commits to one action for improvement.

return on investment (ROI). Monetary benefit of solution divided by the cost of implementing the solution. Jack Phillips is notable in *human performance technology* (q.v.) for introducing ROI as a Level 5 to add to the four levels of the *Kirkpatrick Model* (q.v.).

ROI. See *return on investment.*

root cause analysis (RCA). See *cause analysis.*

Scrum. An *iterative* (q.v.) and *incremental* (q.v.) *Agile* (q.v.) development framework, which can be applied to the production of any feature-based output.

ScrumAlliance. A professional affiliation that supports the community of *Scrum* (q.v.) practitioners and confers a range of professional designations.

scrum master. A *scrum team* (q.v.) member who is responsible for facilitating team events and removing *impediments* (q.v.).

scrum team. A cross-functional group of five to nine people who work together, including two specialized roles, *product owner* (q.v.) and *scrum master* (q.v.).

scrumban. A hybrid work approach that combines a *WIP limit* (q.v.) of *kanban* (q.v.) with the defined *iteration* (q.v.) length of *Scrum* (q.v.).

Serious eLearning Manifesto. A belief system and related principles aiming at a higher level of professional focus, quality, and usefulness, specifically as it relates to the production of web-based training. It was created by Michael Allen, Julie Dirkson, Clark Quinn, and Will Thalheimer; any like-minded person may sign it.

source code. Instructions written in a programming language that make software work.

sprint backlog. The list of *stories* (q.v.) to which a *development team* (q.v.) has committed to complete during the current *iteration* (q.v.).

sprint. An *iteration* (q.v.) in *scrum* (q.v.), typically one, two, or four weeks in duration.

sprint planning. A *Scrum* (q.v.) event that takes place at the beginning of *iteration* (q.v.), during which the *product owner* (q.v.) presents the highest priority *product backlog items* (q.v.), and the team estimates the effort required to complete each item before committing to it.

sprint retrospective. See *retrospective* (q.v.).

sprint review. A *Scrum* (q.v.) event where the team demonstrates its work output to the *customers* (q.v.).

standup. See *daily standup* (q.v.).

story. An item in the backlog on which a team will work to create a product feature.

story points. A method for estimation in *Scrum* (q.v.), where the relative effort is somewhat arbitrarily assigned to each *work item* (q.v.). The scale for these estimates is particular to a *development team* (q.v.) and cannot be compared across teams.

summative evaluation. Measurement and assessment done after a solution is implemented.

sustainable pace. A speed of work effort that can be maintained indefinitely. Expecting a team to work faster is a one-ingredient recipe for burnout, disgruntlement, and poor performance.

sustaining team. A group of software engineers dedicated to paying back *technical debt* (q.v.).

TDD. See *test-driven development.*

team. See *development team.*

team actualization.* The achievement of full potential for high performance, the product of refined technical and *Agile* (q.v.) practices.

team velocity. See *velocity.*

technical debt. The accumulation of *defects* (q.v.) in software. Every time a customer accepts piece of software with defects, it is like borrowing money. Eventually you have to pay it back, with interest. The more technical debt you have, the greater portion of your resources is spent reducing it instead of developing new features.

test-driven development (TDD). An *agile engineering practice* (q.v.) in which a test is created and fails before any *code* (q.v.) is written. The goal of the code is to pass the test.

test automation. The use of specialized software, rather than manual inspection, to look for *defects* (q.v.) within *source code* (q.v.).

tester. See *quality assurance engineer.*

time to productivity. How long it takes for an employee to start contributing, counting days, weeks, or years from hire until the person is competent and productive.

turnover. The number of employees who leave an employer, either voluntarily or involuntarily.

user story. See *story.*

value perception.* A measure of effective collaboration between the *customer* (q.v.) and the *product owner* (q.v.), which can be ascertained by asking the customer directly how helpful the product owner's consulting is.

velocity. Estimated number of *story points* (q.v.) or other unit that the team completes within an *iteration* (q.v.); the measure of team productivity in *Agile* (q.v.).

waterfall. An end-to-end sequential design process where all work is preplanned and each phase is completed before the next one begins; a dirty word to *agilists* (q.v.).

WIP. See *work in process.*

WIP limit. A team rule that caps the number of *stories* (q.v.) to which a person or team can commit at a time.

work in process (WIP). The number of *stories* (q.v.) to which an individual or team is committed a one time.

work item. See *story.*

work iteration. See *iteration.*

work (or iteration) flow.* The journey of backlog items through the *agile performance improvement system* (q.v.), from the *product owner* (q.v.) to the *development team* (q.v.) to the *customer* (q.v.).

workforce efficacy. Measures that refer to how effectively employees perform, on an individual, team or business unit basis, the metrics of which include employee capabilities, productivity, and for new employees *time to productivity* (q.v.).

worth. The value of an accomplishment in consideration of the cost of implementing a solution, precisely defined by Thomas F. Gilbert in his most famous book, *Human Competence.*

XP. See *extreme programming.*

Recommended for Further Study

Chapter 1: Agile and HPT, The Twain Shall Meet

McCarthy, Jim. *Culture Hacking: Jim McCarthy at TEDxHarambee*. Retrieved March 9, 2015, from TEDx page on YouTube: `http://bit.ly/1GkoRSu`, 2013.

> Jim McCarthy delivers an offbeat 22-minute presentation about software and "the fruit of the Enlightenment." Find out what culture, the Beatles, and hippies have to do with Agile.

Rummler, Geary. *Geary Rummler on Performance Engineering*. Retrieved November 9, 2014, from Guy Wallace YouTube channel: `http://bit.ly/1AYDYMN`, 1986.

> Geary Rummler, one of the most esteemed figures in the history of HPT, provides timeless ruminations on management, performance engineering, and training. Professorial and humorous, Rummler holds court while explaining his "transparencies"—it's 1986—and processing the human performance implications of excess baggage charges at the airport.

Chapter 2: The Basics of HPT

Gilbert, Thomas F. *Human Competence: Engineering Worthy Performance, Tribute Edition.* New York: Pfeiffer, 1995.

> Gilbert's *chef d'oeuvre* is on the short list of greatest nonfiction books that I've read. In addition to its monumental contribution to the HPT field, it is at once eloquent, witty, and profound.

ISPI. *CPT Performance Standards.* Retrieved December 10, 2014, from International Society for Performance Improvement: `http://www.ispi.org/pl/cpt/CPT-Performance-Standards.pdf`, 2013.

> This document details the standards for the Certified Performance Technologist (CPT) designation, and it is the authoritative guide for HPT practitioners.

Chapter 3: The Performance Consultant's Toolkit

Harless, Joseph H. *An Ounce of Analysis (Is Worth a Pound of Objectives).* Newnan, GA: Harless Performance Guild, 1970.

> The title of Joe Harless's most famous book is inviting and eminently quotable. Unfortunately, this little classic is out of print and rare.

Robinson, Dana G., and James Robinson. *Performance Consulting: A Practical Guide for HR and Learning Professionals,* 2nd ed. San Francisco: Berrett-Koehler, 2008.

> First published in 1996, this book essentially defined the profession of performance consulting. With splendid insights on overcoming the frustrations of extracting a business focus out of a learning function, the Robinsons provide a panoply of useful interpersonal and analytical techniques.

Chapter 4: The Basics of Agile

Fowler, Martin, and Neil Ford. *Explaining Agile—Martin Fowler and Neil Ford at USI.* Retrieved March 9, 2015, from USI Events YouTube channel: `http://bit.ly/1poaKq3`, 2013.

> This 45-minute video is an entertaining and insightful chat explaining agile concepts in a way that nonsoftware people can readily understand.

Martin, Robert C. *The Land that Scrum Forgot.* Retrieved October 18, 2014, from the Robert C. Martin Talks YouTube playlist. `http://bit.ly/1AbbWOo`, 2011.

In this keynote address from the 2011 Norwegian Developers Conference, Robert C. Martin warns of the perils of overindulging in Scrum and forgetting to develop the technical disciplines required to reap the fruit of Agile. This mesmerizing video stars the intense and erudite Uncle Bob.

Sutherland, Jeff, and Ken Schwaber. *Scrum Guides.* Retrieved March 2, 2015, from ScrumGuides.org: `http://www.scrumguides.org/scrum-guide.html`, 2013.

As the dictionary is to the game of Scrabble, this 16-page paper is to the practice of Scrum. It settles arguments. Anyone starting out in Scrum needs to read this authoritative rulebook maintained by the inventors of the practice. It's short, it's free, and it's online.

Chapter 5: The Agile Software Engineer's Toolkit

Fowler, Martin. *Refactoring: Improving the Design of Existing Code.* Boston: Addison-Wesley, 1999.

This is a hardcore software engineering book, but it rewards the persistent lay reader. In it, Martin Fowler and other contributors provide a comprehensive treatise on refactoring. The chapter on code smells, coauthored with Kent Beck, is alone worth the price.

Martin, Robert C. *Agile Software Development: Principles, Patterns, and Practices.* Upper Saddle River, NJ: Prentice Hall, 2003.

Nonsoftware people might be put off by Uncle Bob Martin's copious software code examples, but the first 63 pages are the most cogent and entertaining written description I have seen of the principles of Agile.

Chapter 6: Agile Performance Improvement

Mager, Robert F. *Preparing Instructional Objectives, Second Edition.* Belmont, CA: Fearon, 1975.

This excellent little (136-page) book showcases the thought of Bob Mager, an under-recognized beacon in the learning and development field. His thinking blazed a trail for Agile and HPT folks, who need to be reminded to start with the outcome and work backward from there. This book is out of print, but used copies are available.

Woody, Zuill. *Mob Programming Time-Lapse Video—A Day of Mob Programming.* Retrieved October 10, 2014, from Mob Programming: `http://bit.ly/1lFPDOC`. 2012.

This video condenses a workday into 3 minutes, 15 seconds. You see a team working in Mob Programming, an extreme form of collaboration where an entire team shares one computer for all programming.

Chapter 7: Proving Value

Corporate Executive Board. *Driving Performance and Retention Through Employee Engagement: A Quantitative Analysis of Effective Engagement Strategies.* Retrieved March 9, 2015 from University of Southern California: `http://www.usc.edu/programs/cwfl/assets/pdf/Employee engagement.pdf`, 2004.

This presentation gives a thorough treatment of employee engagement and the usefulness of data surrounding it. Engagement—a cousin to employee commitment, happiness, and satisfaction—is a difficult concept to grasp, and this is an excellent resource for those first learning about it.

Philips, Jack J. *Handbook of Training Evaluation and Measurement Methods, Third Edition.* Houston: Gulf Publishing Series, 1997.

Jack Philips is best known for appending a level 5 (return on investment) to the original four Kirkpatrick levels. This book is an oldie-but-goodie—a valuable resource to me when I first learned about the measurement and evaluation of training. Practitioners will find a healthy mix of common sense and statistical methods.

Chapter 8: Continuous Improvement Lore

Adkins, Lyssa. *Coaching Agile Teams.* Boston: Addison-Wesley Professional, 2010.

Coaching support is indispensable to success with Agile at any scale. Lyssa Adkins's book is a readable and formidable treatment of this important topic, which the present work treats only lightly.

Cohn, Mike. *Agile Estimating & Planning,* Upper Saddle River, NJ: Prentice Hall, 2005.

Mike Cohn, one of the leading thinkers in Agile and a fine writer, breaks down the nuances of the vexing task of accurately sizing stories. That the book is considered one of the classics of the genre is a testament to the difficulty that Agile teams have in estimating the size and complexity of work items.

I

Index

Q

R

S

T, U

V

W, X, Y, Z

Printed in the United States
By Bookmasters